COMPARISONS IN GLOBAL SECURITY POLITICS

Representing and Ordering the World

Edited by
Thomas Müller, Mathias Albert
and Kerrin Langer

BRISTOL
UNIVERSITY
PRESS

First published in Great Britain in 2024 by

Bristol University Press
University of Bristol
1–9 Old Park Hill
Bristol
BS2 8BB
UK
t: +44 (0)117 374 6645
e: bup-info@bristol.ac.uk

Details of international sales and distribution partners are available at bristoluniversitypress.co.uk

British Library Cataloguing in Publication Data
A catalogue record for this book is available from the British Library

ISBN 978-1-5292-4183-9 paperback
ISBN 978-1-5292-4185-3 ePub
ISBN 978-1-5292-4184-6 OA PDF

Cover design: Hayes Design and Advertising
Front cover image: Alamy/Heritage Image Partnership Ltd
Bristol University Press uses environmentally responsible print partners.
Printed and bound in Great Britain by CPI Group (UK) Ltd, Croydon, CR0 4YY

FSC
www.fsc.org
MIX
Paper | Supporting
responsible forestry
FSC® C013604

Contents

List of Figures and Tables

Figures

Tables

Notes on Contributors

Mathias Albert is Professor of Political Science at the University of Bielefeld. His research interests are in the history and sociology of world politics, in polar science and politics, as well as in youth studies, where he has been one of the leaders of the German *Shell Youth Survey* for more than 20 years. Latest book publications include *The Social Evolution of World Politics* (2023, with Hauke Brunkhorst, Iver B. Neumann and Stephan Stetter; transcript) and *Svalbard Imaginaries. The Making of an Arctic Archipelago* (2024, ed. with Dina Brode-Roger and Lisbeth Iversen, Palgrave).

Paul Beaumont is Senior Researcher at the Norwegian Institute of International Affairs. His research interests include International Relations (IR) theory, hierarchies in world politics, and the (dis)functioning of international institutions. Paul's research has featured in several leading IR journals, including the *European Journal of International Relations*, *International Studies Review* and *Third World Quarterly*. He has published two monographs: *The Grammar of Status Competition: International Hierarchies and Domestic Politics* (2024, Oxford University Press) and *Performing Nuclear Weapons: How Britain Made its Bomb Make Sense* (2021, Palgrave).

Christian Bueger is Professor of International Relations at the University of Copenhagen, where he leads the Ocean Infrastructure Research Group. He is also one of the directors of SafeSeas – the research network for maritime security and ocean governance (www.safeseas.net). In his research he focuses on IR theory, global ocean politics and maritime security as well as epistemic practices. Bueger holds a PhD from the European University Institute. Across his career he has held positions at Cardiff University, Greenwich Maritime Institute, University of Malta and National University of Singapore. With Tim Edmunds, he is the author of *Understanding Maritime Security* (2024, Oxford University Press). Further information is available on his personal website: www.bueger.info

Bastian Giegerich is the Director-General and Chief Executive of The International Institute for Strategic Studies (IISS). Prior to assuming the

Directorship in October 2023, Bastian served as Director of the Institute's Defence and Military Analysis research programme (2015–23). From 2010–15, he worked for the German Federal Ministry of Defence in research and policy roles, while also serving as an IISS Consulting Senior Fellow for European security. He initially joined the IISS in 2005 on a post-doctoral fellowship to work on European military crisis-management efforts.

James Hackett is Head of the Defence and Military Analysis Programme at the IISS. He leads the team's research and analysis agenda, including the delivery of consulting projects and the production of IISS Military Balance products. He has interests in global conflict, military and security affairs, and in defence technology. He co-leads IISS research on Russian military issues. Before his current role, he was Editor of *The Military Balance*.

Lena Herbst is Lecturer and PhD candidate at the Institute of International Relations at Technical University Braunschweig. Her research interests include security studies, peace and conflict studies, as well as international organizations. Her PhD dissertation examines the role of non-state actors in United Nations (UN) cybersecurity governance.

Anja P. Jakobi is Professor of Political Science and International Relations at Technical University Braunschweig. Her research focuses on actors and processes of global governance, in particular related to crime and security. Among her book publications are *Crime, Security and Global Politics. An Introduction to Global Crime Governance* (2021, Bloomsbury) and *Common Goods and Evils? The Formation of Global Crime Governance* (2013, Oxford University Press). Her articles have been published in *Environmental Politics, Crime, Law and Social Change, British Journal of Politics and International Relations*, and *Journal of International Relations and Development*, among others.

Keith Krause is Professor of International Relations at the Geneva Graduate Institute, and Director of its Centre on Conflict, Development and Peacebuilding (CCDP). Until 2016, he was also Programme Director of the Small Arms Survey, an internationally recognized research non-governmental organization (NGO) he founded in 2000. His research concentrates on international security and political violence, as well as post-conflict peacebuilding and security governance. He has published *Arms and the State*, edited or co-edited *Critical Security Studies, Culture and Security*, and *Armed Groups and Contemporary Conflicts*, as well as having authored dozens of journal articles and book chapters, and consulted for governments and NGOs.

Kerrin Langer is Research Associate at the Department of Social Sciences at TU Dortmund University. Her research interests include naval policy, arms dynamics, and status competition, as well as the relationships between the military, the public, and politics during the late 19th and the first half of the 20th century. In her PhD project, she studied practices of naval force comparisons and their role in and impact on naval armament policies, arms dynamics and arms control between 1889 and 1922. Recent articles have been published in the *Zeitschrift für Internationale Beziehungen* and in the *Journal of International Relations and Development*.

Thomas Müller is Senior Lecturer at the Faculty of Sociology at Bielefeld University. He co-leads a research project on the history of power comparisons in the Collaborative Research Centre 1288 *Practices of Comparing*. His research interests are great power politics since the 18th century, world political change and the production of knowledge in world politics. His latest articles have appeared in *Global Society*, the *European Journal of International Security* and the *Journal of International Relations and Development*. He recently co-edited with (Janne Mende) a special issue on 'Publics in Global Politics' in *Politics and Governance*.

Paul Musgrave is Assistant Professor of Political Science at the University of Massachusetts Amherst. He studies US foreign policy, International Relations theory, and how oil and politics mix. His research has appeared in *International Organization*, *International Studies Quarterly*, *Security Studies*, *Presidential Studies Quarterly* and *Comparative Political Studies*, and he has written for *The Washington Post*, *Foreign Policy* and other outlets. In 2019–20, he was an American Political Science Association fellow working for a member of Congress on Capitol Hill. He holds a PhD in Government with a focus on International Relations from Georgetown University.

Madeleine Myatt is a political scientist by training who works as security analyst for Continental AG and serves as academic expert on cyber at the European Center for Countering Hybrid Threats since 2019. Throughout her career in and outside academia, Madeleine has been involved in different research projects in the field of cybersecurity, digital diplomacy and right-wing populism in the digital age. Her research and expertise focus on public–private collaboration in cybersecurity, cyber-based hybrid threats and threat intelligence with an actor-centric focus.

Nike Retzmann is Research Associate in the Collaborative Research Centre 1288 *Practices of Comparing* and a PhD candidate at the Faculty of Sociology at Bielefeld University. Her research interests include the study of narratives, comparative practices and the role of technologies in world politics. Her dissertation project centres on the interplay of power comparisons and technology narratives as part of foreign policy discourses in the US and Canada.

Gabi Schlag is Senior Lecturer at the University of Tübingen. Her research interests are in visual global politics, violence and conflict studies. In addition, she is interested in the formation of security communities, such as the North Atlantic Treaty Organization (NATO), and digital public spheres. Latest publications include 'Socialmedia actors: shared responsibility 3.0?' (2022, in *Routledge Handbook on Responsibility in International Relations*, edited by H. Hansen-Magnussson and A. Vetterlein, Routledge) and 'Visual discourses of identity formation: NATO's image on social media' (2024, in *Oxford Handbook on the North Atlantic Treaty Organisation*, edited by M. Webber and J. Sperling, Oxford University Press).

Hans-Joachim Schmidt holds a PhD from Goethe University in Frankfurt am Main and worked as a senior researcher and project leader at Peace Research Institute Frankfurt (PRIF) from 1982 to 2017. After his retirement he has become an Associate Fellow at PRIF. His main interests are conventional arms control and military confidence building in Europe. One of his latest articles is 'How the Russia–Ukraine war could end, and its impact on conventional arms control' (*IAI Papers*, May 2023).

Steven Ward is Assistant Professor of International Relations in the Department of Politics and International Studies at the University of Cambridge, and a Fellow of Pembroke College. His research focuses broadly on international security, and in particular on status in world politics, coercive diplomacy, and on the relationship between international and domestic politics. He is the author of *Status and the Challenge of Rising Powers* (2017, Cambridge University Press).

Acknowledgements

This volume is the product of two workshops held in 2021 and 2022 to which we invited researchers working on various forms of comparative practices in global security politics to reflect on a possible common research agenda. We are very grateful to all participants for the stimulating and productive discussions. We want to say thank you to our student assistants Mareike Borger, Henrike Brandes and Alina Reschke who helped us organize the workshops and prepare the manuscript. We are also grateful to the anonymous reviewers for their valuable and constructive feedback. A special thanks goes to Steven Curtis for his excellent copy editing. The open access publication was funded by Bielefeld University and the Collaborative Research Centre 1288 *Practices of Comparing*, funded by the Deutsche Forschungsgemeinschaft (DFG, German Research Foundation), as well as the Bundeswehr Centre of Military History and Social Sciences. Last but not least, we would like to thank Stephen Wenham, Zoe Forbes and her colleagues at Bristol University Press for their superb support during the review process and the production of this volume.

Thomas Müller
Mathias Albert
Kerrin Langer
February 2024

Introduction: Practices All the Way Down? Comparisons in Global Security Politics

Thomas Müller, Mathias Albert and Kerrin Langer

Comparisons are a ubiquitous practice in global security politics. State and non-state actors routinely estimate and evaluate differentials in capabilities, power and status. Comparative assessments underpin visions of international order – for instance as a balance of power or a multipolar global order – and fuel competitive dynamics such as arms races and status competition. Comparative practices moreover describe developments in the field of global security – for instance, patterns and trends in the worldwide arms trade, in cyberattacks, in transnational crime or in maritime security. Such practices help to define security phenomena as governance objects and to make them amenable to various governance efforts, ranging from arms control through transnational policing to United Nations (UN) missions and programmes. Comparative techniques such as benchmarking and ranking are not only crucial for mobilizing political support for these efforts but often also underpin the evaluation of their implementation.

Despite the ubiquity of comparative practices, however, the field of International Relations (IR) has not so far developed a substantial interest in those that underpin and shape global security politics. Research on the subject touches upon various comparative practices, but it generally does not treat them as the main object of study. There is consequently not much systematic research done on the evolution and variety of the comparative practices that state and non-state actors use, or on the processes and politics through which certain practices and standards of comparison come to be prominent and influential in global security politics.

The aim of the present volume is twofold: to initiate a dialogue about the various comparative practices that underpin and shape global security politics and to foster a more systemic study of how comparative knowledge is produced, becomes politically relevant and shapes world politics. The present chapter develops a framework for this endeavour. It first discusses the separate streams in the study of comparisons in global security politics, highlighting two dominant approaches. It then conceptualizes comparisons as a special type of knowledge practice that emphasizes similarities and differences between objects. On this basis, it outlines three questions that can guide the debate among the different research streams: How is comparative knowledge produced? How does it become politically relevant? How do comparative practices shape security politics? The chapter concludes by presenting the structure of the book.

Two approaches to the study of comparisons

To avoid misunderstandings: we do not claim that comparisons have been ignored in the research on global security politics. This research knows and shows that comparisons are integral to most, if not all, phenomena in global security politics. Rather, the problem is, on the one hand, that this research tends to focus on aspects of these phenomena other than comparative practices, and, on the other, that when it does indeed focus on these practices, it tends to study the phenomena separately rather than treating them as part of a common research agenda. There is generally little to no debate across research streams – those, for example, on balance of power politics, status competition or the quantification of trans- and international governance – about the comparative practices that underpin the phenomena in question. In the following paragraphs, we briefly chart the research that focuses on comparisons and highlight two distinct approaches, one originating in realist research on balance of power politics and arms dynamics, and the other dominating constructivist and practice theory research on knowledge production in global security politics.

For a long time, IR understood security politics primarily in terms of military security (for a history of security studies see Buzan and Hansen, 2009). The key problematic of interwar and Cold War IR was interstate wars and their prevention. Realist approaches came to dominate the debates on this problematic and made military capabilities central to the study of global security politics. For realists then and now, world politics was characterized by a competition over power among states. States strove to enhance their power both to ensure their security and to be better able to realize their aims. States relatedly care about differentials in power and 'spend a lot of time estimating one another's capabilities, especially their abilities to do harm' – that is, their military capabilities (Waltz, 1979: 131). Realist solutions for the problematic of war consequently centre on the management of the competition over power through practices such as the maintenance of a balance of power and the stabilization of arms dynamics through arms control.

The realist emphasis on the competition for power is de facto an argument about how pivotal comparisons are in world politics. Comparisons fuel the competition over power and also form the basis for its management. In their research during the Cold War, though, realists were more interested in the balancing strategies that states pursued than in the underlying comparative practices. Practices of power comparison were 'generally little studied and poorly understood', one scholar noted near the end of the Cold War (Friedberg, 1988: 3). For all their differences, nonetheless, realists shared the same approach to the effects of the comparisons: They treated the comparative practices as means through which states – sometimes accurately, sometimes wrongly – assessed a materially given distribution of power. For realists, the comparative practices shaped how states perceived, and thus reacted to, the evolving distribution of power, but they did not shape – or for that matter constitute – the distribution itself.

In other words, realists generally assumed that there was a real distribution of power that existed independently of the comparative practices through which it was assessed. Some scholars doubted this assumption, emphasizing that the distribution was elusive and open to multiple interpretations, which made accurate evaluations of 'real' power practically impossible. Prevalent perceptions of power, not the distributions of power itself, shaped the policies of states (see Wohlforth, 1993). Realists readily acknowledged that the distribution of power was not always easy to measure and that states could misjudge it. Although some scholars enquired into the factors contributing to these misperceptions (see May, 1984), the realist tendency to conceptualize the arms dynamics as a security dilemma resulted in a 'focus on misjudgments of intentions rather than misjudgments of situations' (Jervis, 1988: 677). Questions about misperceptions were at the heart of the realist approach to comparisons, not questions about the shifting prevalence of certain ways of representing and problematizing the distribution of power.

After the Cold War a broader understanding of security politics gained ground in IR. This had both empirical and theoretical reasons. The security agendas of trans- and international governance institutions became more expansive. Besides interstate wars and military security, they worked more and more on matters such as fragile states, transnational terrorism, transnational crime or maritime security. Besides, new theoretical approaches – most prominent among them securitization theory (see Buzan et al, 1998) – argued that phenomena were not inherently security issues, but became such through discursive processes. The broader understanding of security politics went hand in hand with an increasing interest in the knowledge practices and infrastructures that undergird global security politics (see Balzacq, 2008;

Berling and Bueger, 2015; Bueger, 2015; de Goede, 2018; Neumann and Sending, 2018; Berling et al, 2022).

While diverse in its approaches, this research generally treats knowledge practices and infrastructures as co-constitutive of the phenomena they purport to describe. Knowledge practices and infrastructures turn phenomena into governance objects that are, to varying degrees, amenable to political action (see also Sending, 2015; Allan, 2017). These knowledge practices involve comparisons if they map differences among actors or seek to trace developments over time – which they generally do. The research, though, often does not conceptualize the knowledge practices as comparative ones. To give two examples: Aradau and Blanke (2018: 1) approach algorithmic practices of searching for criminals and terrorists through anomaly analysis as 'modes of othering'[1] while de Goede (2018) foregrounds the 'chain of security' through which this analysis takes place.

A research stream that explicitly treats knowledge practices as comparative practices is the literature on the quantification of world politics. This literature highlights the proliferation of 'comparative evaluation techniques' (Broome and Quirk, 2015: 820) such as indicators, benchmarks, targets and rankings over the past 30 years. Although security politics is sometimes described as a field less affected by this trend than others (see Kelley and Simmons, 2019: 494, 503), we argue that comparative practices do, in fact, also permeate security politics (see Andreas and Greenhill, 2010), one example being benchmarks in defence planning, such as the North Atlantic Treaty Organization's (NATO) goal that its members spend at least 2 per cent of their gross domestic product on defence by 2024 (see Müller, 2022). Other examples include efforts to measure the global level of crime (see Jakobi, 2020: 159–62), to determine the fragility of states or to evaluate 'human security' through indices such as the Human Development Index (see Homolar, 2015). In fact, security politics has a long tradition of quantifying comparisons. Notably, the use of numerical comparisons became a prominent part of balance of power politics in the 18th century (see Allan, 2018: 75–138) and has remained central to it until today. Security politics relatedly constitutes a fertile starting point for broadening the study of quantification beyond regularly published rankings – which are the main focus of recent studies of quantification (see Broome and Quirk, 2015; Malito et al, 2018; and Kelley and Simmons, 2020) – and for probing into both the variety and combinations of non-quantitative and quantitative comparisons that underpin and shape world politics.

---

[1] This is not to say that 'modes of othering' are not comparative. They are inasmuch as they are enacted through distinctions – and hence comparisons – between actors.

A research stream that sits somehow between the realist approach to comparisons and the broader approach underpinning research on knowledge practices and infrastructures is the literature on status competitions and hierarchies in world politics (for example, Paul et al, 2014; Renshon, 2017; Ward, 2017; MacDonald and Parent, 2021). This literature usually pays more attention to how status concerns fuel conflict in world politics than to the practices through which actors build knowledge about the status hierarchy in the first place. Status researchers have a tendency to map the status hierarchy themselves – a prominent proxy is the extent of the network of diplomatic representations that states maintain (see, for example, Renshon, 2016; Roren and Beaumont, 2019) – rather than to study how politicians, diplomats and other actors compare status (for an exception, see Beaumont, 2024). That said, the literature nonetheless stresses that status is positional and perceptual and consequently conceptualizes status hierarchies as intersubjective understandings of how status is distributed (see Renshon, 2017: 33–7; Ward, 2020: 166). Put differently: status hierarchies only exist if there is a socially shared practice of comparing status.

The broader approach did not, however, displace the older, realist one. Two main approaches to comparisons thus co-exist in the current research on global security politics (see Table 1.1). They can be distinguished by their epistemological stances: the first presupposes that comparisons produce knowledge about independently existing phenomena, while the second posits that comparisons form part of the knowledge processes through which the phenomena are constructed and imbued with meaning.[2] Both could, in principle, be applied to diverse phenomena, though usually only the second one is: the first focuses predominantly on the distribution of capabilities and power.[3]

The first approach, still dominating realist and rationalist research (see Fearon, 1995; Glaser, 2010; Lobell, 2018), understands comparative practices as mapping tools. Actors use comparative practices to make sense of the structural conditions – such as the distribution of power – which shape world politics. Comparative practices produce abstract representations of these structural conditions. The structural conditions exist prior to these representations, though the representations may trigger efforts to change the structural conditions, for instance – to continue the example of the distribution of power – through balancing practices. These efforts are usually explained as resulting from structural pressures, rather than being

---

[2] Desrosières (2001) offers a useful discussion of different epistemological positions on the relation between comparative knowledge – in his case, statistics – and reality.

[3] For research using the second approach to study comparative practices in the context of the distribution of power, see Albert (2016), Guzzini (2009), Allan (2018) and Müller and Albert (2021).

Table 1.1: Two approaches to comparisons

	Mapping tools	Ordering tools
Relation between comparisons and security issues	Security issues exist independent of comparative practices → if done well, comparative practices reveal the crucial patterns that characterize and shape the issues	Comparative practices contribute to the constitution and ordering of security issues → relations are patterned through comparative practices
Research interest	How well do the comparative practices capture the key structural characteristics?	How do certain comparative practices become central to (security) politics?
Typically found in	Realist research on the distribution of power and on arms dynamics	Constructivist and practice theory research on the knowledge practices underpinning (security) politics

triggered by knowledge practices, though there is an acknowledgement that knowledge practices have an impact on how states react to structural pressures. This research relatedly focuses on how accurate and prescient comparative practices are – that is, on how well they capture and anticipate systemic conditions and developments.

The second approach understands comparative practices as ordering tools. Structures are patterned relations. For researchers favouring this approach – among them constructivist and practice theory researchers – comparative practices do not simply reveal patterns but contribute to their making. Knowledge practices make phenomena knowable by patterning them – by postulating that certain elements that form part of phenomena, for example actors, things or events, are crucial to them – and by specifying the relations among these elements. Comparative practices are a prominent mode of specifying these relations. Moreover, by framing phenomena in certain ways, knowledge practices shape the political debate about them and, in particular, foster political demands for particular ways of (re)ordering them – for example, demands that an 'unbalanced' distribution of power should be brought into 'balance'. The systemic pressure is, in this sense, an effect of the knowledge practices. This research is therefore interested in how certain ways of representing the phenomena emerge, become politically dominant and for some time shape how the phenomena are debated and governed.

Comparative practices

Both mapping tools and ordering tools approaches provide valuable insights into the comparative practices that underpin global security politics. While we favour the constructivist and practice theory approach because it is more attentive to the hybrid – socio-material – nature of security issues, we nonetheless think that, rather than debate which approach is right/better, it is more productive to develop a common analytical framework and empirical research agenda. This section makes the first step towards such a framework by discussing what 'comparative practices' are.

Comparisons are an object of study in various disciplines, including philosophy, literary studies, sociology and history (see Espeland and Stevens, 1998; Stoler, 2001; Epple and Erhart, 2015; Steinmetz, 2019). There is no uniform definition of comparisons, but most researchers focus on the following characteristics: (a) the assessment of two or more objects – whether actors, things, events or other entities – according to (b) one criterion or a set of criteria, in order to (c) discern and highlight similarities or differences between these objects. The objects are sometimes called 'comparata', the criteria 'tertia'. Some researchers also emphasize another characteristic. The actors comparing the objects assume that the objects are comparable – that is, that they form part of a set of objects to which the same criterion or set of criteria can be applied (see Heintz, 2016: 307).

In line with this research, we conceptualize *comparative practices* as *ways of doing and saying through which actors produce knowledge about similarities and/or differences between two or more objects.* Comparative practices put objects into relation with one another, either by emphasizing what they share (object x is similar to object y with respect to feature z), or by emphasizing what distinguishes them (object x is different from object y with respect to feature z), or by a combination of both. The knowledge that comparative practices produce – which we call comparative knowledge – is thus relational. Moreover, comparative practices are selective. The actors that compare make several choices, including, in particular, the selection of the objects, the features of these objects that are assessed, and the criterion or set of criteria through which they are assessed. They also opt for certain ways of representing and communicating the comparative knowledge they acquire, for instance in the form of statistics or visualizations.

This conceptualization is compatible with both the approaches to comparisons outlined earlier. The two approaches differ on whether comparative practices reveal pre-existing relations between objects (mapping tools) or co-produce the objects and their relations (ordering tools). But they both treat comparative practices as practices that produce knowledge about similarities and differences between objects. Although the first approach usually does not use the notion of knowledge practices, both approaches conceive of comparative practices as elements of knowledge production processes regarding international phenomena, whether power shifts, arms races, fragile states, transnational crime or cybersecurity.

Comparative practices are a particular type of knowledge practice. They assess objects and are, in this sense, distinct from knowledge practices that are geared towards data collection (for example, reporting mechanisms) or storage (for example, the building of databases). Knowledge practices such as these nonetheless often form the basis for comparative practices. For instance, to compare the number of piracy attacks over time, one needs first to build a database that lists attacks at different points or phases in time, for example per week, month or year. Moreover, comparative practices specify the relations between objects in a particular way: in terms of similarities and differences. This is, however, not the only way of specifying the relations between objects. Another prominent way is to posit causal relations: changes in object x cause changes in object y. Knowledge practices geared towards explaining why objects have certain features or why certain developments happened are, in this sense, different from comparative practices. That said, comparative practices may very well be components of such knowledge practices. Statistical regression analysis, for instance, would not work without the measurement of differences between the data points and the modelled data. Narratives are another example. The practice of telling narratives involves comparisons of objects over time, but it also involves 'emplotment' (Krebs, 2015: 11): an explanation, usually a causal one, of why objects changed or did not change. The currently prominent narrative of a 'rising China', for instance, combines a comparative argument – that China is gaining in power – with causal arguments about why China is rising (for example because its economic growth is increasing its international clout) and how this rise reshapes world politics (for example, by bringing about the end of the Western-dominated liberal international order).

Comparative practices are thus not the only knowledge practices through which politicians, diplomats, scholars, civil society activists and other actors make sense of international phenomena. But we would nonetheless argue that they are integral to many, if not all, knowledge production processes. Both in security politics and beyond, the debate about and governance of international phenomena generally involves at least one and often several of the following forms of comparative knowledge:

- *Distribution assessments* describe the relation between objects in terms of bigger/smaller shares of some features that are deemed important. Examples are analyses of differences in the military capabilities of states, the classification of states as types of powers (for example superpowers, great powers, middle powers and small powers) and the mapping of the number of cyberattacks on different states.
- *Trend assessments* emphasize continuities or changes in objects over time. Examples are diagnoses of power shifts in world politics and analyses of the number of wars or the level of transnational crime in different years.
- *Scenario assessments* are planning practices that imagine different (future) situations to evaluate which strategies work best to achieve certain

aims. Such practices combine two sorts of comparison: they analyse the implications of variations in the possible future development of a phenomenon and evaluate the viability of different political strategies for dealing with the phenomenon as it evolves. An example is the wargaming of anticipated military conflicts.

- *Performance assessments* evaluate how good or bad actors are at dealing with a phenomenon. They describe the relation between the objects in terms of better/worse performances. Examples are the Human Development Index, state fragility indices and the ranking of NATO's members according to how well they fulfil the alliance's 2 per cent goal.

A framework

For all its differences, the diverse research on comparisons in global security politics shares an interest in the same set of questions: How is comparative knowledge produced? How does it become politically relevant? How does it shape global security politics? We therefore propose to organize the study of comparisons in global security politics around these three questions. We now discuss each question in turn and outline the contours of a joint debate across the various streams of research.

How is comparative knowledge produced?

The cast of actors studied by research on comparisons has expanded over time. Realist research on power comparisons has retained its traditional focus on the political elites shaping the foreign policies of states, in particular, the most powerful states. In the past two decades, however, research drawing on global governance, constructivist and practice theory approaches has argued for a much broader perspective. This research shows that a variety of actors are involved in the production of comparative knowledge on matters of global security, including, besides states and foreign policy elites, international organizations, non-governmental organizations (NGOs), think tanks and companies.

As already mentioned, this broadening reflects an empirical trend, an expanding security agenda in global governance in the past decades. Does it also reflect a change in the mode of knowledge production? The two models of knowledge production that Friedberg (1988: 12–17) distils from realist research on power comparisons are a useful starting point for tackling this question. The 'calculative model' assumes that states continuously collect and analyse data, often in statistical form, about the capabilities and power of other states that they regard as relevant to their own fate. The statistics reveal systemic developments – for example changes in the distribution of power – and provide for a constant updating of comparative knowledge.

The 'perceptual model', by contrast, argues that political elites are guided more by perceptions – for example a narrative that their state is in relative decline – than by statistics. Political elites draw on statistics to substantiate their arguments about systemic developments, but their beliefs about how world politics works and what matters in it shape how they interpret these statistics. The model assumes that perceptions are sticky, not very sensitive to slowly unfolding systemic developments, and only change in the wake of significant events such as wars or crises.

This distinction points to two themes for exploring changes in the modes of knowledge production. The first theme is institutionalization. The calculative model presupposes 'epistemic infrastructures' (Bueger, 2015: 2), that is, institutionalized arrangements for the regular production of comparative knowledge on an issue. Friedberg (1988) – in line with most research on power comparisons – describes the two models with national epistemic infrastructures in mind. For a number of issues, however, there are also trans- and international epistemic infrastructures, and these – whether international organizations publishing rankings on matters such as state fragility, regional networks and centres for tracking piracy incidents, or cybersecurity companies compiling statistics on changes in cyberattacks – have gained in prominence and importance in global security governance in the past decades. For which security issues do such epistemic infrastructures exist and for which not? How has the nature of these epistemic infrastructures changed over time?

The second theme is the interplay between quantitative and non-quantitative modes of knowledge production. The calculative model is a reminder that quantification – that is, the use of numbers to depict and analyse phenomena – has been an important part of the production of comparative knowledge for quite some time. Statistics were, for instance, used to rearrange the territorial balance of power in Europe at the Congress of Vienna in 1814–15, fuelled the naval arms race of the late 19th century and were integral to 20th-century arms control (see Allan, 2018: 75–138; Albert and Langer, 2020; Müller et al, 2022: 14–21). At the same time, the perceptual model is a reminder of the salience of non-quantitative forms of comparative knowledge. Narratives of the rise and fall of powerful states are one example (for example Hagström and Gustafsson, 2019; Zarakol, 2019). When ranking military powers, to give another example, some analysts combine quantitative as well as qualitative factors (see Giegerich et al, 2018). In addition, diplomats have what Pouliot (2016: 72–79) calls a 'sense of place': a tacit knowledge about the relative standing of their states. Research usually focuses on explicit forms of comparative knowledge, but such tacit forms matter as well, and should receive more attention than they currently do.

While the expansion of epistemic infrastructures contributes to the further quantification of comparative practices, it does not necessarily entail a decline in the importance of non-quantitative forms of comparative knowledge. In other words, a mix of different modes of knowledge production and dissemination will remain. It seems productive, therefore, to study the evolving mix of these modes. We have already mentioned two: quantification and narratives. Visualization would be another. Statistics are often depicted in the form of tables and graphs. Moreover, images – for example of military parades, terrorist attacks or UN Security Council meetings – are crucial elements of discourses about security politics (see Schlag and Geis, 2017). How are these modes combined in multi-modal modes of knowledge production and dissemination?

Besides the evolving modes of knowledge production, there is another dimension to the question of how actors produce comparative knowledge: the conditions that influence their comparative practices. Some conditions have constraining effects: Disputes among states over the governance of issues can hamper the establishment of international epistemic infrastructures. Moreover, the characteristics of some issues make it difficult to compile reliable data on them. Examples are the opacity of transnational crime and the secrecy regimes that some states build around their military capabilities. Other conditions, by contrast, have enabling effects. In particular, the more comparative knowledge there is already available on an issue, the easier it is to produce new comparative knowledge. Davis et al (2012: 85) note, for instance, that the 'use of indicators may be a self-reinforcing phenomenon: as more indicators are produced, aggregations of indicators become more reliable, more indicators are used, more indicators are produced and so on'. Moreover, there may be isomorphic effects at play that make the practices of the various actors producing comparative knowledge more similar (see DiMaggio and Powell (1983) for an influential discussion of different processes of isomorphism). To give but two examples: epistemic infrastructures may establish standardized procedures for producing comparative knowledge on a given security issue. Actors may copy the comparative practices of other actors that they deem to be good at initiating and shaping debates about security issues.

How does comparative knowledge become politically relevant?

Comparative knowledge can be said to be politically relevant when it influences the debates about security issues and the ways in which they are governed. But how does it become politically relevant? To structure the joint debate, this question can be divided into two subquestions: the first is whether comparative knowledge is produced in response to security issues or to producing the security agenda. The second is why some representations come to dominate the debate on a given security issue.

One answer is that security issues prompt the production of comparative knowledge and shape the evolution of comparative practices. This answer notably informs realist research. For realists, the competition over power and security among states makes certain comparative practices – those assessing differentials in power and military capabilities – key to the conduct of the foreign policies of states. Put differently: systemic structures and pressures shape which comparative practices are salient. What is more, the competition shapes how the comparative practices evolve. Foreign policy elites adjust their comparative practices when they deem new developments – for example new technologies – are affecting and changing the dynamics of the competition. From time to time, significant events such as wars or crises provide insights into how well different states are faring in the competition, which enables foreign policy elites to recalibrate their comparative practices. Realists, though, tend to qualify the calibrating effects. As Wohlforth (1993) emphasizes, states may diverge in their interpretations of systemic structures and developments – and hence in their comparative practices – if their foreign policy elites differ in their beliefs about how world politics works and what matters in it. Moreover, significant events are often not conclusive enough to vindicate only one interpretation.

The converse answer is that comparative practices shape which security issues matter. This argument is made notably by constructivist and practice theory scholars. For them, knowledge practices shape which developments are regarded as politically relevant and important and which not. These knowledge practices are comparative: development *a* is more important than development *b*, phenomenon *c* is more threatening than phenomenon *d* and so on. These assessments are susceptible to contestation and political debate. And they change over time. Arms dynamics – especially the East–West arms race – were widely regarded as the key problem in global security politics during the Cold War. The broadening of the security agenda after the Cold War can be interpreted as a re-evaluation of the relative importance of security issues, with arms dynamics remaining an important item on the agenda but losing their dominating status and becoming one item alongside several others such as transnational crime, terrorism, maritime security, cybersecurity and pandemics. In short, comparative practices are involved in the ordering of the security agenda and this ordering in turn shapes the salience of comparative practices such as assessing differentials in military capabilities or tracking the frequency of cyberattacks over time.

This answer implies that political battles over the governance of issues, rather than systemic pressures, shape which representations come to be dominant. The battles are likely to involve struggles over comparative practices, with actors promoting those that they deem beneficial to their aims and contesting those that they deem detrimental (see Pouliot, 2016: 79–82). As Wohlforth (1993: 303) stresses in his study of power comparisons: '[S]ince many interpretations are always possible, state leaderships in a competitive situation will tend to interpret particular changes opportunistically'. In her study of casualty statistics, Greenhill (2010: 132, 133) similarly notes that 'funding and policy decisions tend to be driven by the perceived size and significance of a problem'. Hence, if 'those producing the numbers believe the issue at hand is a big problem that warrants greater resources and attention, they want a big number; if not, they want a small one'.

In these battles, two types of authority play a role (Zürn, 2018: 50–3). One is political authority. The actors that control the institutions that govern the issues are in a crucial position to choose certain representations of the issues over others and to establish them as the basis for the governance of the issues. The other is epistemic authority: the recognition by other actors that some actors produce and possess special knowledge – expert knowledge – with regard to a phenomenon. Actors consequently 'compete with each other to be recognized as authorities on what is to be governed, how, and why' (Sending, 2015: 11). Being a publisher of well-known comparative statistics can be an asset in this competition. But what counts as good and relevant comparative knowledge can also become a point of contention, for instance when there is a debate about whether accurate statistics can be compiled at all (for the case of transnational crime, see Jakobi, 2020: 159–62) or if some actors claim to have better, 'more relevant' knowledge than other actors (see Krause, 2017: 91).

These answers, to sum up, outline two mechanisms by which some representations, rather than others, come to underpin the governance of issues. The answer favoured by realists emphasizes the isomorphism-fostering and innovation-driving effects of a common competitive environment that shapes the prevalent repertoire of comparative practices. The answer favoured by constructivist and practice theory scholars instead emphasizes political battles that give rise to temporarily dominant representations. The two mechanisms, though, are not mutually exclusive. As mentioned, realists acknowledge that there are limits to the effects of the competitive environment. If, however, multiple interpretations remain possible and plausible, then political battles can erupt over which representations are most relevant and the distribution of political and epistemic authority will be key to the outcome of these battles. Furthermore, the two mechanisms are probably not the only ones. Representations can become dominant through competitive processes, with some actors winning the competition over authority, or cooperatively through negotiations in which actors develop a shared set of comparative practices. Arms control is an example of such negotiation processes.

How do comparative practices shape security politics?

At first glance, research on comparisons in global security politics seems to be divided into two camps with contrasting perspectives on the effects of comparative practices. Research subscribing to the mapping tools approach treats security phenomena as independent of the comparative practice through which they are made knowable. Comparative practices can then prompt political action that manipulates security phenomena, but their effects are indirect and mediated through this political action. Research subscribing to the ordering tools approach assumes, by contrast, that knowledge practices – including comparative practices – co-produce the phenomena they purport to measure and analyse. The process of making security phenomena 'known' (Bueger, 2015) involves the definition of what counts as part of the phenomena – and what not – as well as the choice of particular ways of measuring, representing and assessing them. The knowledge practices thus turn the phenomena into governance objects, that is, distinct political issues that can be debated as well as ordered and manipulated through political action (see Allan, 2017). From this perspective, comparative practices have both direct and indirect effects: direct effects, both constitutive and enabling, by creating governance objects and indirect effects by prompting and steering political action that manipulates the phenomena.

At a second glance, therefore, while research on comparisons disagrees on whether or not comparative practices also co-*produce* the phenomena they observe, there is agreement that they have (at least indirect) *effects* on these phenomena. The joint debate can be structured around which effects occur under which conditions. Besides the turning of phenomena into governance objects, we propose to distinguish between at least three effects: the promotion of policies, the shaping of distributional outcomes and the manipulation of competitive dynamics.

Comparative practices can, first, influence whether and how issues are governed. They play a role in both agenda setting and the promotion of policies for dealing with security issues. By publishing statistics on, for instance, inequalities in the distribution of military capabilities, increases in piracy attacks or cyber incidents, political actors can both problematize these issues and raise public attention for them. Such statistics, moreover, help these actors to substantiate calls for political action, for example more military capabilities to redress the inequalities, more resources to combat piracy or new cybersecurity policies. These attempts are successful when they increase public attention for the issues and lead to changes in their governance.

Comparative practices can, second, shape the distributional outcomes that the governance – or non-governance – of issues generates. Governance involves the allocation of rights, duties and resources to different actors (see Fehl and Freistein, 2020) and comparative knowledge such as statistics are routinely used to decide on this allocation. Examples include the allocation of permanent seats to the group of great powers when the UN Security Council was established, the use of state fragility indices to decide on the distribution of development aid and the establishment of limits and ratios for major weapons in arms control treaties. All these cases involve choices for certain representations – of the hierarchy of powers, of the ranking of states in terms of their fragility, of the military balance – and these choices entail distributional consequences.

Comparative practices can, third, underpin and shape competitive dynamics. Competitions are central to the study of global security politics, whether in the form of rivalries, arms races or status competitions (see Mahnken et al, 2016; Renshon, 2017; Myatt, 2021). As contests over scarce goods, competitions would not work without comparative practices that represent the distribution of these goods. The effects of comparisons on competitive dynamics merit further research, though. For a start, some comparative practices seem more prone to fuel competitive dynamics than others. Notably, relative standards of comparisons are more likely to generate competitive dynamics than absolute ones (Towns and Rumelili, 2017). Moreover, while comparisons may drive competitions, they may also contribute to their taming. A prime example is arms control. Arms control agreements involve various kinds of comparison, from the evaluation of the stability and mutual acceptability of different distributions of military capabilities to the fixation of limits and ratios to the monitoring that the actual distribution of military capabilities stays within the agreed parameters.

These effects can occur in combination. When actors problematize a distribution of military capabilities by pointing at 'imbalances', they may generate political support for armament policies which in turn may give rise to or further escalate an arms race. When non-state actors shame the arms control policies of certain states, this may influence the reputation and status of these states which, in turn, may prompt them to adapt their policies in order to have a positive influence on their reputation and status (for the arms trade, see Erickson, 2015).

Before proceeding to outline the structure of the book, and in order to avoid misunderstanding, we wish to also emphasize what this book is *not* about: it is *not* a book about comparative methods, understood as either a general analytical tool across a wide range of disciplines (see Ragin, 2014), or more narrowly as a subdiscipline-defining tool such as in comparative politics (see Caramani, 2011). While some of the individual chapters draw on comparative methods to varying degrees, the book as a whole is not about them, but about the uses and effects of comparisons as a practice in security politics. This is where this book's novelty lies.

The structure of the book

Comparative practices and their effects may vary across both time and issues. Given how ubiquitous comparative practices are in global security politics, a book can only cover a sample of them. The present volume accounts for their variety in two ways: first, by exploring not only contemporary comparative practices, but past ones as well; second, by looking both at traditional security issues such as arms competition and arms control and at security issues that have gained in importance in global security politics over recent decades, such as maritime security, state fragility, global crime and cybersecurity.

The book is structured in three parts. Part I outlines several ways in which comparative practices can be analytically teased out and traced. Part II highlights that comparisons are not merely 'aspects of' security governance, but in fact constitute specific security governance objects. Part III shows how comparisons are not static practices, but reshape competitive dynamics. Needless to say, many contributions also address issues pertinent to the other parts of the book; their inclusion in one specific part rather than another simply reflects their primary focus.

Part I, 'Teasing Out Comparative Practices', starts with a chapter by *Paul Beaumont* that proposes an approach for grasping and analysing the comparisons that underpin status politics. Arguing that status research in IR tends to map status hierarchies rather than study their construction, he proposes to shift the analytical focus to the socially negotiated rules that underpin status competitions. Reconstructing the US debate on the Strategic Arms Limitation Talks (SALT) nuclear arms control negotiations in the 1970s, he highlights how assumptions about status comparisons were instrumental in the US shift from an acceptance of unequal numerical limits in SALT I to an insistence on equal numerical limits in SALT II.

In Chapter 3, *Bastian Giegerich* and *James Hackett* provide an insiders' account of the production of comparative knowledge on military capabilities. They discuss the history of one of the key publications on military capabilities, namely *The Military Balance* issued annually by the International Institute for Strategic Studies. They unpack the methodological questions underpinning the calculation of military expenditures and the counting of weapon systems. Moreover, they reflect on the drivers of the changes in comparative practices, highlighting, besides technological developments in weapon systems and geopolitical changes, the possibilities that new technologies offer for developing more sophisticated comparative practices, such as digital databases enabling quicker and more complex comparisons.

Gabi Schlag, in Chapter 4, turns to the visual dimension of comparative practices: the charts and maps that are used to visualize the distribution and deployment of military capabilities. She conceptualizes these visual representations as technical images and proposes a visual discourse analysis for probing into how they are used and (re)shape the discourse on security politics. To illustrate the approach, she analyses the visual elements in two pamphlets NATO published in the first half of the 1980s to substantiate its claims that there was an imbalance in the military balance in Europe and to legitimize its own military build-up as an attempt to redress this imbalance.

Chapter 5 proposes an experimental survey approach to teasing out politically relevant comparative knowledge. *Paul Musgrave* and *Steven Ward* study status comparisons in the field of space exploration and politics. They demonstrate how research on comparative practices can move past a focus on political elites and how an experimental survey approach can help to explicate the status comparisons of political audiences. Their findings suggest that status comparisons are influenced by a set of general and field-specific status markers and that they differ among groups within audiences.

After outlining the wide range of approaches through which comparative practices can be found in the security field, Part II, 'How Comparisons Constitute Governance Objects', demonstrates how objects of security governance are actually 'made' through comparative practices. In Chapter 6, *Christian Bueger* argues that the increasing political attention paid to maritime security is closely related to the emergence and proliferation of epistemic infrastructures that produce knowledge about trends in maritime incidents such as piracy. The databases that these epistemic infrastructures assemble form the basis for comparative practices that identify, analyse and emphasize trends in maritime incidents. There is, however, little standardization and consolidation taking place between the various epistemic infrastructures, which contributes to a messiness of the available comparative knowledge about trends in maritime incidents.

State fragility is another security issue that has gained considerable political attention in the past decades. In Chapter 7, *Keith Krause* shows that comparative practices have been integral to the discourse on the subject. Analysing four prominent attempts to map state fragility, he highlights how the related comparative practices promote and reify certain understandings of stability and fragility, thus contributing to the construction of state fragility as an object of security governance. In addition to ordering security politics, comparative practices have also had an impact on development politics, reshaping the patterns of development assistance.

In Chapter 8, *Anja Jakobi* and *Lena Herbst* explore the use of statistics in global crime governance. They show that the production of various forms of quantitative comparative knowledge has expanded over time, driven by a turn towards evidence-based policy making. Yet, the very nature of the governance object – the opacity of most crimes – makes it difficult to impossible to produce accurate statistics. The result is an array of inaccurate and incoherent statistics which often do not realistically map the crimes or the effectiveness of measures to combat them. The statistics are nonetheless used politically to order the governance of the crimes, including for decisions on which crimes are the most pressing problems and in need of more political action.

Madeleine Myatt and *Thomas Müller* study the comparative practices underpinning the governance object of cybersecurity in Chapter 9. They identify three clusters of publishers of comparative knowledge in the cybersecurity ecosystem, each with a distinct logic of comparison and focusing respectively on patterns of cyber threats, the cybersecurity capacities of states and their cyber power. They argue that two characteristics of the ecosystem help to explain the differences in the types of actors prevalent in each cluster: inequalities in resources, particularly those relating to the monitoring of cyber threats, as well as political struggles that effectively leave the second and third cluster to non-state actors.

Part III, 'How Comparisons Reshape Competitive Dynamics', zooms in on another key effect of comparative practices besides the constitution of governance objects: the impact on competitive dynamics that comparative practices have had in various historical periods. In Chapter 10, *Kerrin Langer* explores the comparative practices underpinning the naval arms competition in the late 19th and early 20th century. Focusing on Great Britain, France and Germany, she shows that comparative knowledge about the capabilities and relative standing of the various naval powers was used strategically to legitimize and delegitimize naval armament policies. The outcome was that naval power came to be regarded as a crucial status marker and, as a corollary, that concerns over relative standing fuelled naval arms competition among the great powers.

Chapter 11 looks at how comparative practices were used to tame competitive dynamics at the end of the Cold War. *Hans-Joachim Schmidt* teases out the comparative practices underpinning the negotiations for, and the renegotiation of, the Treaty on Conventional Forces in Europe in the late 1980s and early 1990s. He shows that the conclusion of the treaty involved a standardization of the comparative practices for the assessment of the conventional military balance in Europe. In addition, he highlights an interplay between comparative practices and geopolitical change. During the negotiations, the comparative practices were reworked – notably by replacing an alliance-to-alliance balance with national limits as a comparative framework – to manage the politico-military implications of reunification of Germany, the dissolution of the Warsaw Pact and the end of the Soviet Union.

Nike Retzmann in Chapter 12 explores how comparative practices contribute to the framing of technological developments as matters of competition. She focuses on recent US debates about the security political implications of the rise of artificial intelligence (AI) to highlight the interplay between narratives and comparative practices that imbues technological developments with competitive dynamics. For that purpose, she reconstructs the narratives promoted by the US National Security Commission on Artificial Intelligence and discusses their impact on subsequent US policy decisions. She shows how the commission reinforced a narrative of an AI arms race between the US and China that has come to shape US policy, thus further fuelling the competitive dynamics.

The concluding chapter reflects on the insights provided by the various chapters. It summarizes and synthesizes the arguments made by the chapters with regard to the three guiding questions. Taken together, the chapters show that traditional security issues and newer ones are – for all their differences – not so dissimilar in their production of comparative knowledge, the dynamics through which that knowledge gains political relevance and the effects that comparative practices have on global security politics.

References

Albert, M. (2016) *A Theory of World Politics*, Cambridge: Cambridge University Press.

Albert, M. and Langer, K. (2020) 'Die Geschichte des Streitkräftevergleichs in der internationalen Politik: Machtvergleiche und die Macht des Vergleichens', *Zeitschrift für Internationale Beziehungen*, 27(2): 34–64.

Allan, B.B. (2017) 'Producing the climate: states, scientists, and the constitution of global governance objects', *International Organization*, 71(1): 131–62.

Allan, B.B. (2018) *Scientific Cosmology and International Orders*, Cambridge: Cambridge University Press.

Andreas, P. and Greenhill, K.M. (eds) (2010) *Sex, Drugs, and Body Counts: The Politics of Numbers in Global Crime and Conflict*, Ithaca, NY: Cornell University Press.

Aradau, C. and Blanke, T. (2018) 'Governing others: anomaly and the algorithmic subject of security', *European Journal of International Security*, 3(1): 1–21.

Balzacq, T. (2008) 'The policy tools of securitization: information exchange, EU foreign and interior policies', *Journal of Common Market Studies*, 46(1): 75–100.

Beaumont, P. (2024) *The Grammar of Status Competition: International Hierarchies and Domestic Politics*, Oxford: Oxford University Press.

Berling, T.V. and Bueger, C. (eds) (2015) *Security Expertise: Practice, Power, Responsibility*, London: Routledge.

Berling, T.V., Gad, U.P., Petersen, K.L. and Wæver, O. (2022) *Translations of Security: A Framework for the Study of Unwanted Futures*, London: Routledge.

Broome, A. and Quirk, J. (2015) 'Governing the world at a distance: the practice of global benchmarking', *Review of International Studies*, 41(5): 819–41.

Bueger, C. (2015) 'Making things known: epistemic practices, the United Nations, and the translation of piracy', *International Political Sociology*, 9(1): 1–18.

Buzan, B. and Hansen, L. (2009) *The Evolution of International Security Studies*, Cambridge: Cambridge University Press.

Buzan, B., Wæver, O. and de Wilde, J. (1998) *Security: A New Framework for Analysis*, London: Lynne Rienner.

Caramani, D. (ed) (2011) *Comparative Politics*, 2nd edn, Oxford: Oxford University Press.

Davis, K.E., Kingsbury, B. and Merry, S.E. (2012) 'Indicators as a technology of global governance', *Law & Society Review*, 46(1): 71–104.

De Goede, M. (2018) 'The chain of security', *Review of International Studies*, 44(1): 24–42.

Desrosières, A. (2001) 'How real are statistics? Four possible attitudes', *Social Research*, 68(2): 339–55.

DiMaggio, P.J. and Powell, W.W. (1983) 'The iron cage revisited: institutional isomorphism and collective rationality in organizational fields', *American Sociological Review*, 48(2): 147–60.

Epple, A. and Erhart, W. (eds) (2015) *Die Welt beobachten: Praktiken des Vergleichens*, Frankfurt am Main: Campus.

Erickson, J.L. (2015) *Dangerous Trade: Arms Exports, Human Rights, and International Reputation*, New York, NY: Columbia University Press.

Espeland, W. and Stevens, M.L. (1998) 'Commensuration as a social process', *Annual Review of Sociology*, 24: 313–43.

Fearon, J.D. (1995) 'Rationalist explanations for war', *International Organization*, 49(3): 379–414.

Fehl, C. and Freistein, K. (2020) 'Organising global stratification: how international organisations (re)produce inequalities in international society', *Global Society*, 34(3): 285–303.

Friedberg, A.L. (1988) *The Weary Titan: Britain and the Experience of Relative Decline, 1895–1905*, Princeton, NJ: Princeton University Press.

Giegerich, B., Childs, N. and Hackett, J. (2018) 'Military Capability and International Status', 4 July, www.iiss.org/blogs/military-balance/2018/07/military-capability-and-international-status [Accessed 21 July 2021].

Glaser, C.L. (2010) *Rational Theory of International Politics*, Princeton, NJ: Princeton University Press.

Greenhill, K.M. (2010) 'Counting the cost: the politics of numbers in armed conflict', in A. Peters and K.M. Greenhill (eds) *Sex, Drugs, and Body Counts: The Politics of Numbers in Global Crime and Conflict*, Ithaca, NY: Cornell University Press, pp 127–158.

Guzzini, S. (2009) *On the Measure of Power and the Power of Measure in International Relations*, DIIS Working Paper, 28, Copenhagen: Danish Institute for International Studies.

Hagström, L. and Gustafsson, K. (2019) 'Narrative power: how storytelling shapes East Asian international politics', *Cambridge Review of International Affairs*, 32(4): 387–406.

Heintz, B. (2016) '"Wir leben im Zeitalter der Vergleichung": Perspektiven einer Soziologie des Vergleichs', *Zeitschrift für Soziologie*, 45(5): 305–23.

Homolar, A. (2015) 'Human security benchmarks: governing human wellbeing at a distance', *Review of International Studies*, 41(5): 843–63.

Jakobi, A.P. (2020) 'Wo endet wissenschaftliche Verantwortung für Daten und deren Effekte? Eine Problematisierung der Datenproliferation im Kontext politischer Entscheidungen', *Zeitschrift für Internationale Beziehungen*, 27(2): 153–66.

Jervis, R. (1988) 'War and misperception', *The Journal of Interdisciplinary History*, 18(4): 675–700.

Kelley, J.G. and Simmons, B.A. (2019) 'Introduction: the power of global performance indicators', *International Organization*, 73(3): 491–510.

Kelley, J.G. and Simmons, B.A. (eds) (2020) *The Power of Global Performance Indicators*, Cambridge: Cambridge University Press.

Krause, K. (2017) 'Bodies count: the politics and practices of war and violent death data', *Human Remains and Violence*, 3(1): 90–115.

Krebs, R.R. (2015) *Narrative and the Making of US National Security*, Cambridge: Cambridge University Press.

Lobell, S.E. (2018) 'A granular theory of balancing', *International Studies Quarterly*, 62(3): 593–605.

MacDonald, P.K. and Parent, J.M. (2021) 'The status of status in world politics', *World Politics*, 73(2): 358–91.

Mahnken, T., Maiolo, J. and Stevenson, D. (eds) (2016) *Arms Races in International Politics: From the Nineteenth to the Twenty-First Century*, Oxford: Oxford University Press.

Malito, D.V., Umbach, G. and Bhuta, N. (eds) (2018) *The Palgrave Handbook of Indicators in Global Governance*, Cham: Palgrave Macmillan.

May, E.R. (ed) (1984) *Knowing One's Enemies. Intelligence Assessment before the Two World Wars*, Princeton, NJ: Princeton University Press.

Müller, T. (2022) 'Self-binding via benchmarking: collective action, desirable futures, and NATO's two percent goal', *Global Society*, 36(2): 170–87.

Müller, T. and Albert, M. (2021) 'Whose balance? A constructivist approach to balance of power politics', *European Journal of International Security*, 6(1): 109–28.

Müller, T., Albert, M. and Langer, K. (2022) 'Practices of comparison and the making of international orders', *Journal of International Relations and Development*, 25(3): 834–59.

Myatt, M. (2021) 'Small, smart, powerful? Small states and the competition for cybertech security in the digital age', in D. Russ and J. Stafford (eds) *Competition in World Politics: Knowledge, Strategies and Institutions*, Bielefeld: Transcript, pp 233–60.

Neumann, I.B. and Sending, O.J. (2018) 'Expertise and practice: the evolving relationship between the study and practice of security', in A. Gheciu and W.C. Wohlforth (eds) *The Oxford Handbook of International Security*, Oxford: Oxford University Press, pp 29–40.

Paul, T.V., Welch Larson, D. and Wohlforth, W.C. (eds) (2014) *Status in World Politics*, Cambridge: Cambridge University Press.

Pouliot, V. (2016) *International Pecking Orders: The Politics and Practice of Multilateral Diplomacy*, Cambridge: Cambridge University Press.

Ragin, C. (2014) *The Comparative Method: Moving Beyond Qualitative and Quantitative Strategies*, Oakland, CA: The University of California Press.

Renshon, J. (2016) 'Status deficits and war', *International Organization*, 70(3): 513–550.

Renshon, J. (2017) *Fighting for Status: Hierarchy and Conflict in World Politics*, Princeton, NJ: Princeton University Press.

Røren, P. and Beaumont, P. (2019) 'Grading greatness: evaluating the status performance of the BRICS', *Third World Quarterly*, 40(3): 429–50.

Schlag, G. and Geis, A. (2017) 'Visualizing violence: aesthetics and ethics in international politics', *Global Discourse*, 7(2–3): 193–200.

Sending, O.J. (2015) *The Politics of Expertise: Competing for Authority in Global Governance*, Ann Arbor, MI: University of Michigan Press.

Steinmetz, W. (ed) (2019) *The Force of Comparison: A New Perspective on Modern European History and the Contemporary World*, New York, NY, Oxford: Berghahn.

Stoler, A.L. (2001) 'Tense and tender ties: the politics of comparison in North American history and (post) colonial studies', *The Journal of American History*, 88(3): 829–65.

Towns, A.E. and Rumelili, B. (2017) 'Taking the pressure: unpacking the relation between norms, social hierarchies, and social pressures on states', *European Journal of International Relations*, 23(4): 756–79.

Ward, S. (2017) *Status and the Challenge of Rising Powers*, Cambridge: Cambridge University Press.

Ward, S. (2020) 'Status, stratified rights, and accommodation in international relations', *Journal of Global Security Studies*, 5(1): 160–78.

Waltz, K.N. (1979) *Theory of International Politics*, New York, NY: McGraw-Hill.

Wohlforth, W.C. (1993) *The Elusive Balance: Power and Perceptions during the Cold War*, Ithaca, NY: Cornell University Press.

Zarakol, A. (2019) '"Rise of the rest": as hype and reality', *International Relations*, 33(2): 213–28.

Zürn, M. (2018) *A Theory of Global Governance: Authority, Legitimacy and Contestation*, Oxford: Oxford University Press.

PART I

Teasing Out Comparative Practices

2

The Construction of Status in Security Politics: Rules, Comparisons and Second-Guessing Collective Beliefs

Paul Beaumont

One of this volume's core analytical wagers is that bringing constructivist insights to bear on the comparative mapping practices within security politics will shed considerable new light on how these practices order international relations. This chapter's mandate in this endeavour is to explore and problematize how comparative knowledge underpins international status dynamics and thereby informs and shapes security politics.[1] In the process, the chapter will reflect upon International Relations (IR) status research's comparative practices. Status research is understood here as an umbrella term for all research that explores the causes and consequences of states' efforts to maintain or improve their position in international social hierarchies. This research agenda has proven highly successful over the course of the last decade in documenting how states often prioritize status over wealth or security (see Larson and Shevchenko, 2003; 2019; Deng, 2008; Wohlforth, 2009; de Carvalho and Neumann, 2014; Barnhart, 2017; Beaumont, 2017; Ward, 2017; Murray, 2018). However, this chapter will expand on the analytical costs of what the editors of this volume correctly highlight as status research's curious commitment to treating status hierarchies as a mind-independent phenomenon amenable to careful mapping (see also Müller et al, 2022).

---

[1]   This research was undertaken with the help of funding from the Research Council of Norway's WARU project (project number: 300923).

Indeed, the modus operandi of most – if not all (see Naylor, 2018; Dunton, 2020; Røren, 2023) – status research has been to map the status hierarchy on its subjects' behalf and attempt to identify whether a given state responds to the status hierarchy in a manner consistent with their preferred status theory (Zarakol, 2017: 7). While the proxies used by status researchers vary from the crude to the complex and a healthy, if contentious, debate has ensued about their validity (Duque, 2018; Røren and Beaumont, 2019; Ward, 2020; MacDonald and Parent, 2021; Buarque, 2023), these works assume that states know their status in the international hierarchy, even if they consider it unfair and wish to revise it (see Mercer, 2017). This underpins the methodological goal of identifying as accurately as possible this widely shared, mind-independent status hierarchy and exploring its systematic effects (Beaumont, 2024). As a result, although status research reconceptualizes the international structure in terms of *status* hierarchies, it typically shares the philosophical realism of the IR realist scholarship it typically seeks to contest.

That philosophical realism is so dominant within status research is curious because the latter's conventional definition of status is decidedly constructivist, or at the very least is highly amenable to constructivist inquiry: status treated as 'collective beliefs about a given state's ranking on valued attributes (wealth, coercive capabilities, culture, demographic position, socio-political organization, and diplomatic clout)' (Larson et al, 2014: 7). To the (thick) constructivist, these valued attributes do not come ready valued and thus imply that the quest for status also involves a battle over how status is assessed or status comparisons are made (Pouliot, 2014). Yet, as Paul Macdonald and Joseph Parent's (2021: 7) recent review essay complains, for all status researchers' differences their agenda lacks answers to the fundamental (constructivist) questions such as: 'Who decides which attributes are prized and how?' By jumping straight to the proxies they identify for policy makers, states and publics, status researchers further presume an intersubjective international agreement around the status hierarchy,[2] and foreclose the study of the multiple rival hierarchies that are in use and contested at the same time.[3] As a result, status research is dominated by a peculiarly *thin* constructivism that agrees that status is

---

[2] It should be noted that given collective beliefs are unobservable and famously difficult to measure, status research's commitment to philosophical realism bequeathed a formidable task. As Gilpin (1981: 33) noted, prestige is so difficult to assess that it was ultimately 'imponderable'.

[3] Some readers might object that social identity theory (see Larson and Shevchenko, 2003; 2010; 2019) captures this with social creativity. However, within its rendering, social creativity is a strategy for attempting to change a pre-existing status hierarchy that is widely shared, it does not imply that different actors understand the international hierarchy differently in the first place.

socially constructed, but eschews inquiring into the processes of social construction (Beaumont, 2024).

This chapter explores some of the unfortunate consequences of status research's philosophical realism, thin constructivism and commitment to *mapping* status hierarchies at the expense of studying their construction and contestation. Its goal is to show how this foreclosure can be fruitfully addressed by tapping into IR status research's own lineage, which can provide the theoretical warrant for studying international status dynamics via the rules underpinning status comparisons and thus status hierarchies. Such a move allows us to pose questions such as how do rules governing status competitions emerge, why do some rules become agreed upon and others contested, and what are the consequences of these processes of rule formation? While developing a framework for studying status dynamics through the production and contestation of rules requires an ontological gestalt switch for conventional status research (which has tended to focus on variance in motivations), this chapter argues that it is possible to do as much while remaining consistent with status research's core definition of status (collective beliefs about rank).

To make this case, the chapter proceeds in three steps. Section one takes stock of the existing status literature and identifies two common limitations that inhibit the elaboration of a (thick) constructivist – rule-centred – status approach: (1) the psychological underpinnings of much of IR's status research, which conceives of status as a discrete motivation distinct from security; and (2) the penchant for mapping status hierarchies and thereby eliding the study of the construction of international hierarchies. This bundle of assumptions, I argue, has also led many status researchers to draw an unnecessarily stark line between status and security explanations. I then show how Robert Gilpin's (1981) influential theorization of prestige can provide the basis for a constructivist account of status – one that does not treat status as a distinct motivation – even if this potential has largely been eschewed by those inspired by his framework. To bring out Gilpin's latent constructivism, section two then revisits an underappreciated chapter in Nicholas Onuf's *World of Our Making* to underline and conceptualize the rule-based nature of status comparisons and status hierarchies. When considered alongside Elena Esposito and David Stark's (2019) work on the social function of public rankings, the section elaborates why states may compete according to the rules embodied in public rankings even when they consider them to provide an inaccurate picture of reality. Taken together and put into security politics, these works provide a framework for studying how comparisons that ostensibly map the distribution of power can *become* co-constitutive of status hierarchies and how their symbolic function can *become* their strategic utility.

Section three illustrates the usefulness of this approach via a short historical vignette on the US's negotiating strategy during the Strategic Arms Limitation Talks (SALT) in the 1970s. Briefly put, I illustrate how over the course of the negotiations one questionable means of mapping the nuclear balance – in terms of aggregate launchers – *became* the benchmark by which the government expected domestic and international audiences to evaluate the treaty and assess the superpowers' status in the nuclear competition. Ultimately, the chapter shows how making the rules of comparison their analytical focus can enable status scholars to shed new light on core concerns of security studies – power maximization, extended deterrence and domestic legitimation – without needing to (necessarily) forgo their assumption that states are primarily motivated by security. Indeed, convincing one's allies and citizens that one is not losing the nuclear arms race is a rational goal for a security-maximizing state, even if it means competing in a symbolic competition. While the framework has broader applicability, I will suggest that it should prove particularly useful for negotiating the well-known methodological difficulty of differentiating status from security concerns.

From motivations and mapping to rules and ordering

Contemporary status scholarship in IR has many predecessors and relates to security in different and often contradictory ways. For those grounded in social identity theory and psychology, status is a distinct motivation that prompts states to pursue foreign policies that go against their security or economic interests (Barnhart, 2017; 2020; Larson and Shevchenko, 2019). Similarly, those that ground their theory in Thorstein Veblen's sociology contend that status symbols are constituted by visible, reckless waste (Gilady, 2018) as opposed to prudent or rational utilities. Meanwhile, others draw upon classic political philosophers – for example Hobbes, Machiavelli, Thucydides and Rousseau – to posit that glory, honour or pride are timeless human passions (for example de Carvalho and Neumann, 2014; Gilady, 2017). These approaches differ in vocabularies and frameworks, but they share the assumption that states place an *intrinsic* value on their status in the international system: actors value status for its own sake. Since status re-emerged as a theoretical and empirical research agenda in the 2000s (Larson and Shevchenko, 2003; Wohlforth, 2009; Volgy et al, 2011), the dominant methodological modus operandi for these approaches has been to show how policies that make little sense from a conventional rational perspective, can readily be explained if one assumes status as a *motivation*. Status is thus usually *juxtaposed* with security and deemed a dangerous and irrational pursuit, one that states would be wise to forgo or at least temper. This strand of status research has quickly established how a great deal of international politics makes a lot more sense if one assumes big, small, middling, rising and declining powers are all partly driven by status concerns.

The problem with this agenda is not the lack of compelling evidence, but how the status/material interest[4] binary curtails more sociological inquiries into the status hierarchy itself and focuses instead on parsing the motivations of the actors within it (Beaumont, 2024).[5] Using the same conventional definition of status – social position in ranking defined by collective beliefs – it is possible to identify status hierarchies (and their consequences) while remaining ambivalent about whether any actor responding to the hierarchy in question is motivated by status or something else. To take an easy example, the Olympic games provides a paradigmatic example of international status competition: players (representing nation states) are ranked in a hierarchy of position based on their performance in various activities requiring skill. 'Status' will assuredly motivate some of those taking part, but it need not: some may compete for the material prizes (sponsorship, government funding), others to please their pushy parents; meanwhile, the state governments involved may not care about status themselves but recognize that their electorates do and invest accordingly (see Ward, 2017). Whatever the motivation for taking part, it has little to say about whether the status hierarchies that result from the games are indeed status hierarchies (collective beliefs about rank). What is interesting about the Olympics is not that it is a particularly important case, but that, because it is self-consciously designed to be a well-functioning status competition, the crucial constitutive features of a status competition are so visible: rules (Beaumont, 2024). Indeed, it is the rules of the game(s) that define a status hierarchy and status competition, not the motivation of players involved. At a minimum, this implies that beyond parsing variance in status motivation (see Renshon, 2017), we could potentially study other sorts of status competition through variance in the rules of the game. After all, although Olympic rules are institutionalized and therefore mostly stable, the rules in most international status competitions are not. The major advantage of studying status competitions through the rules of the game would be that it avoids trapping status research in the dastardly difficult quest to ascertain motivations.

While psychological theories of status assume it to be a distinct motivation that can be parsed from more conventional material motivations, the realist-inspired wing of status research emerging from 19th-century Realpolitik avoids this pitfall. This strand of scholarship posits status (or in its terminology,

---

[4] Often but not always conflated with the rational/irrational binary and warning against the wasteful pursuit of status (see Mercer, 2017).

[5] See Towns (2010), Pouliot (2014), Naylor (2018; 2022), Beaumont (2021), Dunton (2020) and Røren (2023) for notable exceptions to this tendency.

'prestige') to be *instrumentally* valuable to states as a means to an end. That is, states do not care about status for its own sake, but because it helps them pursue other interests. The seminal work in this school is Gilpin's *War and Change in World Politics* (1981), in which prestige is defined as 'reputation for power'. Although this conception is sometimes trivialized as merely an intervening variable, for Gilpin (1981: 31) the intervening it does is fairly crucial: 'Prestige, rather than power, is the everyday currency of international relations, much as authority is the central ordering feature of domestic society.' Prestige is 'enormously important' because 'if your strength is recognized, you can generally achieve your aims without having to use it' (Gilpin, 1981: 31). Those with high prestige can expect others to defer to them and accommodate their interests without the need for the use of force or even explicit threats. Put differently, being secretly powerful would be extremely inefficient in world politics because it would require a state to use, prove and thus exert resources to get its way. As the famous movie *Dr Strangelove* attests, even a doomsday machine cannot influence enemies' behaviour if kept a secret. While the instrumentalist school has primarily been concerned with hierarchies of prestige narrowly defined in terms of reputation power, the instrumentalist logic can also be applied to other domains: wherever a state enjoys a prestigious position, that position may come with instrumentally valuable trappings that may provide part of the motivation for seeking it in the first place. Ultimately, this school posits that high status within a hierarchy of one's peers can provide tangible benefits.

As this short discussion indicates, the Gilpin school of status research enables the way in which prestige – 'reputation for power' – is determined, is earned and informs world politics to be investigated without being tied to status as a distinct motivation driving anyone or any state seeking it. However, Gilpin's initial theorization to some extent pre-structured and prematurely narrowed this agenda by asserting that 'prestige was ultimately imponderable' and could only be settled by war, which would then temporarily clarify the hierarchy of power. Hence, prestige scholarship has largely been preoccupied by studying how wars have been waged to retain or pursue status/prestige (see Mercer, 2017, for a critical discussion). For instance, Jonathan Renshon (2017) claims that states that suffer from a mismatch between material power and status recognition have been more prone to wage war to remedy their 'status deficit' over the last 200 years. Moreover, he suggests that waging war has generally proven effective at improving recognition and therefore is a rational strategy for a status-concerned state. Notwithstanding the debates about the empirical merits of this research (see Røren and Beaumont, 2019; Ward, 2020), taking inspiration from Gilpin, these works have generally paid less attention to how hierarchies of prestige are constructed, and even organized and maintained in peacetime, by establishing agreed upon public rankings of power and thus prestige.

This is beginning to be redressed. In perhaps the most significant restatement of this research agenda, Yuen Foong Khong (2019) argues that Chinese and American rivalry is better understood as a competition for prestige rather than security. As Khong (2019: 120) explains, China 'seeks the top seat in the hierarchy of prestige, and the United States will do everything in its power to avoid yielding that seat, because the state with the greatest reputation for power is the one that will govern the region'. This competition is not explained by reference to psychology but because the winner 'will attract more followers, regional powers will defer to and accommodate it, and it will play a decisive role in shaping the rules and institutions of international relations' (Khong, 2019: 120). Notably, Khong suggests that this competition is not 'imponderable' but can be assessed with careful mapping of relevant indicators. He goes on to suggest that the Asia Power Index provides the most comprehensive measure available for assessing prestige in the region:

> [The] Asia Power Index (API) may have succeeded in meeting these challenges [of measuring power/influence] *better than most*. Published in May 2018, the API is a remarkably comprehensive and rigorous ranking of the overall power of 25 Asian countries (including the United States and Russia). Countries are assessed along eight weighted dimensions: economic resources (20 per cent), military capability (20 per cent), resilience (7.5 per cent), future trends (7.5 per cent), diplomatic influence (10 per cent), economic relationships (15 per cent), defence networks (10 per cent) and cultural influence (10 per cent). (Khong, 2019: 126, emphasis added)

While the API may indeed provide a useful window into the relative prestige of countries in Asia, Khong (2019: 122–3) remains uninterested in why particular indicators of military power become important or crucial as measure of status/prestige or why each indicator was weighted in the way it was. Moreover, and in line with the assumption of 'mapping' comparisons discussed in the introduction, he elides the potential ordering effects of picking one indicator (and thus one principle of comparison) over another, and presumes the existence of an invisible hierarchy of power and prestige that could theoretically be evaluated for accuracy. To reemphasize, there is nothing wrong with such philosophically realist efforts at mapping prestige, but it is also quite possible that such efforts may themselves influence and even co-constitute the status hierarchies they purport to measure.

Indeed, while the API is probably not yet sufficiently significant to have much in the way of ordering effects, as Kerrin Langer's chapter in this volume reveals, power-mapping practices have been quite influential in structuring the competition for reputation for power (prestige). Indeed, Langer documents how early 20th-century great powers semi-institutionalized a ranking for assessing sea power in terms of number of battleships and tonnage that stood in as a workable and generally agreed upon proxy for power. By virtue of its conventional usage by other powers, this ranking could therefore provide not only a map of the material capabilities of other states, but a reasonable proxy for reputation for power (prestige) as well. Hence, what this metric may have lacked in terms of utility for assessing outcomes in war (it elided the value of submarines, for example), it made up for in providing a shared standard for assessing and thereby ordering the hierarchy of prestige, thus serving the purpose of indicating who should defer to whom without recourse to war. The downside, of course, was that these rules structured and thereby enabled an intense arms race in battleships, and due to its privileging of their number and tonnage as rules of comparison, an ostensibly excessive number of heavy and highly costly ones.

Who sets the rules of the game?

Ultimately, despite the necessary *ontological* centrality of comparisons in status and prestige seeking, status scholarship has devoted relatively little analytical attention to studying how states actually compare their status (Mercer, 2017). Rather, as the introductory chapter notes, status researchers tend to ascertain the nature of the status hierarchies without studying how states and other actors themselves go about assessing status. Hence, while these scholars often insist that status is perceptual, intersubjective and cultural (see Renshon, 2017: 33–7), they nonetheless – often tacitly – assume (1) that states agree about the rules of the game and (2) that, as observers, they can ascertain those rules without too much ado. Hence, Renshon measures 'objective status' over 200 years via the CINC measure, meanwhile Khong (2019) suggests without critical reflection that the API can serve the same purpose. The result is that contemporary status scholarship is dominated by a thin constructivism that presumes that rules governing international status hierarchies are sufficiently stable and agreed upon for us to be able to study their independent effects – the status seeking it incentivizes – while bracketing the processes of social construction that produce the status hierarchies in the first place. An unfortunate side effect of the tendency for status scholars to map status hierarchies on behalf of the agents of world politics prior to analysis is that both the intrinsic and the instrumental school have largely neglected to empirically investigate or theorize how actors engage in mapping international status (see Mercer, 2017), let alone whether and how those efforts at mapping produce ordering effects. This is unfortunate because, as the editors of this volume note in their introductory chapter, 'status hierarchies only exist if there is a socially shared practice of comparing status'.

Studying the rules of status competitions

The previous section has undertaken a ground-clearing exercise. It has shown how psychological approaches to status use an analytical strategy that relies upon establishing status as an intrinsic motivation, distinct from security and other material motivations. It then identified how Gilpin's conception of status as instrumentally useful provided an alternative that could escape this binary (status/material motivations). However, Gilpin-inspired approaches have largely eschewed studying how reputations for power are co-constituted by comparative practices that pretend to merely map. Yet, as Langer in this volume illustrates, these mapping practices can and do influence the object of their assessments by providing a conventionalized – and thus well-shared – understanding of what counts as power. The following section sets out to show how we can study both the social construction of mapping practices and understand how and why they can generate ordering effects. This can be done by marrying the Gilpin's instrumentalism with an analytical focus on the rules governing any given status competition and on how and why these rules are liable to become conventionalized in public rankings. For the first I draw upon Onuf's unfortunately overlooked chapter on standing in *World of Our Making*, before turning to Esposito and Stark's theorization of why even inaccurate rankings serve useful purposes for status assessments.

To begin, let us first sketch out Onuf's theorization of the rule-governed nature of interests, which can enable us to differentiate the rules governing status comparisons from other kinds of comparison. For Onuf, at the highest level of abstraction there are only three possible interests and these align with three possible *grounds of comparison*: what he calls internal, binary and global comparisons. The first, internal comparison, should be immediately familiar as the liberal preference for absolute gains and what Onuf calls an interest in *wealth*. Though by 'wealth' he does not mean just money, but anything of value one can desire and enjoy more of: money, love, knowledge or anything else. For Onuf (1989: 266), this involves comparing 'any state of affairs in which other people's attributes, preferences, choices count only as a resource for or obstacle to choice'. For instance, a husband wishing to decide whether to eat porridge or a croissant for breakfast will need to order his preferences, whether it be via taste, cost, health or some other concern. To make this order he needs some kind of rule of comparison, otherwise his preference will be random. What makes this *internal*, for Onuf, is that others only feature in the comparison as an obstacle or a resource: the husband's partner may pay (provide resources) for or oppose or endorse one or other breakfast, but that has no necessary relationship to the ordering of preferences in the first place; what others prefer need not be taken into account. Onuf's second ground of comparison is binary, which Onuf labels interest in *security*. Here, the grounds for comparison are associated with a realist understanding of relative gains vis-à-vis a single opponent. Here, clearly, one cannot know how much one needs without comparing oneself with the significant other on the relevant criteria.

Finally, and most pertinently, Onuf theorizes that concern for standing must always be founded upon *global comparison*. By 'global' Onuf means a comparison with more than one other entity, rather than one that is global in the geographic sense. This mode of rationality can be understood as analogous to an Olympics: one seeks to do better than the other(s) at a given game with the ultimate goal of being best. Like binary comparison, this mode of rationality is necessarily relational: one cannot aim to be better or best at something without reference to one or more other participants. However, unlike binary comparison, this mode of rationality requires the construction of a ranking system: 'The set, or whole, then consists of a series of positions occupying a complete and transitive ordering: first place, second place … last place. Furthermore, the places in such an ordering come with cardinal values. … Only now can she say: I want to be best' (Onuf, 1989: 267). While also relational, unlike binary comparison, global comparison does not involve wanting what the other has in a zero-sum game, but to want to do better than others in some socially valuable thing(s). In order to say that state X is number one in power, democracy or fly-fishing, one needs to have some criteria: is it most tanks or missiles, most fish or biggest fish that matters? Moreover, in order for the hierarchy to be a *social* hierarchy and for one to be able to plausibly strategize to move up and avoid moving down, some degree of intersubjective agreement on those rules of comparison will be required. Hence, Onuf explicates how any status hierarchy – defined by collective beliefs to do with rank – necessarily depends upon some shared understanding of the rules of comparison. If there were no rules underpinning high/low status, one would not know how to compete for it (Onuf, 1989: 267) and status seeking would be a crapshoot.

Onuf allows us to rephrase the question facing status researchers: 'How can we ascertain collective beliefs?' to 'How are the rules governing "collective beliefs" about rank formed? How do these "collectives", whoever they are and wherever they may be, construct their ranking system?' The difficulty of this task for any single individual may at first make the researcher despair; how can we empirically investigate how these people construct their systems for global comparison. But it is precisely the difficulty involved in constructing a ranking – selecting the right rules or gathering the evidence – that gives rise to the shortcuts provided by society. We tend not to do it ourselves but instead outsource the task and rely upon conventions, that is, socially standardized modes of comparison: for instance, GDP is a widely accepted means of ranking states according to wealth or development, even though many if not most of those using it would agree that it is an imperfect measure. If one simply wanted accuracy, one might be tempted to develop one's own bespoke system of comparison that departed from the convention. Yet, utilizing a bespoke ranking system in a world where others respond to and act on the basis of the conventional ranking is potentially costly: for instance, if other states use tonnage to assess naval power while one state cleverly pioneers a ranking based on submarines, that state's cleverness may lead it into avoidable conflict as others seek to exploit its apparent weakness by conventional standards. It pays to follow the herd in other words, and public, conventionalized rankings provide a window into the herd's collective beliefs.

Indeed, Esposito and Stark (2019) highlight the broader social function of public rankings (rather than to accurately map reality), which can account for the persistent popularity of inaccurate rankings. For them (2019: 4), public rankings are not popular because they adequately describe the 'independent world (for which they are inevitably flawed …)' but because they 'provide an orientation about what *others* observe'. Indeed, they contend that public ranking systems – especially conventional ones – are best understood as social technologies that allow us to ascertain – or second-guess with confidence – audience beliefs. While Esposito and Stark do not make the link explicit, they provide grounds for believing that international rankings – when conventionalized – operate as a window into collective beliefs about a state's status in the phenomenon that the ranking purports to measure. Moreover, if the herd's assessment can help or harm the rankees, then they would have a Gilpinian interest in pursuing a position in that ranking even if they know it to be inaccurate. Hence, from a status perspective, when mappers debate the accuracy of widely recognized power rankings, they miss the point: it is not the accuracy of the measure but the *extent* of its *use – where, by whom and for what purpose* – that makes it valuable for ascertaining '*collective* beliefs' about rank. Ultimately, Onuf and Esposito and Stark provide a theoretical warrant for studying status hierarchies – and their effects – via the prevalence, contestation and conventionalization of concrete public modes of comparison and ranking.

The US's SALT strategy: how status became security

To illustrate how public efforts at mapping objective hierarchies conventionalize the rules of comparison enabling actors to make educated and consequential guesses about status, I turn to the case of the Strategic Arms Limitation Talks (SALT). In particular, the case study explores the backstage process through which the United States determined its negotiating position from SALT I to SALT II and specifically how it determined which rules – grounds of comparison – to assess the nuclear balance by, and how and why it settled upon aggregate number of launchers. Besides practical reasons, the US side of the negotiation is selected because it provides a harder case for my approach: Russia's status obsession is already well documented, whereas the US has received considerably less attention. Moreover, although I would argue that the high visibility, public salience and exclusivity of nuclear weapons makes arms control likely to become imbricated with status concerns, security scholars tend to contend that the high politics of arms control is dominated by hardheaded strategic analysis. Therefore, if the rules the US used to assess the strategic balance when forming their negotiating strategy were dictated by third-party audiences rather than their own strategic analysis, then it would help convince security scholars that similar processes could be at work in lower politics too.

SALT was premised upon the idea that the superpowers shared an interest in reducing the risk of nuclear war by implementing more stable force structures and reducing the costs of strategic arms racing that would leave neither side safer, only poorer. The SALT processes spanned a decade and three presidencies (Richard Nixon's, Gerald Ford's and Jimmy Carter's) and initially seemed successful. 'SALT I' led to the signing and ratification in 1972 of the ABM treaty (Treaty between the United States of America and the Union of the Soviet Socialist Republics on the Limitation of Anti-Ballistic Missile Systems), which limited each side to two anti-ballistic missile sites apiece, and the 'Interim Agreement' (Interim Agreement between The United States of America and The Union of Soviet Socialist Republics on Certain Measures with respect to the Limitation of Strategic Offensive Arms), which froze for five years the level of submarine-launched ballistic missiles (SLBMs) and land-based intercontinental ballistic missiles (ICBMs) at 1972 levels. The SALT II process would eventually lead to the SALT Treaty (Treaty between the United States of America and the Union of Soviet Socialist Republics on the Limitation of Strategic Offensive Arms), which limited both sides to 2,250 strategic nuclear missiles, and 1,320 missiles equipped with multiple re-entry vehicles (MIRVs). However, the SALT II Treaty took over six years and three US presidents to negotiate and, while it was eventually signed in 1979, it never reached the Senate for ratification because the administration cancelled the vote following the Soviet invasion of Afghanistan. The conventional story has it that SALT II was hamstrung by fears of cheating, a mutual obsession with letting the other side achieve relative gains and thereby enabling them to gain political or military advantages in crisis situations. If this were the case, we would expect that the negotiations strategy of the United States would use systems of comparison by which to assess dyadic outcomes: political (the ability to make the other side back down) or military (for example, the ability to 'win' a nuclear war).

Instead, as I have shown in my research elsewhere (Beaumont, 2024), although the Americans did strive for relative military advantages, in SALT II they prioritized achieving equality in the number of nuclear launchers. While at first blush this might appear like the same thing: was prioritizing the number of launchers not the same thing as seeking military advantages (or avoiding disadvantages)? Not exactly. But to understand why is to recover the reason why this mode of comparison (launchers) was ultimately settled upon as the most important means of measuring equality. First of all, it is important to clarify that this method of measuring the balance was only one of several plausible candidates. As Henry Kissinger pointed out early in the process of SALT II, equality could mean several different things:

> Everyone agrees that one of our most fundamental objectives in SALT Two is equality. The real question is, how do we define equality. Do we mean (1) equality in first-strike capability, (2) equality in second-strike capability, (3) equality in numbers of launchers and re-entry vehicles, or (4) equality in assured destruction capability. (FRUS, 1973: 50)

In fact, during SALT I talks, as national security advisor to the president, Henry Kissinger strongly opposed demands for an agreement with equal numerical aggregates. He argued that not only did the various US capabilities that fell outside the agreement (MIRVS, forward-based systems such as bombers in Europe) offset any numerical disparity, but, given that the US lacked plans to build either new SLBMs or ICBMs, any freeze on the Soviet side would be to the US's advantage. Kissinger would defend SALT I along similar lines throughout SALT II. Thus, it was better to limit the Soviets than do nothing; the US would make relative gains regardless of the perception of inequality. Ultimately, the military did not get their way: the interim agreement that emerged out of SALT I froze the SLBMs and ICBMs at levels whereby the US were permitted fewer submarine and land-based launches. Kissinger would see this result as a remarkable negotiating feat. As he put it, the US had not been 'stopped' from doing anything they had planned, while the Soviet's build-up had been halted. In fact, Kissinger considered it 'miraculous' that the US had managed to limit submarines and ICBMs 'when we had next to no chips' (FRUS, 1972: 957). Here we can clearly see how Kissinger's concern for relative gains did not necessarily mean being allowed more launchers than the Soviets under the treaty or even the same number, but was calculated relative to what would have transpired without a treaty.

Yet, disquiet among allies and domestic opposition to SALT I became increasingly apparent through the negotiations of SALT II. The result was that, despite Kissinger still doubting the merit of insisting on equal aggregate launchers, the US ultimately made this the hill it would die on in the negotiations. While he might well have had other motivations, Secretary of Defense James R. Schlesinger was vociferous in making the case for insisting on equal aggregates for SALT II. Crucially, he did not emphasize the strategic case for equality of numbers, but leant instead upon the presumed opposition of domestic critics, who, he asserted, considered numbers of launchers the crucial measure of equality:

> Inherently, this kind of decision is simple to make. The question is whether militarily, diplomatically, and politically, you want to move rapidly toward the Soviet proposal of giving the U.S. inferiority in numbers. This would be very difficult to justify. Unequal numbers would not have much Congressional support, and would violate the Jackson Amendment which requires equal numbers. It would be difficult to persuade the American public that any position other than equal aggregates, especially as our going-in position, is the correct one. (FRUS, 1974b: 330)

Note the role of the Jackson Amendment here in providing a plausible window into how domestic audiences would assess the balance and therefore a window into how the US reputation for nuclear power among domestic audiences would be affected by the agreement. It was named after the hawkish senator, Henry Jackson, who had publicly spoken out against the SALT I Interim Agreement's provisions, arguing that the freeze froze the United States into a position of 'sub-parity' and would put the United States at a disadvantage (*New York Times*, 1972). Jackson thus sought to attach a Congressional understanding to the interim agreement. The Jackson Amendment, as it became known, demanded that any future SALT agreement must have 'equal numbers of intercontinental strategic launchers taking account of throw weight'.

While the amendment itself was non-binding and the government would later consider breaching it, by accepting the amendment, they legitimated the criterion of aggregate number of launchers as a means of comparing the nuclear powers arsenals in SALT II, and therefore of how equality should be assessed. Hence, despite its inadequacy as a measure of nuclear balance, which Schlesinger and other advocates of equal launchers freely admitted backstage (for example, FRUS 1974b: 332; FRUS, 1974c: 374), it served the purpose that Esposito and Stark (2019) attribute to public rankings: providing an 'orientation about what *others* observe', in this case what, or perhaps *how* domestic audiences would assess the outcome of a future strategic arms limitation treaty. Indeed, Jackson's amendment was frequently used as a reference point and evidence for gauging how domestic audiences would assess a treaty (see FRUS 1974a: 364; 1974b: 330).

However, numerical equality was not the only grounds of comparison the administration expected the domestic audience to use to assess SALT II, the fallout from SALT I led them to believe it was how their allies would assess the treaty. For instance, during his backstage campaign for prioritizing numerical equality in launchers, Schlesinger recounted a conversation he had had with the Japanese minister of defence about SALT I, as evidence for why equal aggregates were crucial: 'He asked me why we accepted an unequal agreement in 1972. I answered him that we had a technological advantage. But this is to point out that the perception is there in third parties' (FRUS, 1974a: 364). But, Schlesinger went on, it was not only the Japanese, 'there is a problem of *appearance* in Europe. The agreement is perceived as unequal' (FRUS, 1974a: 364, emphasis added). Backing up Schlesinger, the Joint Chiefs of Staff (JCS) frequently emphasized the importance of perceptions of equality rather than the importance of equality per se. As the backstage debate surrounding how to assess equality heated up, Schlesinger expressed the priority of diplomatic and political advantages even more bluntly. For instance, rounding off his contribution to one acrimonious National Security Council (NSC) meeting on SALT II he argued that '[on] the question of equal aggregates, it is politically and diplomatically crucial. Perhaps, *it is the most critical feature.* We can live with an increase in instability, but it would be difficult not to come up to their level' (FRUS 1974a: 367, emphasis added). Finally, Presidents Ford and Nixon both also raised concerns about how various audiences would interpret any deal that did not appear equal. At an NSC meeting in 1973, President Nixon asserted that the US must take into account how SALT '*appear[s]* to other countries, since this is what affects our foreign policy' (FRUS, 1973: 50, emphasis added).

Hence, between SALT I and SALT II equality in aggregates *became* a priority in the negotiations and this was justified primarily in reference to how key audiences would assess the outcome of the treaty. As I have highlighted elsewhere (Beaumont, 2024), the prioritization of exact equality of aggregates, against their own strategic assessments, slowed down negotiations and removed a bargaining chip from both hawks, who aspired to limit the Soviet heavy bombers, and doves, who wished to achieve significant cuts in the arsenals.

Conclusion

The preceding discussion and vignette have sought to speak to the volume's core theoretical concerns: how can comparative knowledge become salient in international security politics, and how and why should IR research foreground comparative practices? First, the vignette illustrated how public efforts at objectively mapping the nuclear balance – by counting launchers – could be turned into a rule for making educated guesses about the status implications of a potential SALT agreement. Indeed, as we saw, the Japanese foreign minister's view of SALT I and the Jackson Amendment served as compelling evidence backstage to predict what rule of comparison domestic and international audiences would use to assess the nuclear balance in the wake of an agreement. They thus provided a plausible window into how the status implications of any treaty would vary according to how the agreement performed according to this rule of comparison. Second, the fact that equality in launchers only *emerged* as the key rule of comparison out of the backlash against SALT I indicates the value of historically investigating how mapping practices become constituted as reference points for status. Conversely, it illuminates the danger of attempting to retrospectively use the same proxy for status across time and space, as some large N status scholarship has been wont to do (see Volgy et al, 2011; Renshon, 2017). Third, on the advantages of studying status through comparative practices, the chapter has argued that foregrounding how rules of comparison for status emerge, change or are contested enables us to study status dynamics without needing to parse security and status motivations. Indeed, although the US side's eventual prioritization of equality in launchers was explicitly legitimated by reference to domestic and international audiences, this certainly does not rule out security as a motivation.[6] Convincing their domestic audiences and allies that the US did not 'lose' as a result of the SALT II Treaty would be consistent with a motivation for security broadly understood. To paraphrase Gilpin, the US was merely maximizing the everyday currency of international politics.

Finally, this chapter also allows us to mount a defence of the dogmatic army general of popular imagination. Generals are always preparing to fight the last war, the old aphorism runs. As conservative as they are dogmatic, they prepare to attack on horses when they should practise sitting in trenches. This tendency is usually deemed at best inefficient and at worst tragic. Yet, the preceding analysis can shine a more sympathetic light on our imaginary generals. Deterring enemies requires they appreciate the implications of waging war. Maintaining allies requires they appreciate the *potential* of one's military power. Indeed, deterrence and deference do not depend upon what would *really* happen in war. Instead, they are social outcomes: they depend upon what others expect would occur and this may not be the same thing. If your enemies and allies are preparing for the last war, then deterrence of the enemy and ally loyalty will require the prudent general to do so too. Indeed, although the US military and Secretary of Defense accepted that the relative aggregate number of launchers was a suboptimal means of assessing the nuclear balance and the treaty, they could

---

[6]   Nor does it mean that the protagonists involved did not have ulterior motives. For instance, General Snowcroft wrote to Kissinger that he suspected 'that the JCS don't want an agreement and will pursue any convenient argument to prevent it' (FRUS, 1976: 572).

not afford to ignore it because this was the system of comparison by which international and domestic audiences evaluated the military position. In short, the US generals had to prepare for the last war *and* the next war at the same time.

References

Beaumont, P. (2017) 'Brexit, retrotopia and the perils of post-colonial delusions', *Global Affairs*, 3(4–5): 379–90.

Beaumont, P. (2021) *Performing Nuclear Weapons: How Britain Made Trident Make Sense*, Cham: Palgrave Macmillan.

Beaumont, P. (2024) *The Grammar of Status Competition: International Hierarchies and Domestic Politics*, Oxford: Oxford University Press.

Barnhart, J. (2017) 'Humiliation and third-party aggression', *World Politics*, 69(3): 532–68.

Barnhart, J. (2020) *The Consequences of Humiliation: Anger and Status in World Politics*, Ithaca, NY: Cornell University Press.

Buarque, D. (2023) *Brazil's International Status and Recognition as an Emerging Power Inconsistencies and Complexities*, Cham: Palgrave Macmillan.

De Carvalho, B. and Neumann, I.B. (eds) (2014) *Small State Status Seeking: Norway's Quest for International Standing*, London: Routledge.

Deng, Y. (2008) *China's Struggle for Status: The Realignment of International Relations*, Cambridge: Cambridge University Press.

Duque, M.G. (2018) 'Recognizing international status: a relational approach', *International Studies Quarterly*, 62(3): 577–92.

Dunton, C. (2020) 'Willing to serve: empire, status, and Canadian campaigns for the United Nations Security Council (1946–1947)', *International Journal*, 75(4): 529–47.

Esposito, E. and Stark, D. (2019) 'What's observed in a rating? Rankings as orientation in the face of uncertainty', *Theory, Culture & Society*, 36(4): 3–26.

Foreign Relations of the United States (FRUS) (1972) '327: Conversation among President Nixon, Senator John Stennis, the President's Assistant for National Security Affairs (Kissinger), the Assistant to the President (Haldeman), and the President's Deputy Assistant for Legislative Affairs (Korologos) Washington, June 13, 1972', pp 957–61 in FRUS 1969–1976, vol. 32, SALT I, 1969–1972.

FRUS (1973) '14: Minutes of a Meeting of the National Security Council Washington, March 8, 1973, 10:10–11:30 p.m.', pp 45–60 in FRUS 1969–1976, vol. 33, SALT II, 1972–1980.

FRUS (1974a) '81: Minutes of a Meeting of the National Security Council Washington, October 18, 1974, 3:40–5:45 p.m.', pp 349–67 in FRUS 1969–1976, vol. 33, SALT II, 1972–1980.

FRUS (1974b) '77: Minutes of a Meeting of the National Security Council Washington, October 7, 1974, 2:55–4:35 p.m.', pp 321–37 in FRUS 1969–1976, vol. 33, SALT II, 1972–1980.

FRUS (1974c) '85: Memorandum from the President's Assistant for National Security Affairs (Kissinger) to President Ford Washington, undated' [c. 27 October 1974], pp 373–79 in FRUS 1969–1976, vol. 33, SALT II, 1972–1980.

FRUS (1976) '120. Message from the President's Assistant for National Security Affairs (Scowcroft) to Secretary of State Kissinger Washington, January 22, 1976', pp 570–2 in FRUS 1969–1976, vol. 33, SALT II, 1972–1980.

Gilady, L. (2017) 'Triangle or "trilemma": Rousseau and the "Kantian Peace"', *Journal of International Relations and Development*, 20(1): 135–61.

Gilady, L. (2018) *The Price of Prestige: Conspicuous Consumption in International Relations*, Chicago, IL: University of Chicago Press.

Gilpin, R. (1981) *War and Change in World Politics*, Cambridge: Cambridge University Press.

Khong, Y.F. (2019) 'Power as prestige in world politics', *International Affairs*, 95(1): 119–42.

Larson, D.W., Paul, T.V. and Wohlforth, W.C. (2014) 'Status and world order', in T.V. Paul, D.W. Larson and W.C. Wohlforth (eds) *Status in World Politics*, Cambridge: Cambridge University Press, pp 3–29.

Larson, D.W. and Shevchenko, A. (2003) 'Shortcut to greatness: the new thinking and the revolution in Soviet foreign policy', *International Organization*, 57(1): 77–109.

Larson, D.W. and Shevchenko, A. (2010) 'Status seekers: Chinese and Russian responses to US primacy', *International Security*, 34(4): 63–95.

Larson, D.W. and Shevchenko, A. (2019) *Quest for Status: Chinese and Russian Foreign Policy*, New Haven, CT: Yale University Press.

MacDonald, P.K. and Parent, J.M. (2021) 'The status of status in world politics', *World Politics*, 73(2): 358–91.

Mercer, J. (2017) 'The illusion of international prestige', *International Security*, 41(4): 133–68.

Murray, M. (2018) *The Struggle for Recognition in International Relations: Status, Revisionism, and Rising Powers*, Oxford: Oxford University Press.

Müller, T., Albert, M. and Langer, K. (2022) 'Practices of comparison and the making of international orders', *Journal of International Relations and Development*, 25(3): 834–59.

Naylor, T. (2018) *Social Closure and International Society: Status Groups from the Family of Civilised Nations to the G20*, London: Routledge.

Naylor, T. (2022) 'Social closure and the reproduction of stratified international order', *International Relations*, 36(1): 23–39.

New York Times (1972) 'Jackson's SALT Ploy', *New York Times*, 7 August, p 26.

Onuf, N. (1989) *World of Our Making: Rules and Rule in Social Theory and International Relations*, Colombia, SC: University of South Carolina Press.

Pouliot, V. (2014) 'Setting status in stone: the negotiation of international institutional privileges', in T.V. Paul, D.W. Larson and W.C. Wohlforth (eds) *Status in World Politics*, Cambridge: Cambridge University Press, pp 192–215.

Renshon, J. (2017) *Fighting for Status*, Princeton, NJ: Princeton University Press.

Røren, P. (2023) 'The belligerent bear: Russia, status orders, and war', *International Security*, 47(4): 7–49.

Røren, P. and Beaumont, P. (2019) 'Grading greatness: evaluating the status performance of the BRICS', *Third World Quarterly*, 40(3): 429–450.

Towns, A.E. (2010) *Women and States: Norms and Hierarchies in International Society*, Cambridge: Cambridge University Press.

Volgy, T., Corbetta, R., Grant, K. and Baird, R. (2011) *Major Powers and the Quest for Status in International Politics: Global and Regional Perspectives*, New York, NY: Palgrave Macmillan.

Ward, S. (2017) *Status and the Challenge of Rising Powers*, Cambridge: Cambridge University Press.

Ward, S. (2020) 'Status from fighting? Reassessing the relationship between conflict involvement and diplomatic rank', *International Interactions*, 46(2): 274–90.

Wohlforth, W. (2009) 'Unipolarity, status competition, and great power war', *World Politics*, 61(1): 28–57.

Zarakol, A. (2017) 'Theorizing hierarchies: an introduction', in A. Zarakol (ed) *Hierarchies in World Politics*, Cambridge: Cambridge University Press, pp 1–15.

3

Defence Analysis and Military Data at the IISS: How to Count and When is a Tank Modern?

Bastian Giegerich and James Hackett

Defence and military data and the IISS

The International Institute for Strategic Studies (IISS) celebrated its 60th anniversary in 2018. Initially called the Institute of Strategic Studies (the word 'International' was adopted in the early 1970s), the then ISS was created in 1958, enabled by an initial three-year grant from the Ford Foundation, to consider issues including defence and military strategy after the advent of nuclear weapons and to provide objective information on the military balance of power in the context of Cold War confrontation. The IISS was not conceived as a think tank that would primarily send papers with policy recommendations to governments, but rather as an organization that would help to create the basis for assessments that could underlie decision making by providing data and analysis (see Howard, 2020) independent of government or political affiliation.[1] Its ethos since then has been focused more on helping analysts and practitioners with the question of how to think about a problem rather than telling them what to think.

Within the context of this edited volume, the IISS forms part of the epistemic infrastructure in the area of defence and military matters. It has instituted a range of processes and publications that consciously aim to produce data and knowledge about the phenomena encountered in this field

---

[1] As Howard (2020: 283–286) explains, in the run-up to establishing the institute some of the founding fathers of the IISS originally envisioned a stronger focus on what he refers to as the 'moral issues' around nuclear weapons and the conduct of limited nuclear war.

of enquiry and policy. However, the methodologies employed by the IISS in its defence assessment work should not be considered as an abstract evolution of comparative methodologies. They form part of comparative practices that are informed by, and ultimately reflect judgements on, the evolution of wider political landscapes, and thus relevance criteria with regard to what should be counted and compared, and how this should be accomplished.

One of the major products the IISS produces to achieve this is *The Military Balance*, published for the first time in 1959 and annually since. At the time it was a thin 11-page document containing information on the defence holdings and policies of 15 states, collated essentially by the founding director of the IISS, Alasdair Buchan. Today the book covers 173 states and territories, is some 500 pages strong every year, and is created by a growing team of professional defence analysts based in several IISS offices and organized in its Defence and Military Analysis Programme (DMAP). The underpinning general idea, that better data could (not would) lead to better decisions and that a reliable independent-of-government reference source might help to avoid misunderstandings and increase transparency, remain essentially the same. With reference to the project that gave rise to this edited volume, *The Military Balance* helps to map important elements of military capability across units of analysis – in this case nation states – and across time.

The 1959 edition noted in its foreword that the publication was intended as 'a contribution to the growing concern that is developing throughout the world about the arms race' – there would be value in bringing together available information 'into one simple comparative analysis ... in order to provide a firmer basis, not only of the discussion of "the balance of terror", but of the problems of disarmament' (ISS, 1959: Foreword). The 1961 foreword suggests 'the demand for previous editions ... has shown that [*The Military Balance*] fills an important gap in public knowledge, and is considered useful as a guide to the strategic balance between the great powers and their allies and of the orders of magnitude involved in the problem of disarmament' (ISS, 1961: 1). Later versions, such as the one published in 1990 (IISS, 1990), carried a disclaimer that was actually titled 'WARNING' in capital letters. This advisory note, written to help readers interpret what they were seeing, explained that the data in *The Military Balance* provided a quantitative assessment of personnel strengths and equipment inventories, but not an assessment of military capability. It went on to suggest that 'those who wish to do so can use the data provided to construct their own force comparisons' (IISS, 1990: 10). Indeed, it was recognized within the Institute that the very title of the book reflected not only this distinction between quantitative and qualitative assessments, but also the challenges that a product like *The Military Balance* could create for analysts. According to Sir Michael Howard, one of the founders of the Institute, Alasdair Buchan and his successors were 'later to lament that they had got themselves stuck with the title *The Military*

Balance, providing as it does so stark and conceptually misleading an idea of the complex nature of military power'. But, he continued, 'stuck they are, and "MilBal" has become the Institute's flagship' (Howard, 2020: 287).

Unlike the first editions, the 2022 edition does not explicitly explain why the IISS produces the book and collects data but instead provides extensive notes on how this is done and how the data and analysis contained in it should be interpreted (see IISS, 2022a). The modern editions all clarify that *The Military Balance* is an open-source work, based on either the most accurate data available or on the best estimate that can be made and that, while the cooperation of governments has been sought and in many cases received, the Institute's judgements contained in *The Military Balance* are its own: 'The data presented reflects judgements based on information available to the IISS at the time the book is compiled' (IISS, 2022a: 511) – a statement contained in the methodology statements in the book and database and that has changed little in recent years.

Since 2017, the IISS has published the Military Balance Plus, a searchable electronic database that contains the dataset and text and graphics content contained in the *Military Balance* books, as well as additional data the IISS possesses but cannot include in the book, and additional pieces of analysis including some from related IISS research (see IISS, 2023b).

The database is updated continuously throughout the year, and this now represents the latest assessment available from the IISS at any given point in time, whereas the book continues to be published annually. While the database removes many constraints on the data the IISS can provide – including volume and pace of update – an electronic database that users can interrogate according to their needs will likely also change patterns and practices of interaction with the dataset provided. In very simple terms, extracting a tailored response covering multiple data years, multiple countries and multiple capability categories – for example – can now be achieved in seconds rather than the hours, or possibly even days, that would be required to manually extract the same information from multiple volumes of the book. If users know they can test hypotheses or assumptions much more rapidly, they will achieve results faster but also are likely to ask more questions, enabled by the gain in productivity. Users are also able to export data or results of a complex query into preformatted Excel sheets which facilitate integration of this dataset with other sources or existing datasets held by the user. Because the database introduces functionality and datasets not present in the print book, it opens to subscribers the chance to interrogate datasets in complex ways and juxtapose data to produce insightful conclusions (one example is to produce dissimilar datasets, such as combat aircraft against air defence systems in potential adversary countries). At the same time, subscribers are able, in calls with IISS account managers, to suggest to the IISS new functionalities, data sets and user journeys (linking up data sets according to their interests) that they would find useful and that go beyond what is included in the database. Within resource and technological constraints, DMAP considers this feedback in future development and update cycles. As a result, the database has created a feedback loop between the creators of the data and those using it that is much deeper and wider than before.

Drawing on the work conducted in the context of *The Military Balance* publication and database, this chapter will examine a range of defence economic and military capability metrics that have been implemented by the IISS DMAP in order to enable the practice of international military comparisons. Specifically, it will present different metrics to measure defence expenditure and discuss their advantages and effects, illustrate changing naval equipment classifications over time, and present a methodology to classify military equipment by degree of modernity. These examples can serve to illustrate the challenges but also the evolving nature of the practice of comparison in the field *The Military Balance* covers. The chapter will conclude with a section analysing the drivers that influence the way the IISS produces military data and assessments, or, in the language of the present volume, comparative knowledge.

Show me the money: defence spending

On the face of it, the question of how much a government spends on defence each year should be straightforward to answer. However, internationally there is no shared understanding of what constitutes a defence budget. Some countries do not even release a defence budget publicly, others classify parts or all of it, and yet others use line items in other budgets to supplement defence activity. So, for international defence spending comparisons, the first problem is what to include.[2] NATO includes in its official definition of defence expenditure the defence budget, pensions, costs of peacekeeping and humanitarian operations, and R&D costs. Where possible, the IISS seeks to follow this approach internationally. *Military Balance* products list three different measures of basic defence spending data: the official defence budget figure provided by the government (where it exists), an additional measure referred to as defence expenditure where additional outlays for defence not covered in the official defence budget are known to exist or can be estimated and, for NATO countries, a defence expenditure figure as reported by NATO

---

[2] For a case study of how different approaches to countries that lack transparency and are rather opaque when it comes to their defence spending lead to different outcomes, see Nouwens and Béraud-Sudreau (2020).

(converting local currencies using International Monetary Fund (IMF) exchange rates). Of these, the second defence expenditure figure is thus an estimate that is relevant where the IISS assesses the official budget to be an incomplete picture of the total financial effort devoted to defence. Therefore, the defence expenditure figure can be expected to be higher than the official budget for the same year.

There are additional challenges beyond definitions and transparency, such as the sector-specific impact of inflation on defence spending or the utility and feasibility of applying purchasing power parity (PPP) to defence – both aspects that have wide ranging implications for the interpretation of the data and what kind of output can be generated (see McGerty, 2022). Hence a seemingly simple question like 'how much did Russia spend on defence in 2021?' has in fact multiple answers (figures taken from IISS, 2022a):

a. The official Russian defence budget at market exchange rates: US$45.8 billion
b. Defence expenditure at market exchange rates: US$62.2 billion
c. Defence expenditure in purchasing power parity: US$178 billion

This matters for policy discourse, for example on threat perceptions and regional security dynamics. European policy makers regularly ask how much of a conventional military threat Russia really can be to EU and NATO member states if its defence budget is less than US$50 billion. However, if examined via a PPP measure the story is somewhat different, with Russian spending in the above 2021 example close to the combined expenditure of France, Germany and the UK.

The Military Balance uses market exchange rates based on IMF data. The limitation of this approach is that it does not consider the cost basis – personnel, equipment and investment – that might differ quite dramatically between countries. Converting figures from local currency to US dollars at market rates masks the fact that these input costs will be lower in some countries. An alternative approach would be to make conversions using PPP exchange rates. However, the appropriateness of PPP conversions depends on the extent to which a country is self-sufficient in developing and producing the armaments required by its armed forces.

PPP conversions have utility in reaching a more nuanced understanding of the defence expenditure of China and Russia, as imported systems play almost no role in Russia's case and only a small and decreasing one in China's. As a consequence, the IISS began to include a PPP-based expenditure figure for both countries several years ago. However, PPP conversions are less suitable when assessing the spending of countries such as India and Saudi Arabia, which rely heavily on imports of military equipment from relatively high-cost producers. For those countries it would be necessary to adopt a hybrid approach to determine defence expenditure in dollars, with the market exchange rate used for converting defence procurement and the PPP conversion rate applied to all other defence expenditure (personnel, operations and so on). So, to produce standardized international comparisons, PPP conversions would have to be applied to all countries (IISS, 2023a: 491).

Moreover, using PPP exchange rates creates its own analytical challenges, not least because defence-specific PPP rates are unlikely to be the same as the general GDP-based PPP rates widely used in economics. The latter reflect mostly civilian goods and services, whereas a measure more relevant to defence spending would need to take into account defence input unit costs which are difficult to establish principally because of transparency issues. Creating defence-specific PPP measures is thus a very resource-intensive undertaking, which so far has prevented their widespread use beyond a few particularly relevant countries.

Inflation presents a similar challenge to the PPP discussion. *The Military Balance* provides, as part of its national economic statistics included in the country entries, an inflation data point which represents the year-on-year change in consumer prices in that country. However, it is reasonable to assume that defence inflation, and thus an inflation figure tailored to defence activity, would be different from consumer price changes because it would cover very different goods. The UK Ministry of Defence (2022) has found that defence inflation has been significantly higher than inflation faced by the consumers in the general population: 4.1 per cent in the 2020–21 period compared to 0.6 per cent (since then consumer inflation has risen to a 40-year high in the UK, peaking at the end of 2022). It has furthermore found that 36 per cent of defence inflation is related to labour-cost inflation but 63 per cent is driven by contract-related inflation (UK Ministry of Defence, 2022). While efforts exist to assess defence-specific inflation, there is so far no shared methodology and approach that would enable international comparison.

A second set of problems concerns what metrics to use when making comparisons: absolute spending in local currency or in USD (or some other currency)? Defence spending as a percentage of GDP or a percentage of overall government spending? These metrics generate very different results. In absolute terms the US ranks number one in the world, but in terms of defence spending as a percentage of GDP, it was 18th in 2022, with Oman being at the top of the board. Of course, it makes a difference what data sources are used for GDP data. For instance, the World Bank, Organisation for Economic Cooperation and Development (OECD) and European Commission all present differing figures. This makes it important also to examine, in turn, the methodologies used by these data providers. Indeed, as the US State Department's World Military Expenditure and Arms Transfers publications have shown, there are several different methodologies to covert expenditure from local currencies into US dollars, all with somewhat different outcomes.[3]

The Military Balance Plus database provides additional datapoints with relevance for defence economics, most notably budget breakdown data and defence budget forecasts. The budget breakdown data provide totals in local and USD terms (current and constant) as well as a percentage of defence investments as part of the entire defence budget in order to indicate how much of a defence budget is devoted to defence research and development and weapons procurement. This, in turn, can be used as an input into assessment of defence modernization processes and equipment recapitalization across countries. In July 2020, the IISS launched a forecasting tool in the database to determine future defence budget trends for some 30 countries covering some 90 per cent of global defence spending. The IISS defence budget forecast uses a Bayesian network-based model. The IISS determined the most important factors that shape defence budget allocations and, together with a data-driven model based on historical data, developed an econometric forecast model. The algorithm was developed in partnership with data scientists at Objective Computing Limited, a UK-based developer. Up to 45 variables are considered for each country model. Input variables include macroeconomic factors (gross domestic product, government expenditure), demographics (dependency ratio), defence economic data (corruption, arms trade, military aid, defence-industrial complex, official spending targets), regime type (democratic, military rule), and war and international relations dynamics (years of warfare, alliance membership, missions and deployments). Certain variables are logged based on plot evaluation and analyst discussion of variable behaviour. These forecasts can be used to identify plausible defence budget trends which can, for example, be compared to defence policy and procurement ambitions.

Classifying and categorizing equipment, and moving to qualitative judgements

A key goal the IISS pursues with *The Military Balance* publication, both in database and book form, is to provide an authoritative reference point for military and defence data. It allows examination of national forces and equipment, and also international comparisons across groups of countries. It is used by a diverse audience ranging from government officials, the armed forces, the private sector, media and members of the analytical community;

---

[3]   Because of a change in legislation, the US Department of State has ceased the production and publication of the *World Military Expenditures and Arms Transfers* report following its 2021 edition, a development that will certainly not help with transparency in this area.

all these audiences have somewhat different requirements and interests. *The Military Balance* includes data on state armed forces equipment holdings both for the active fleet (the available inventory) and, where possible, equipment held in storage (even though equipment held in store is not counted in the main inventory totals published by the IISS). IISS data is necessarily selective. It does not cover small arms and light weapons. These are of course central to many conflicts, but their ubiquity makes any assessment of numbers and organization a highly fluid and complex endeavour. Because of this, IISS data encompass crew-served weapons and above. The same analytical challenge is presented by other munitions such as missiles and bombs, but in these cases the IISS assesses numbers of missile launchers, and types of air-launched missiles and bombs.

Technological evolution and the changing character of armed conflict also influence the roles in which military platforms are employed. These roles can, in turn, affect equipment classifications. For the IISS, it is not of overriding importance how a certain country classifies its equipment – or what name it gives it – but where a platform fits into the IISS equipment classification. The IISS classification system is designed to enable international comparisons, based on a defined set of criteria. As technology and the character of conflict evolve, these parameters might need to be revised, creating possible reclassification issues.

Classifying naval vessels according to role – the function they perform– is a complex undertaking. A post-war consensus on primary surface combatants revolved around a distinction between independently operating cruisers, air defence escorts (destroyers) and anti-submarine-warfare escorts (frigates). However, ships are increasingly performing a range of roles. Also, modern ship design has meant that the full-load displacement (FLD) of different warship types has evolved and, in some cases overlaps, further eroding what once were relatively clear distinctions. For these reasons, *The Military Balance* now classifies vessels by an assessed combination of role, equipment fit and displacement.

Principal surface combatants are multi-mission combat ships capable of complex warfighting and open ocean and task group operations, with an FLD above 2,200 tonnes. Cruisers sit above 9,750 tonnes FLD. Destroyers range from 4,500 to 9,749 tonnes FLD and will have principally a medium or an area air defence equipment fit and role, designed primarily for task group operations. They will generally be carrying a heavier armament than frigates. Frigates can range from 2,200 to 9,000 tonnes FLD and will have principally an anti-submarine warfare or general-purpose equipment fit and role. In the IISS classification, principal aviation-capable combat vessels are included among principal surface combatants. Full-size aircraft carriers have above 35,000 tonnes FLD, are conventionally or nuclear powered and capable of simultaneously mounting offensive and defensive operations with a fixed-wing aircraft group (conventional or short take-off and vertical landing (STOVL)).

This means that designations used by countries, for instance for their frigates or destroyers, in many cases match IISS designations, but sometimes they do not. For example, Japan's *Hyuga* and *Izumo* ship-classes – listed by the Japan Maritime Self-Defence Force as helicopter-carrying destroyers – are classified by the IISS as helicopter carriers, reflective of their assessed role. As the conversion of the *Izumo* class to embark the F-35B combat aircraft approaches completion, the IISS will again reclassify the *Izumo* class as the vessels' role changes. In 2020–21 the maritime data team working on *Military Balance* data undertook to reassess and, where necessary, reclassify data on the above parameters. This led to some movement between IISS maritime data classifications, as seen in in Table 3.1.

However, these assessments still lead to primarily quantitative outcomes. But many users across government, the armed forces, academia and the private sector have an analytical interest not just in understanding numbers of platforms and the roles they can perform, but also to get a measure of the capability of one type of platform versus another within a given platform classification. This requirement has led to a significant change in the type of defence data that *The Military Balance* provides. IISS data teams still produce hard facts around numbers and types of organizations and equipment, but now add a qualitative assessment of capability.

Of course, a host of input measures, including policy, doctrine, funding, maintenance and training, influence military capability. Nonetheless, judgements can be made which provide important indicators of capability. For example, there is a vast difference between a modern main battle tank

Table 3.1: Selected reclassifications in the IISS dataset of French naval vessels

Class	Designation prior to 2021	Current designation	Reason for designation/change
Cassard	Destroyer	Destroyer	No change: primary air defence role
Forbin	Destroyer	Destroyer	No change: primary air defence role
Georges Leygues	Destroyer	Frigate	Change: general purpose/ anti-submarine warfare role
Aquitaine	Destroyer	Frigate	Change: general purpose/ anti-submarine warfare role
Floreal	Frigate	Frigate	No change: light armament, 3,000 tonnes FLD
La Fayette	Frigate	Frigate	No change: general purpose/ anti-submarine warfare role

Source: IISS

and a main battle tank that is obsolete in capability terms. Indeed, while NATO member states' inventories include more than 9,000 main battle tanks, in 2021 the IISS assessed some 40 per cent of them as either ageing or obsolete.

The IISS has conducted work to add assessments of equipment capability to its data set, adding new data (in the form of an analytical judgement made by DMAP staff) and delivering new functionality to users of the Military Balance Plus database in 2022. Subscribers can now query elements of the dataset based on the level of modernity of platforms. Through this step the IISS now provides data indicating the relative level of quality and capability of the equipment in the database. The IISS is incrementally increasing these judgements across its dataset, to cover a larger volume of data. Subscribers can view these judgements on the Military Balance Plus dashboard alongside an appropriate equipment record. For instance, the display for the Greek army's main battle tanks indicates that the *Leopard* 2A6HEL is judged as 'modern (+)', the *Leopard* 2A4 as 'modern' while the *Leopard* 1A5s are 'Ageing (+)' and the army's M48A5 *Pattons* are obsolescent. Aside from providing qualitative capability assessments that add a new dimension to force comparisons between countries, doing this also allows the IISS to better track the modernization of equipment inventories, in terms of both a current snapshot and a trendline over time. While primarily a feature of the database, the resulting output will also be included in graphics and charts in the *Military Balance* book.

The solution designed by DMAP aims to assign a numbered capability category to all equipment records in particular equipment classifications. For DMAP analysts engaged in assigning judgements on the internal *Military Balance* content management system, the value '1' represents obsolete equipment and '5' represents advanced equipment. This assignment needs to be based on technical characteristics specific to each equipment classification, as what makes a main battle tank obsolete or advanced naturally differs from what makes a fighter-ground attack aircraft obsolete or advanced. The capability judgement based on these specific characteristics generates a value for the numbered category which in turn translates into a label such as 'obsolete' or 'advanced' on the subscriber-facing Military Balance Plus dashboard. So, while the basic framework of making platform capability judgements needs to be applied across the domains (such as air, land, sea) and use identical language, the relationship between the characteristics observed and the capability judgement reached needs to be unique in order to yield useable information.

While the capability categories will remain fixed, the characteristics that lead to a particular capability judgement will evolve over time: what might be modern now will likely be obsolete at some point in the future. It is also necessary to capture upgrades and interim capabilities that lead to some types of equipment falling between capability categories, possessing some but not all of the technical characteristics required for a particular category. In a database format, where upgrades move equipment in the direction of a higher capability category, these instances can be displayed through symbols like plus signs ('+'). Since this approach has been implemented, Military Balance Plus users have new functionality available that allows them to search classifications such as 'main battle tanks' for judgements of equipment capability. These judgements are available in the Military Balance Plus data tools module (where users can select multiple countries and equipment classifications for their searches) and are also displayed in the relevant 'country and organization' and 'equipment' modules. The search returns a breakdown of capability categories for one or more countries against the selected classifications, both in table form and as a colour-coded stacked bar chart.

The five categories the IISS is using for this judgement are 'obsolete' (1), 'obsolescent' (2), 'ageing' (3), 'modern' (4) and 'advanced' (5). It is important to underline that these judgements are based on a platform's technical characteristics, not its physical age, remaining service life or the ability of the country that owns it to operate it successfully. Within these, IISS analysts have detailed lists to aid decision making, for instance as to which precise characteristics mean that the levels of protection for a set of equipment lead it to be assigned a particular category, be it obsolete, advanced or something in between (see Table 3.2).

Factors driving change in military data and defence assessments

The evolution of the IISS's military and defence data and assessments process reflects a blend of the Institute's original mission, availability of data, available resources, technological developments and the requirements of the three core audiences in government, the private sector, and the expert and opinion-forming communities. If the starting point in the late 1950s was to create one simple comparison, the journey since has been one of increasing complexity. More countries are covered now, more data areas are included and in greater depth and detail, more written analysis is provided and, whereas the first *The Military Balance* was essentially produced by a team of one, at the end of 2022, DMAP consisted of more than 20 full-time defence analysts. But the aim is still to provide the best possible open-source assessment based on the available information in order to inform the public policy debate.

New military technologies have emerged and a number of technologies that were developed in the civilian realm turned out to have military applications, either intended and unintended. Some, like cyber capabilities, have turned into their own domains of military competition and conflict. Armed forces have set up cyber commands and units at various levels

Table 3.2: Overview of selected technical characteristics informing IISS platform capability judgements

	Land	Maritime	Air
Characteristics	• Level of protection • Main armament • Fire control • Optics	• Crew-to-displacement ratio • Primary missile armament • Sensor suites • Signature reduction • Propulsion	• Avionics • Weapons • Signature management • Upgrades

Maritime example of a platform capability judgement

A principal surface combatant will be considered to be obsolete if it shows the following characteristics:

• FLD–crew ratio low

• No primary missile armament or only limited missile armament with trainable launchers

• No or limited aviation facilities

• Basic radar and/or sonar suite

• No significant signature reduction

• Steam or basic diesel propulsion

Source: IISS

to conduct defensive and offensive cyber operations. The rise of this domain and the military capability of nation states to operate in it needs to be captured in *The Military Balance* as well. The IISS started out with prose assessments of key developments in cyber strategy, doctrine and organization at the national level. It has since built a methodology for assessing, principally relating to indicators of militarily owned cyber capability and will in the coming years integrate the resulting new metrics into the dataset. Both *The Military Balance 2021* and *The Military Balance 2022* carried short chapters outlining the emerging thinking on this domain at the IISS (IISS, 2021a: 503–6; IISS, 2022a: 507–10). Another research team at the IISS, focused on cyber power and future conflict, is conducting wider assessments of national cyber power, beyond the military realm, that informs and contributes to the efforts within DMAP (see for example IISS, 2021b). A principal challenge for DMAP analysts is that capability in this area is opaque; equipment cannot be assessed as in other domains and so indicators of cyber capability are the focus of research attention. Moreover, the organizations pursuing activity in this area operate across the boundary between civil and military organizations. Signals intelligence agencies, for instance, are part of the relevant 'organization' list for countries as much as those organizations formally within the armed forces; in the cyber realm these civil and military organizations are both essential to the delivery of the capability.

Another important area where the boundaries are increasingly blurred relates to space systems. These have traditionally been used by armed forces and defence establishments for early warning, surveillance, and communications. And the cost of accessing space, and indeed of building satellite systems, traditionally restricted the 'user club'. No more. A growing number of countries, and private sector firms, offer access to space at increasingly competitive costs, also offering bandwidth on commercial satellites. This complicates the analytical task, and in future means that when displaying space systems IISS analysis will have to take greater account of non-government and non-military providers; these are increasingly 'militarily relevant'.

Other examples of technological change have triggered notable modifications within existing domains. The emergence, integration and fielding of uninhabited systems, which in its early years centred on the air domain, has long reached into the maritime and land domains as well. This trend generates a new information requirement and the need to create new classification elements capturing the different systems in use by governments. For example, the Uninhabited Aerial Vehicle (UAV) parent classification the IISS uses breaks down further into Combat, Intelligence, Surveillance, and Reconnaissance (CISR); Intelligence, Surveillance, and Reconnaissance (ISR); Electronic Warfare (EW); and Transport (TPT). Some of these are then further subdivided – for example, into heavy, medium and light – to form the full classification tree. Similar efforts are underway for the maritime and land domain. The IISS, to provide another example, also decided to add a 'Loitering & Direct Attack Munitions' classification to break out a category of weapons systems that in public discourse were sometimes grouped together with UAVs but have distinct characteristics. The IISS defined these new systems as air vehicles with an integral warhead that share some characteristics with both UAVs and cruise missiles. They are designed to fly either directly to their target (Direct Attack), or into a search or holding pattern (Loitering).

Another factor that is technology-driven is the ability of analysts to process greater amounts of data and utilize sources of data that would not have been available in the open-source environment until recently. Data scientists work with defence analysts to automate the creation of certain data sets for further assessment, reducing the data collection burden on analysts and creating greater time for interpretation, evaluation and assessment. High-resolution satellite imagery is now nearly ubiquitous, and a number of commercial providers have struck agreements with think tanks and media outlets to trade access to imagery for visibility of their brand (through the time-honoured technique of requesting acknowledgement of the source). The fact that commercial operators can make resources available that would have been reserved to a small number of governments around the world until a few years ago has levelled the playing field to a degree (Strobel and Wall, 2022). It has contributed to an ever-increasing volume of data and assessments offered by open-source analysts. These, in turn, have reinforced government efforts to integrate and exploit open-source material for their own efforts, in many cases mixing it with classified sources. This proliferation of methods, techniques and judgements is naturally of varied quality and sifting through the material to discern what is background noise and what is valuable insight has in itself become a challenge. Even so, government analysts continue to have access to confidential insights provided by diplomats and other government officials with relevant access, as well as classified material acquired by their intelligence agencies, sometimes from highly technical sources (IISS, 2022b). IISS analysts, working in the non-government open-source arena, are able to take advantage of the profusion of open-source data and the increasing range of technical tools to help gather and filter this information. But this change in the 'data landscape' makes more important associated moves within the *Military Balance* team to continue to improve the underlying analytical standards, techniques and processes that underpin its judgements.

That said, the reality of conflict – not least Russia's war of aggression against Ukraine – demonstrates that an abundance of information does not necessarily lead to sound judgement. To simplify greatly, the performance of the Russian armed forces in the first year of the war was worse than external observers anticipated, and that of the armed forces of Ukraine was better (Dalsjö et al, 2022). An important caveat is, of course, that the Russian ground forces were by Moscow's own metrics the least 'modern' of its armed forces and that some elements of the Russian armed forces have been used sparingly (at time of writing). Another caveat is that the assessments were in general not wrong in terms of the existence of equipment or weapons systems but in Russia's ability to deliver the latent capability offered by this equipment. Moreover, the war in Ukraine underlines the importance of qualitative factors in capability assessments (Giegerich and Hackett, 2022). These include human factors such as the will to fight, morale, cohesion, and the quality of leadership, but also plans and training as well as defence-industrial resilience and logistics strategies. Among the many challenges highlighted by these qualitative factors is that while comparative assessments among states, an important function for the IISS *The Military Balance*, are difficult to achieve, their importance cannot be ignored. This also highlights that while instruments and institutions such as *The Military Balance* provide an important and elaborate epistemic infrastructure that informs practices of comparison, the latter can never be entirely reduced to the former. On the contrary, while improvements to methodologies are designed to provide as neutral and sound a basis for military force comparisons as possible, the requirement to compare factors that cannot easily be quantified as well requires constant reflection on both the analytical possibilities as well as the limitations of comparisons such as those in *The Military Balance*.

References

Dalsjö, R., Jonsson, M. and Norberg, J. (2022) 'A brutal examination: Russian military capability in light of the Ukraine war', *Survival*, 64(3): 7–28.

Giegerich, B. and Hackett, J. (2022) 'Military capabilities in Europe: a framework for assessing the qualitative dimension', IISS Research Papers, 4 February, www.iiss.org/blogs/research-paper/2022/02/military-capab ilities-in-europe-a-framework-for-assessing-the-qualitative-dimension [Accessed 6 February 2023].

Howard, M. (2020) 'IISS – The first thirty years: a general overview', in IISS (ed) *A Historical Sensibility: Sir Michael Howard and the International Institute for Strategic Studies, 1958–2019*, Abingdon: Routledge, pp 281–96.

Institute of Strategic Studies (ISS) (1959) *The Soviet Union and the NATO Powers: The Military Balance*, London: ISS.

ISS (1961) *The Communist Bloc and the Western Alliances: The Military Balance, 1961–1962*, London: ISS.

International Institute for Strategic Studies (IISS) (1990) *The Military Balance 1990–1991*, London: Brassey's.

IISS (2021a) *The Military Balance 2021*, Abingdon: Routledge.

IISS (2021b) *Cyber Capabilities and National Power: A Net Assessment*, 28 June, www.iiss.org/blogs/research-paper/2021/06/cyber-capabilities-natio nal-power [Accessed 6 February 2023].

IISS (2022a) *The Military Balance 2022*, Abingdon: Routledge.

IISS (2022b) 'Defence intelligence: maintaining relevance in the open-source era', in IISS (ed) *The Military Balance 2022*, Abingdon: Routledge, pp 14–25.

IISS (2023a) *The Military Balance 2023*, Abingdon: Routledge.

IISS (2023b) Military Balance Plus, www.iiss.org/publications/the-milit ary-balance-plus [Accessed 6 February 2023].

McGerty, F. (2022) *Military Expenditure: Transparency, Defence Inflation and Purchasing Power Parity*, IISS Research Papers, 20 December, www.iiss. org/blogs/research-paper/2022/12/military-expenditure [Accessed 6 February 2023].

Nouwens, M. and Béraud-Sudreau, L. (2020) *Assessing Chinese Defence Spending: Proposals for New Methodologies*, IISS Research Papers, 3 March, www.iiss.org/blogs/research-paper/2020/03/assessing-chinese-defence-spending [Accessed 6 February 2023].

Strobel, W.P. and Wall, R. (2022) 'Ukraine war puts spy satellites for hire in the spotlight', *The Wall Street Journal*, 1 May, www.wsj.com/articles/ukraine-war-puts-spy-satellites-for-hire-in-the-spotlight-11651410002 [Accessed 6 February 2023].

UK Ministry of Defence (2022) *Evidence Summary: The Drivers of Defence Cost Inflation*, https://assets.publishing.service.gov.uk/government/uploads/system/uploads/attachment_data/file/1056623/Evidence_Summary_-_The_Drivers_of_Defence_Cost_Inflation.pdf [Accessed 6 February 2023].

4

Seeing Deterrence and Defence: Visual Representations of Military Force Comparisons between NATO and the Warsaw Pact in the 1980s

Gabi Schlag

Whose soldiers are top trained, who owns the best-serviced nuclear weapons, who deploys the most lethal but ethically responsible drones? Comparing material-military resources and capabilities is a common academic and political practice to assess the power, strength and security of states. Yet very little is known about how technical charts, diagrams and figures shape these discourses on security, power and strength nationally, regionally and globally. How are resources and capabilities envisioned literally? How do such visualizations contribute to the governance of military objects and the politics of security? What are the 'conditions of sensibility' (Austin, 2019) and 'conditions of possibility' (Bleiker, 2014; see also Connolly, 1991) that shape public knowledge of and attitude towards military force?

  This chapter introduces visual discourse analysis as a method of studying visual representations of military force and deployment. It illustrates the necessity and validity of such a perspective by studying a selection of technical images such as diagrams, table charts, icons and maps of a disclosed report on 'NATO and the Warsaw Pact – Force Comparisons' from 1984, authored by the NATO Information Service. I argue that technical images are conditioning the sensible and possible by normalizing the deployment of military force and disciplining anxieties about deterrence and defence. This look is based on spatial divisions, absent people and relational objects. In the case of the booklet, the technical images contribute to the repoliticization of armament, highlighting modernization as an 'inevitable project' to secure the military balance in Europe. To use the distinction made by the editors in their introduction (see Müller et al, Chapter 1), the technical images thus are no mere 'mapping tools' but rather 'ordering tools' that construct the world that they purport to depict.

Seeing force comparisons: world-making and security governance

To compare and contrast is a situated and relational practice (see Müller et al, Chapter 1). While Russia keeps more nuclear warheads than the US, its GDP per capita is three times lower than the US's. In addition, comparison often implies a hierarchization claiming, for example, that in a world of growing tensions military power is much more important than economic wealth. Such practices of comparing frequently make use of numbers, graphs and illustrations to offer evidence and to support truth claims. Numbers are a social convention for objectively measuring, quantifying and thereby relating actors, objects and/or events. In the case of military resources, they are supposed to deliver political messages of power and strength (over 31,000 bombs!) on the one hand, and weakness (nearly 1,000 soldiers killed!) on the other. Technical images like maps, charts and diagrams visualize these numbers by using colours, lines, bars and other design elements. International Relations (IR) scholars are paying increasing attention to the political side of imaginaries enabled through technical devices like satellites and drones (Shim, 2013; Rothe, 2017; Grayson and Mawdsley, 2018; Saugmann Andersen, 2019). The more traditional visual practices of creating a map or bar diagram remind us of the longstanding geopolitical and colonial legacies of such representations (Dodds, 2007; Barney, 2015; Çapan and dos Reis, 2024). Technical images contribute to world-making as much as they enable spaces, people and objects to be governed.

Visual representations of military force, I argue in this chapter, are influential and consequential for imagining and governing worlds 'of our making' (Onuf, 1989). They are influential as they are shaping public visions of 'reality'. This is particularly true for rather clandestine 'realities' such as military force. As they are actively shaping these public visions of reality, visual representations are productive of what we know about the world. While some things become visible, alternative representations and realities remain invisible or become sidelined and hidden. An essential part of this visualization is not only the content ('what is shown'), but also the form ('how it is shown'). It makes a difference whether nuclear weapons are publicly imagined by a photo *or* a diagram, as ways of seeing are entangled with ways of knowing and feeling. Therefore, images are consequential because they define the conditions of possibility, what we are able to know about an actor, object and/or event and what we are able to do about it. This implies that the ability to represent shapes the discursive boundaries of action. It makes the world and its spaces, people and objects governable.

In this chapter, I am interested in visual representations of comparisons of military force. How is military power represented and compared visually? How is comparative knowledge produced by visuals? What modes are used to represent military power visually? What role do signs, icons, colour, lines, bars and compositions play? How do such practices of visual comparison shape public perceptions of security and defence? To illustrate the productivity of visual discourses of military force, I turn to a disclosed report on NATO's capabilities in contrast to those of the Warsaw Pact from 1984, programmatically entitled 'NATO and the Warsaw Pact – Force Comparisons' (NATO Information Service, 1984).

The chapter proceeds with a discussion of discourse analysis and its extension to visual data. After contextualizing disputes over military balance in the 1980s and the booklet's history, I discuss five vignettes of popular visualizations: the bar diagram, the line graph, the timeline chart, the icon (with table chart) and the map. I argue that visuals condition the sensible and possible by normalizing a geopolitical perspective on security and defence. This look is based on spatial divisions, absent people and relational objects. In the case of the booklet, technical images, therefore, are contributing to the repoliticization of forces, highlighting modernization as an 'inevitable project' to secure the military balance in Europe. As Çapan and dos Reis (2024: 154) aptly write '[t]echniqualities render political projects "scientific"' and thus discipline human anxieties associated with deterrence and defence in the case of force comparison between NATO and the Warsaw Pact in the 1980s.

Discourse analysis revisited

Often associated with the work of Michel Foucault, Ernesto Laclau and Chantal Mouffe, or Jacques Derrida, there are not one but many ways to understand discourses. Discourse theory bridges the gap between the micro-level of the (re)production of meaning, that is meaning-in-use, and the macro-level of institutionalized structures that reset the conditions of possibility for such meaningful communicative action. Although many discourse approaches in IR are informed by postmodern and poststructuralist thinking, the two perspectives are not synonymous. Think about Habermas's political discourse theory and ethics as well as the sociological approaches put forward by Ruth Wodak, Teun van Dijk and Norman Fairclough that critically reflect the ideological site of discourses.

Discourse analysts commonly assume that discursive practices are powerful because they constitute meaning in the first place (Wæver, 2004). As Dunn and Neumann (2016: 4) outline: 'Discourses are systems of meaning-production that fix meaning, however temporarily, and enable actors to make sense of the world and to act within it.'

As meaning-in-use, discourses define what can be said, seen and done. Therefore, a discourse is an enabling and constraining entity, and its boundaries are not fixed but historically, socially and culturally contingent. Contingency means that a discourse reproduces its boundaries through its doings, implying that meanings can shift – though they often do not due to forceful sedimented structures and routinized practices. Therefore, power is an essential aspect of discourse analysis to understand why meaningful configurations manifest in specific ways (Hopf, 2004). As Holzscheiter (2014) writes, there are three aspects to the relationship between power and discourse that one should keep in mind. First, power *in* discourse refers to an actors' ability to shape and invoke meaning that is widely accepted, hegemonic and becomes taken for granted. Second, power *over* discourse is defined by access to discourses, that is what and who is included and excluded. Discourses constitute subjects and subject positions enabling agents to speak and act in specific ways. Finally, power *of* discourse identifies the structural features of a discourse, for example the conventions, language games and narratives that actors appeal to. Due to its anchoring in rituals and institutions, some narratives like the 'hero protector' or the 'evil barbarian' are more powerful than others. They shape what audiences can know about an actor, object and/or event and affect how one sees it and feels about it.

Michel Foucault famously states, though, that power goes hand in hand with resistance. While some scholars investigate the relation between hegemonic and counter-hegemonic or subaltern discourses, others assume that a discourse is itself characterized by struggles over the meaning-in-use. Therefore, contestation indicates the flipside of power in, over, and of discourses. Because discourses define what can be meaningfully said, seen and done, 'struggles over setting the limits to discourse' (Diez, 2014: 326) make visible both the instability and the temporal fixation of meaning. Because meaning is contingent, struggles over representation signify the working and productivity of discourses.

The textual, visual and sensible site of discourses

Meaning making often combines modes of communication, for example written text and photo images in a newspaper report, either on- or offline. It is therefore essential to expand the scope of discursive analysis to visual data. Many scholars, though, have emphasized and shown that images have never been excluded from discourse analysis by definition. As Rose

(2001: 137) argues: 'It is possible to think of visuality as a sort of discourse too. A specific visuality will make certain things visible in particular ways, and other things unseeable … and subjects will be produced and act within that field of vision.'

For the last 20 years, the main challenge for IR scholars has been to understand 'the ways in which images may function as communicative acts' (Williams, 2003: 527). Compared to (written and spoken) words, images have specific features, and these features are even more tangible when images are shared globally through social media. First, images are characterized by immediacy through which seeing, feeling, experiencing and thinking intersect. 'Reading an image' is a situated practice shaping our knowledge of what the image means to us and how we feel about it as an individual spectator but also how the collective audience is interpreting it. Second, images have an immanent compositional order. In a metaphorical sense, they are what they are showing – for example, a simplified map of the European continent. Images are not true or false but make visible something as shown, even if it is an abstract picture or a faked depiction. Third, images are not isolated but are linked to other images and other communicative modes, establishing conventional ways of showing and seeing. Such inter-iconicity and inter-modality are established by discursive formations that evolve over time but are culturally contingent. Fourth, images have performative qualities, they do something (literally and metaphorically), they can move us, they can make us think about something, and they make worlds knowable and governable. Finally, digital technologies, devices and the global nature of social media have accelerated the quantity of images produced and shared daily. They have also altered the agency of this kind of production and consumption, making it less controllable and predictable what kind of images are produced, shared and seen by whom.

More broadly understood, regimes of visibility and invisibility are an essential mode of being and knowing (Callahan, 2020). Discourses, therefore, produce realities by setting the conditions of sensibility and possibility through scopes and modes of communication. Institutionalized practices of visibility enable and constrain the discursive production of 'reality' and 'truth'. Visual discourse analysis is a tool to study visual patterns *and* practices (MacKenzie, 2020; Schlag and Heck, 2020). It aims at discovering the power dynamics in play because the ability to represent is a genuinely political act which implies that alternative ways of showing, seeing, knowing and feeling are possible. Making visible, therefore, always implies invisibilities, either intentional or otherwise. And from this extension of discourse approaches to the visual and sensible, six conclusions follow.

First, a discourse is constituted by 'text', broadly understood. Foucault's work already clearly illuminates the multi-modal and multi-media nature of discourses that combine ideational and material sites. Meaning is produced in and by different media, including speaking, writing, showing, sketching and designing, within different institutional settings, for example the university or the prison, it materializes through spaces and objects such as the panopticon or the lecture hall, and thereby becomes a visible and sensible configuration. As W.J.T. Mitchell (1984) argues, the notion of image is multifaceted and ranges from signs to vision. Therefore, using words is as much a textual as it is an auditive, visual and sensible practice (Callahan, 2020).

Second, a discourse is structured and relational. Discursive formations of meaning unravel patterns, although these patterns are not fixed forever. Configurations are dependent on the ways in which meaning becomes effectively produced and reproduced. While patterns indicate the structural side of discourse, meaning is essentially relational. Practices of linking and differencing constitute a web of meanings (Hansen, 2006), which builds upon and enables comparisons. The positioning of subjects and objects vis-à-vis one another through the logic of difference and the logic of linking is key to understanding discursive (in)stability (Laclau and Mouffe, 1985: 127–34). The equivalences created are essential for understanding discursive (in)stability as they cancel out individual differences (Doty, 1996: 11; Hansen, 2006). Meanings are 'used to express something identical underlying them all' (Laclau and Mouffe, 1985: 127). 'Positive' notions of identity are examples of linking and equalizing, for example the articulation that all NATO weapons are defensive. As Laclau and Mouffe (1985: 130) write, the logic of equivalences 'is a logic of the simplification of political space'. The logic of difference, though, positions elements vis-à-vis each other. It 'is a logic of its expansion and increasing complexity' (Laclau and Mouffe, 1985: 130). To continue the example: while all NATO weapons have a defensive purpose, all Warsaw Pact weapons are offensive. Both the logic of equivalence and the logic of difference create relational and comparative meaning that normalizes the distinctive character of weapons. In addition, action is enabled by adding a hierarchical dimension to the web of meanings, claiming that NATO's weapons serve to self-defend its members while Warsaw Pact weapons pose a threat and must be deterred.

Such equivalences and differences are often taken for granted or seem to be so. According to Laclau and Mouffe, discursive nodal points are such partial fixations of meaning. These points limit the productivity and fluidity of discursive practices (or chains of signification in their terminology) and 'make predication possible' (Laclau and Mouffe, 1985: 99). Nodal points, as Diez shows, materialize as meaningful concepts that tie together a number of discourses. By connecting multiple discourses to a broader concept, they temporarily fix meaning (Diez, 2001: 16). Nodal points, however, may entail non-textual data as well, for example iconic images (Hansen, 2011). Discursive nodal points, then, indicate 'a limited fixation of meaning' (Diez, 2001: 17; Doty, 1996: 10) by establishing a 'hidden truth', something that is and must be taken for granted. Obviously, visual representations are contributing to the construction of such truth claims by mediating knowledge and experience.

Third, a discourse is open-ended and incomplete. Because meaning cannot be fixed forever due to the interplay of the logic of equivalence and difference, discursive formations remain instable. Therefore, a discourse possibly changes when the practices of meaning making shift. For example, external disruptions like 'force modernization' can reconfigure subject positions, relations and meanings. Discourse approaches are often less interested in (causally) explaining why these changes occur than in how they are made possible and how consequential they are. Conditions of possibility remind us of the contingent nature of meaningful structures, implying that the world could be a different one. The boundaries of what can be shown and seen (publicly and in private) are constantly being reshaped by the practices of showing, seeing and hiding. This assumption does not imply that discourses are never fixed temporarily but that all discursive formations are characterized by incompletion.

Fourth, a discourse is productive of 'reality', that is 'what can be known and acted upon' (Dunn and Neumann, 2016: 3). The productivity of a discourse refers to its power to create a world that sets the boundaries of what can be said, seen, known, sensed and therefore acted upon. Traditionally, discourse scholars focused on sayings and doings, arguing that saying *is* doing something. Security, for example, is then not a predefined concept, but articulations and performances create its meaning (Wæver, 1995). Performativity means that something comes into being by being said and done. Such productive and performative practices, though, are embedded in conventions, rituals and institutions. Hence, a speech act can misfire if its speaker fails to use the words properly. In addition, visual representations are performative comparable to speech acts (Schlag, 2019a). What can be seen co-defines what can be known and acted upon. A good example of this productive power are technical images, for example charts, tables, models or diagrams. The most displayed and distributed image of climate change has been the world map turned red, making transformations visible that are difficult to detect by our senses only. We know the dramatic impact of climate change because we can see it, symbolized by the red map (Schneider and Nocke, 2014). Legitimate action thus depends to a large extent on the visibility of a reality that we acknowledge as 'real'.

Fifth, a discourse is about the entanglement of knowledge and power, fixing a particular representation and establishing it as '*the* truth'. When legitimate (political) action depends on meaningful representations of the world, then knowing and seeing something is always intertwined with power. Those who can define what is by showing how it is also have the power to shape the scope of legitimate actions. From a discourse approach, knowledge refers to situated practices and not only to scientific knowledge. It's about knowing how to do things. Discursive nodal points and taken-for-granted representations are the visible expression of the nexus between power and knowledge. On the one hand, images can be manufactured or used in a manipulative way as words can. Scepticism towards the epistemic value of images is informed by a century-long tradition of dismissing the visual as a misleading illusion. On the other hand, documentary visual media like photography possess an immediate quality of testifying to a 'real situation' as captured by the camera's 'eyes'. While this 'real situation' might be arranged and staged, it documents a scene that has been present. Although most viewers know that every picture is selective and somehow framed, both professional photojournalism and amateur photography remain the most popularized practices of visualization around the world. In addition, technical imaginaries are obviously not documentary, but articulate knowledge claims with the aesthetic authority of science.

Six, a discourse operates through practices and links ideational and material sites. A discourse is not only a structured pattern but an active and fluid web. The interplay of non-material and material practices of meaning making composes 'realities' that people are acting upon. While material aspects have gained greater attention in recent years associated with practice theory and actor-network theory, along with other scholars like Roland Bleiker, Bill Callahan and Lene Hansen, I argue that discourses also operate through practices that combine the affective, sensible and visual site of meaning-in-use.

A visual methodology for comparing military force

In this chapter, I argue that meaning- and world-making is shaped by words/ language as much as by images/vision (Shim, 2013; Rothe, 2017; Grayson and Mawdsley, 2018). As a text, an image is a source of knowledge, feeling and experience. Images, words and emotions are closely connected, and scholars must take their interplay theoretically and empirically into account. Therefore, a visual methodology is interdisciplinary and builds on insights from visual culture studies, communication and media studies, and cultural and aesthetic theories. It also defines a new field of study as it explicitly investigates the political site of visuals, the visual site of politics and policies, and the global site of both (Bleiker, 2018; Schlag, 2019b). As I have outlined elsewhere (Schlag, 2015), visual discourse analysis is a methodological position that scholars fill with life differently. As the empirical focus of this chapter is on technical images like diagrams, graphs and maps, I will utilize a segment analysis for 'reading' images of force comparison. Technical images are designed images where a creator is adding different graphic elements, that is segments, to convey meaning. By unpacking these segments, the meaning-making practices become visible.

The aesthetics of force comparison

In the remainder of this chapter, I want to support the claim that ways of showing and seeing military force in comparison shape the politics of security. Therefore, 'conditions of sensibility' (Austin, 2019) are inevitably entangled with 'conditions of possibility' (Connolly, 1991). Security is a configuration composed of discursive, material, technological, aesthetic and affective encounters. Visual discourse analysis helps to uncover these configurations, how they mesh performances, technologies, aesthetics and emotions, and how they shape the politics of security. Practices and discourses of force comparison regularly make use of diagrams, charts and maps:

> Technical images are not artistic, instead primarily originating in the fields of science, technology, and medicine; they are predominantly instrument-based or the results of imaging procedures. On the one hand, 'technical' emphasizes the way these specific images are produced (by technical means, apparatuses, instruments, or by hand). On the other hand, images may be thought of as tools or as instruments in their own right. (Bredekamp et al, 2015: 1)

One could argue that NATO's illustrations only partly count as scientific images as they are not accurately made. They convey politically shaped knowledge, not scientific knowledge. They are polysemic, belonging to both the world of geopolitics (content) and the world of scientific representation (form). Like political cartographies, they are applying an aesthetic of spatial divisions, absent people and relational objects.

In general, images have become a powerful tool to envision and share worldviews, to produce knowledge and to mobilize emotional registers. Therefore, they assist in governing the world (as we know it and see it) by configuring the conditions of the sensible and the possible. Technical images, though, mobilize a very specific set of knowledge and affect that often supports naturalization, rationalization and management. Commonly used to illustrate research results, technical images like bar diagrams are performative by generating knowledge and facilitating sensibilities. They make actors, things and events governable. In the case of force representations, for example, they naturalize and depoliticize stockpiles of weapons by representing them as numbers and icons instead of deadly tools to kill people. It's a feeling of control and order they create (Cohn, 1987) and military strategists can deploy and move weapons on an imaginary board.

Aesthetically, a technical image is characterized by its formal design. It is literally made by composing and relating elements, in particular forms and colours. To illustrate different meaning-making layers, I will utilize a visual frame analysis which zooms in and out on specific segments (Breckner, 2015). These segments are the perceptual foci that help to inscribe meaning and thus can be 'read' as meaning-making visual devices.

Contextualization: disputes over military balance in the 1980s

Due to space limitations, I cannot provide an overview and assessment of armament policies in the 1980s. However, as Hans-Joachim Schmidt (Chapter 11) emphasizes in his chapter, the visibility and distinctiveness of military equipment has been and still is a precondition for verification policies. If one does not know which weapons exist, how they function and how systems differ, neither their impact on (in)security nor the necessity to control or even reduce these systems can be evaluated. Information graphics, tables, maps and charts comparing and locating weapons are certainly the most popular way of making weapons visible and assessable.

After the failure of SALT II and the Soviet invasion of Afghanistan, the political debates of the early 1980s centred around the implementation of NATO's double-track decision and the modernization of intermediate nuclear forces (INF). In 1983 US President Ronald Reagan set the tone for the Second Cold War with his 'evil empire' speech, adding a religious and moral side to the already tense relations with the Soviet Union and the Warsaw Pact. It was only in 1987 that the INF Treaty was signed – by Mikhail Gorbachev, who came to power in 1985, and Reagan. The Stockholm International Peace Research Institute's (SIPRI) data on military expenditure indicates that the US increased its spending compared to the 1970s and invested over 6.0 per cent of its GDP in arms and forces from 1982 until 1988 (SIPRI, no date).

Studies show that its European partners had doubts about the US's reliability in case of a conflict with the Soviet Union. Many of them were sceptical about 'Reagan's roller-coaster approach to arms control' (Stuart, 1990: 426). Stuart writes that there was a 'new defence consciousness among key European Allies during the 1980s' (Stuart, 1990: 428). The French government under President Mitterrand, for example, prioritized European self-reliance and French leadership. UK Prime Minister Thatcher enhanced British military capabilities by investing in the Trident programme while confronted with a battle for the Falkland Islands in the South Atlantic. Thomas Risse-Kappen (1991: 483) shows that West Germany changed from an outspoken supporter of US-based nuclear deterrence to a strong advocate of nuclear arms control. Accordingly, public perception of a Soviet threat declined from high levels in the early 1980s (Risse-Kappen, 1991: 495). Military build-up and Reagan's 'evil empire' rhetoric paradoxically 'eroded the public support for his defense policy', Risse-Kappen (1991: 501) summarizes. Anti-nuclear weapon protest grew in the US and Europe and the House of Representatives voted in favour of a nuclear freeze resolution to halt the testing, production and deployment of nuclear weapons in 1983.

Given this political context of the 1980s, campaigns to reunite the US and Western Europe emerged in response to domestic critique and new Soviet policies. The booklets on military force, authorized by the US government, NATO Information Service Brussels and the USSR Ministry of Defence, are certainly part of this effort to regain support at best and to minimize open dissent at least. Editions authorized by the US on *Soviet Military Power* are from 1981, 1983, 1984, 1985, 1986, 1987, 1988, 1989, 1990 and 1991 and booklets on *Whence the Threat to Peace*, published by the USSR are from 1982, 1984, and 1987. The 1982 edition of *Whence the Threat to Peace* was published in English, Russian, French, Spanish, Italian and German, according to Stefanovsky (1983). Although the production and publication context of these booklets remains vague (Herzog and Wildgen, 1986), one can assume that editions in different languages were published to reach a broader population. Maynard Glitman (2006: 133), US diplomat and negotiator of the INF Treaty, reports that the first booklet on *Soviet Military Power* in 1981, 'was a significant event in the campaign for public support'. In combination with the force comparison editions, it provided:

> NATO nations with a common, accurate database from which to argue the Alliance's position both inside the negotiations and in the public arena. Moreover, *Soviet Military Power*'s high-quality color photographs and graphics made it easier for the general public to understand the technical subject matter. *Soviet Military Power* also helped buttress domestic support in the United States for the administration's defense programs. (Glitman, 2006: 133)

In *Soviet Military Review*, Major-General Stefanovsky described the 1982 edition of the comparison of military force between NATO and the Warsaw Pact as a 'pamphlet' and 'yet another attempt to prove that the present international situation is not marked by military-strategic equilibrium between the USSR and the USA ... but by an alleged "overwhelming military superiority" of the USSR and the Warsaw Treaty Organisation' (Stefanovsky, 1983: 53). The journal *Survival* reprinted a four-page excerpt from the 'Whence the Threat to Peace' of 1982. The unattributed introductory paragraph states that this report is a response to the US *Soviet Military Power* of 1981, which is described as 'tendentious' and 'distorted' by cited Russian sources (Survival, 1982: 134).

Technical images of force comparison: exploring five vignettes

The force comparison authored and edited by the NATO Information Service in 1984 takes a closer look at the military capabilities of the Warsaw Pact and the Atlantic Alliance. It is the second edition of a report from 1982 in which all the graphics are the same, only the colouring has changed from black and white to red and blue. According to military conventions, the colours blue and red represent opponents in training exercises. As the reproduced images in this chapter are in black and white, I will clarify in the text which element I am referring to. All images are reproduced under NATO's 'Fair Use' policy.

Technical images are highly prominent in a scientific context and have been conventionalized over decades. There is a standard way to compose a graph with bars, to map a geographical area or to indicate relations by lines, arcs and arrows. Symbols and icons feature prominently to represent weapon systems and forces. Although figures reduce complexities, they claim to be accurate, objective and truthful. They are, in other words, presented as 'mapping tools' that depict the world as it is. Despite their obvious constructedness (they are not natural and documentary pictures), they represent knowledge in a visual-textual mode as a shortcut for often politically and scientifically controversial matters. By doing so, they promote particular visions of the problems that NATO faced – notably an unfavourable military balance – and suggest particular ways in which NATO should address these problems – in this case through sustained armament policies. They thus function as ordering tools. The following discussion of different technical images teases out the tensions between the mapping tools and ordering tools aspects of comparative practices. While supposedly 'technical', the images are in fact political and designed to promote a particular ordering project: NATO's quest to reshape the military balance in Europe.

A *bar diagram* (chart or graph) is a type of graphical representation that uses rectangular bars to display data. In general, the length or height of each bar corresponds to the magnitude or value of the data it represents, making it easy to compare and visualize different categories. The horizontal axis of the chart typically represents the categories being compared, while the other axis represents the values or frequencies of each category. Bar diagrams are widely used and convey information easily.

Figure 4.1 looks like a typical bar diagram, using different colours and adding icons (instead of words) to identify the categories that are compared. The chart presents a quantitative comparison of forces between NATO and the Warsaw Pact. Its visual grammar is easy to read, from left to right and

Figure 4.1: Force comparison

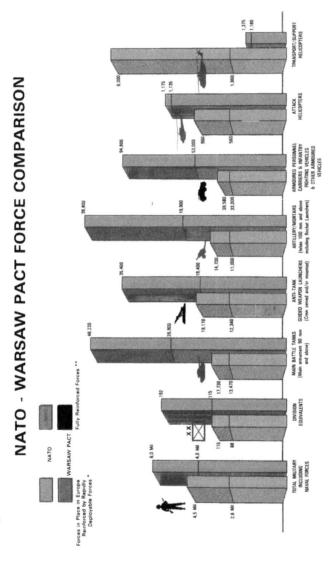

NATO - WARSAW PACT FORCE COMPARISON

Source: NATO Information Service (1984); creator: unknown

bottom to top (and vice versa). Icons for each military branch and equipment as well as colouring help to distinguish the bars. Blue stands for NATO (each bar on the left), red for the Warsaw Pact (each bar on the right), a soldier with a rifle for military personnel. NATO outnumbers the Warsaw Pact in only one category, namely 'transport/support helicopters'.

Diagrams are supposed to be accurate as they represent a key scientific mode of visualizing facts. In Figure 4.1, though, the relations between the force categories are distorted regarding absolute numbers. The bar for Soviet main battle tanks, numbering 46,230, is marginally lower than the bar for Soviet artillery pieces, numbering 38,800.

Bar diagrams are abstract, frequently synonymous with quantifiable and objective depictions of an uncontested and apolitical reality. You cannot argue about numbers, you can only count differently. However, the objectivity of diagrams is a myth as designers create and relate the key visual elements in such a way as to best convey their message.

Line graphs can add a temporal dimension to comparisons. They are a type of chart that displays information as a series of data points connected by straight lines or curves. Line graphs are commonly used to illustrate trends or changes in data over time, although they can also be used to show other types of relationships between variables. In a line graph, the horizontal axis typically represents time or another continuous variable, while the vertical axis represents the value of the data being measured. Each data point is represented by a dot or other symbol, and these points are connected by straight lines to show how the data changes over time or across the range of the independent variable.

In Figure 4.2, a time span from 1973 to 1983 is scaled on the horizontal axis and strategic force parity or advantage (and by implication disadvantage) on the vertical axis. In addition, the horizontal line in the centre is marked 'parity'; it divides the diagram into an upper (blue) and lower (red) rectangle. While it takes some time to decipher the diagram, the visual move obviously represents a decline in NATO advantage with three out of four curves crossing parity.

Visualizations of change and continuity frequently use *timelines*. Figure 4.3 spatializes and temporalizes, in this case the modernization of short and intermediate range delivery systems from 1955 to 1983. On the vertical axis, the scale refers to the categories 'artillery', 'missiles', and 'aircraft'.

In general, the figure conveys modernization as a relational action. If party A introduces a system, party B will follow. However, this representation alone leaves it open who initiated the modernization and whether it counts as an action or reaction.

Icons and symbols are widely used in technical images as a visual shortcut. A symbol can represent an object, concept or action. Icons are often simplified, stylized and easily recognizable, making them effective at

Figure 4.2: Strategic forces: trends in relative advantages

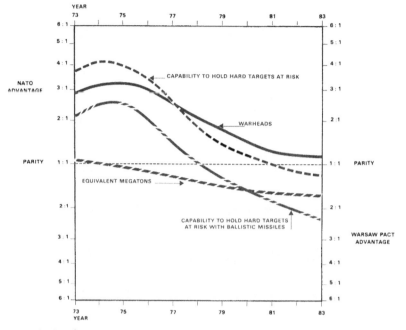

Source: NATO Information Service (1984); creator: unknown

conveying meaning quickly and efficiently. Icons can represent a wide range of concepts, from everyday objects such as a phone or a car to more abstract concepts such as an idea or a feeling as emojis.

Back in the 1980s, conventional icons for military objects were used in the booklets. As Figure 4.4 shows, each missile type is represented by a specific icon which differs in size. Visually, it may remind us of both a bar chart and a phallic symbol. In addition, a table complements the figure listing categories and numbers. The ratio between the icon for the Pershing II (10.61 m) on the right and icon for the SS-20 (16.5 m) on the left looks accurate.

A *map* is a visual representation of an area or a region that typically shows the location of geographic features such as rivers, mountains, cities and roads. Maps can take many forms: topographic maps, political maps, road maps and thematic maps. Figures 4.5 and 4.6 show a map of states in Europe, North Africa, Central Asia and the Middle East. The view is the typical bird's-eye perspective that creates an artificial overview. The image is centred on Moscow. On the left-hand side – or in the west – the map shows the 'Atlantic Ocean' with 'Greenland', 'Portugal', and 'Mauretania' as

Figure 4.3: Short and intermediate range delivery systems modernization comparison (by year)

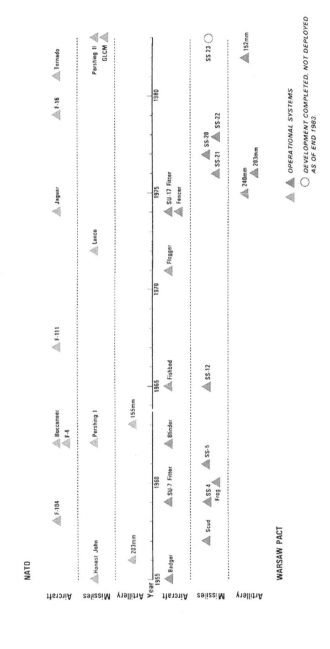

Source: NATO Information Service (1984); creator: unknown

Figure 4.4: Longer-range INF missile systems deployed end 1983

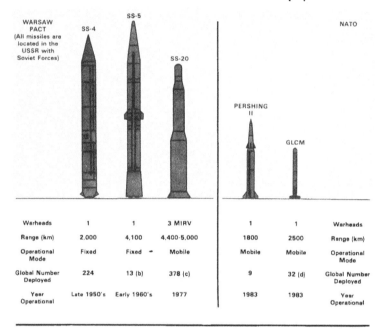

LONGER-RANGE INF MISSILE SYSTEMS DEPLOYED END 1983 (a)

	SS-4	SS-5	SS-20	PERSHING II	GLCM	
Warheads	1	1	3 MIRV	1	1	Warheads
Range (km)	2,000	4,100	4,400-5,000	1800	2500	Range (km)
Operational Mode	Fixed	Fixed	Mobile	Mobile	Mobile	Operational Mode
Global Number Deployed	224	13 (b)	378 (c)	9	32 (d)	Global Number Deployed
Year Operational	Late 1950's	Early 1960's	1977	1983	1983	Year Operational

(a) This table is prepared on the basis of missiles on launchers.
(b) By end 83 all SS-5 missiles were being retired.
(c) Excludes refire missiles.
(d) Not all of the 32 GLCMs had reached initial operational capability at end 1983.

Source: NATO Information Service (1984); creator: unknown

well as non-indicated parts of Western Sahara and Canada. In the east – on the right-hand side – the map is bounded by parts of 'China', 'Nepal', and 'India'. In the north, it extends to parts of Canada, 'Greenland', the 'Soviet Union' and 'China'; in the south to Mauretania, 'Mali', 'Algeria', 'Libya', 'Egypt', the Red Sea, 'Saudi Arabia', and the 'Arabian Sea'.

The representation of territorial size and shape is non-accurate (based on the conventional representation of the Mercator map) and compressed. Names used to indicate the states are shortcuts instead of the official and legal titles. The state borders organize the surface of the image. Three icons of an upright missile, three lines linking these missiles and locations in the south-west, and three light red-coloured arcs overlapping with Greenland, Western Europe, North-East Africa, the Mediterranean and Central Asia have been added to the conventional state map.

Figure 4.5: SS–20 bases

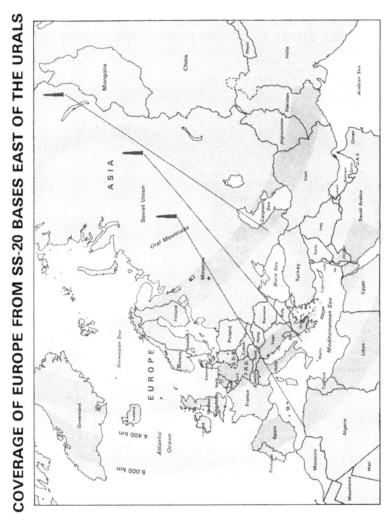

COVERAGE OF EUROPE FROM SS-20 BASES EAST OF THE URALS

Source: NATO Information Service (1984); creator: unknown

The map is informed by conventional geopolitical images of state borders, territorial entities and seas. It is simple and flat. It is structured by lines, contours, four colours (red, grey, white and black), and the three icons of a missile. It is composed of two layers: the layer of states and the layer of missile coverage implying ranges. The representational mode creates relations of entanglement based on a shared space. It distances and connects entities at the same time. Cartography is both a medium and a technology (Barney, 2015: 97), intended to produce spatial knowledge fortified with political meaning.

The combination of a geopolitical layer of state representation and a military-strategic-tactical layer of missile deployment and range illustrates the complexity of the issue at hand. The technical image of the figure with simplified icons, arcs and lines disciplines such complexity. It makes SS-20 bases detectable and thus governable – in principle. However, it also makes visible some contradictions. As shown, SS-20 missiles could reach not only the territory of NATO member states but Iran, Saudi Arabia, Libya, and Tunisia as well. The figure extends the SS-20 'threat' beyond the political boundaries of NATO. It implies that 'we (the states) are all affected'. The fact that missiles could be launched east or north instead of west, though, is not depicted.

Figure 4.6 represents NATO's 'defence line' with the coverage of GLCM (BGM-109G Ground Launched Cruise Missile) and Pershing II missiles. It visualizes that the Russian capital Moscow lies within range and can be reached by GLCMs. These maps illustrate the Europe-centred perspective of military balance. Only two maps illustrate more than the wider European theatre of military confrontation (Figures 1 and 18 in the booklet).

Seen together, but kept in different images, Figures 4.5 and 4.6 represent the relational side of mutual vulnerability. It is telling that the authors did not design one image that blended the coverage of NATO and Warsaw Pact missiles, did not mark the 'Iron Curtain' as a dividing line in Europe and did not indicate alliance membership (which is represented in Figure 20, the last in the booklet).

All in all, the visual frames used to represent military capabilities in comparison are based on objectifying segments. On the one hand, these imaginaries look familiar to scientific ways of visualization. On the other, the implied conclusion to be drawn is highly political, framing a military imbalance between NATO and the Warsaw Pact within the context of mutual vulnerability. Due to the technicalities of the imaginary, anxieties are controlled to support controversial political projects. While force comparison is represented as technical and objective, the visuals reveal the highly political nature of any representation. By using the aesthetics of science, the booklet aptly shows how actors apply specific visual types to represent spaces and objects while leaving the affected people out of sight.

Figure 4.6: NATO's defence line

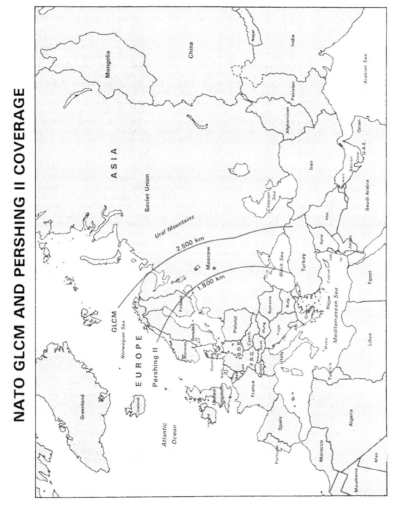

NATO GLCM AND PERSHING II COVERAGE

Source: NATO Information Service (1984); creator: unknown

Seeing deterrence and defence, modernizing forces?

The booklet was part of a broader propaganda campaign through which NATO sought to legitimize its force modernization and arms control positions. There is no clearcut answer to the question of how successfully the booklets shaped public opinion. That said, NATO continued to argue for its interpretation of a military balance in need of rebalancing and this interpretation then influentially underpinned the negotiations for the Treaty on Conventional Forces in Europe, as Hans-Joachim Schmidt shows in Chapter 11. The booklets contributed to the normalization of this interpretation. Visualizations of force comparisons condition the sensible and possible. They are part and parcel of public knowledge, even today as the old booklets have become digitally available. The overall geopolitical imaginary of the booklets represents a 'way of looking' that is 'highly visual' (Dodds, 2007: 4). It creates a 'particular understanding of places, communities and accompanying identities' (Dodds, 2007: 5). Technical images make capabilities visible through an aesthetic of spatial divisions and relational objects. In addition, populations and people are absent and rendered invisible. The human side of military force and security policies is elided.

Technical images are important meaning-making devices to imagine and govern the world (Akerman, 2009; Barney, 2015; Çapan and dos Reis, 2024). IR scholars should pay more attention to these representational modes as they underpin political claims with the aura of scientific authority. By emphasizing the technical side of forces and their comparison, anxieties relating to deterrence and defence are controlled. Visual discourse analysis helps to unpack this nexus between power, knowledge and sensibilities at the intersection of textual and visual representations. Visualization strategies reflect dominant regimes of visibility and invisibility, which may shift due to new technologies and policies. Compared to today's social media world, practices and patterns of visualization look more diverse and contested.

Two trends might be important if we intend to take the analysis of visual representations of force comparison one step further. First, while bar diagrams and maps are still popular, new modes of digital imaginaries like Twitter messages, memes or short videos on YouTube and TikTok are evolving (Baspehlivan, 2024; Duncombe, 2019) – and NATO is quite active here. Booklets have mainly gone, but visual representations of force comparison still prevail. Second, images can be manipulated quite easily; diagrams are not by definition objectively accurate but depend on the aesthetic and political choices of the creator. With the rise of artificial intelligence, it is possible to fabricate a world from scratch. The consequences of this trend are highly uncertain: many people might be more sceptical concerning the authenticity of visual representation while the numbers of images circulated globally and digitally are constantly rising.

References

Akerman, J.R. (ed) (2009) *The Imperial Map: Cartography and the Mastery of Empire*, Chicago, IL: University of Chicago Press.

Austin, J.L. (2019) 'Security compositions', *European Journal of International Security*, 4(3): 249–73.

Barney, T. (2015) *Mapping the Cold War: Cartography and the Framing of America's International Power*, Chapel Hill, NC: University of North Carolina Press.

Baspehlivan, U. (2024) 'Theorising the memescape: the spatial politics of internet memes', *Review of International Studies*, 50(1): 35–57.

Bleiker, R. (2014) 'Visual assemblages: from causality to conditions of possibility', in M. Acuto and S. Curtis (eds) *Reassembling International Theory: Assemblage Thinking and International Relations*, London: Palgrave Macmillan, pp 75–81.

Bleiker, R. (ed) (2018) *Visual Global Politics*, London: Routledge.

Breckner, R. (2015) *Sozialtheorie des Bildes: Zur interpretativen Analyse von Bildern und Fotografien*, Bielefeld: Transcript Verlag.

Bredekamp, H., Dünkel, V. and Schneider, B. (2015) *The Technical Image: A History of Styles in Scientific Imagery*, Chicago, IL: University of Chicago Press.

Callahan, W.A. (2020) *Sensible Politics: Visualizing International Relations*, New York, NY: Oxford University Press.

Çapan, Z.G. and dos Reis, F. (2024) 'Creating colonisable land: Cartography, "blank spaces", and imaginaries of empire in nineteenth-century Germany', *Review of International Studies*, 50(1): 146–70.

Cohn, C. (1987) 'Sex and death in the rational world of defense intellectuals', *Signs: Journal of Women in Culture and Society*, 12(4): 687–718.

Connolly, W.E. (1991) *Identity/Difference: Democratic Negotiations of Political Paradox*, Ithaca, NY: Cornell University Press.

Diez, T. (2001) 'Europe as a discursive battleground: discourse analysis and European integration studies', *Cooperation and Conflict*, 36(1): 5–38.

Diez, T. (2014) 'Setting the limits: discourse and EU foreign policy', *Cooperation and Conflict*, 49(3): 319–33.

Dodds, K. (2007) *Geopolitics: A Very Short Introduction*, Oxford: Oxford University Press.

Doty, R.L. (1996) *Imperial Encounters: The Politics of Representation in North–South Relations*, Minneapolis, MN: University of Minnesota Press.

Duncombe, C. (2019) 'The politics of Twitter: emotions and the power of social media', *International Political Sociology*, 13(4): 409–29.

Dunn, K.C. and Neumann, I.B. (2016) *Undertaking Discourse Analysis for Social Research*, Ann Arbor, MI: University of Michigan Press.

Glitman, M.W. (2006) *The Last Battle of the Cold War: An Inside Account of Negotiating the Intermediate Range Nuclear Forces Treaty*, Basingstoke: Palgrave Macmillan.

Grayson, K. and Mawdsley, J. (2018) 'Scopic regimes and the visual turn in international relations: seeing world politics through the drone', *European Journal of International Relations*, 25(2): 431–57.

Hansen, L. (2006) *Security as Practice: Discourse Analysis and the Bosnian War*, London: Routledge.

Hansen, L. (2011) 'Theorizing the image for security studies: visual securitization and the Muhammad cartoon crisis', *European Journal of International Relations*, 17(1): 51–74.

Herzog, R.J. and Wildgen, J.K. (1986) 'Tactics in military propaganda documents: a content analysis of illustrations', *Defense Analysis*, 2(1): 35–46.

Holzscheiter, A. (2014) 'Between communicative interaction and structures of signification: discourse theory and analysis in international relations', *International Studies Perspectives*, 15(2): 142–62.

Hopf, T. (2004) 'Discourse and content analysis: Some fundamental incompatibilities', *Qualitative Methods*, 2(1): 31–3.

Laclau, E. and Mouffe, C. (1985) *Hegemony and Socialist Strategy: Towards Radical Democratic Politics*, London: Verso.

MacKenzie, M. (2020) 'Why do soldiers swap illicit pictures? How a visual discourse analysis illuminates military band of brother culture', *Security Dialogue*, 51(4): 340–57.

Mitchell, W.J. (1984) 'What is an image?', *New Literary History*, 15(3): 503–37.

NATO Information Service (ed) (1984) *NATO and the Warsaw Pact. Force Comparisons*, Brussels: NATO.

Onuf, N.G. (1989) *World of our Making: Rules and Rule in Social Theory and International Relations*, London: Routledge.

Risse-Kappen, T. (1991) 'Public opinion, domestic structure, and foreign policy in liberal democracies', *World Politics*, 43(4): 479–512.

Rose, G. (2001) *Visual Methodologies: An Introduction to Researching with Visual Materials*, London: Sage.

Rothe, D. (2017) 'Seeing like a satellite: remote sensing and the ontological politics of environmental security', *Security Dialogue*, 48(4): 334–53.

Saugmann Andersen, R. (2019) 'Military techno-vision: technologies between visual ambiguity and the desire for security facts', *European Journal of International Security*, 4(3): 300–21.

Schlag, G. (2015) 'Imaging security: a visual methodology for security studies', in G. Schlag, J. Junk and C. Daase (eds) *Transformations of Security Studies*, London: Routledge, pp 173–89.

Schlag, G. (2019a) 'The afterlife of Osama bin Laden: performative pictures in the "war on terror"', *Critical Studies on Terrorism*, 12(1): 1–18.

Schlag, G. (2019b) 'Thinking and writing *Visual Global Politics* – A review of R. Bleiker's visual global politics (2018, Abingdon and New York: Routledge)', *International Journal of Politics, Culture, and Society*, 32(3): 105–14.

Schlag, G. and Heck, A. (2020) *Visualität und Weltpolitik: Praktiken des Zeigens und Sehens in den Internationalen Beziehungen*, Wiesbaden: Springer.

Schneider, B. and Nocke, T. (eds) (2014) *Image Politics of Climate Change: Visualizations, Imaginations, Documentations*, Bielefeld: Transcript Verlag.

Shim, D. (2013) *Visual Politics and North Korea: Seeing is Believing*, London: Routledge.

SIPRI (Stockholm International Peace Research Institute) (no date) *SIPRI Military Expenditure Database*, www.sipri.org/databases/milex [Accessed September 2023].

Stefanovsky, G. (1983) 'Who threatens peace?', *Soviet Military Review*, (1): 53–4.

Stuart, D. (1990) 'NATO in the 1980s: between European pillar and European home', *Armed Forces & Society*, 16(3): 421–36.

Survival (1982) 'Documentation: Whence the Threat to Peace', *Survival*, 24(3): 134–8.

Wæver, O. (1995) 'Securitization and desecuritization', in R.D. Lipschutz (ed) *On Security*, New York, NY: Columbia University Press, pp 46–86.

Wæver, O. (2004) 'Discursive approaches', in T. Diez and A. Wiener (eds) *European Integration Theory*, Oxford: Oxford University Press, pp 197–216.

Williams, M.C. (2003) 'Words, images, enemies: securitization and international politics', *International Studies Quarterly*, 47(4): 511–31.

5

What Drives Status Comparisons? An Experimental Study of Status Attribution in the Field of Space Exploration

Paul Musgrave and Steven Ward

The insight that practices of comparison matter for international security is at the centre of the fast-growing literature on status in world politics.[1] Status refers to an actor's position in a hierarchy, understood either as rank along a consensually valued dimension of comparison or as membership in an exclusive, elite club. Individuals and groups value favourable social comparisons, and compete to establish and maintain relative standing (Tajfel, 1978; Hogg and Abrams, 1988). To hold a particular status requires the possession of a symbolically significant marker or the performance of a similarly meaningful practice, together with recognition by relevant audiences. The last element is critical, as it suggests that measuring status is a complicated endeavour.

Over the past two decades, scholarship on status in world politics has accumulated rapidly (Dafoe et al, 2014; Paul et al, 2014; Götz, 2021; MacDonald and Parent, 2021). This work draws on a rich range of theoretical perspectives, including social psychology, sociology, social theory and others, and employs a variety of methods (Larson and Shevchenko, 2010; Renshon, 2015; 2016; Duque, 2018; Murray, 2018; Musgrave and Nexon, 2018; Røren and Beaumont, 2019; Ward, 2019; Barnhart, 2020). Research has established that states care about status comparisons; that status anxiety

---

[1] Among other work cited below, see, from this volume, Langer, Chapter 10 and Beaumont, Chapter 2.

can contribute to belligerence; and that states can also seek status in more peaceful and productive ways (Renshon, 2017; Wohlforth et al, 2018). The status motive is theoretically distinct from material calculations, and may thus explain competitions for dominance or position even in the absence of compelling strategic justifications (Larson and Shevchenko, 2010; Barnhart, 2016; Ward, 2017).

Understanding how states compete for position is a central concern for scholars working in this area. Some authors view status acquisition as a matter of demonstrating material power. Jonathan Renshon (2016) argues that states gain status by sending public signals about their willingness (or ability) to fight wars. Similarly, Deborah Welch Larson and Alexei Shevchenko (2010) contend that the relevant dimensions for states competing to join the 'great power' club involve instantiations of material power. Others suggest that status symbols constitute instances of 'conspicuous consumption': states gain status by displaying expensive or unusual attributes and practices (Gilady, 2018). These authors stress the social construction of status symbols, which means that status markers may manifest differently over time, as with the changing symbolic value of empire over the last century (Barnhart, 2020).

Recent work has also developed propositions about how comparative practices related to status may influence security politics. Negative comparisons with a relevant other can spur investment to improve a state's position in the hierarchy (Renshon, 2016; Larson and Shevchenko, 2019; Ward, 2019). One particularly dangerous consequence may be the production of deeply revisionist foreign policy orientations (Ward, 2017). Positive comparisons may also influence behaviour. Some authors have suggested that accommodating status aspirations, thereby effectively elevating a state's status, might foster its cooperation in promoting order (Paul, 2016). Positive comparisons may also bring about negative consequences, however: they may promote sensitivity to loss, thus contributing to the pursuit of costly policies aimed at defending deference (Onea, 2014; Fettweis, 2018; Butt, 2019).

In sum, recent research has suggested many links between status comparisons and foreign and security policy. Yet status comparisons are difficult to study empirically. Indeed, status is likely to be even harder to measure than the notoriously slippery concepts such as power or wealth at the heart of other research agendas (Jerven, 2013; Beckley, 2018). This is because status is intrinsically social and perceptual. A state's status depends not on how much of a symbolically significant attribute it possesses, but on how relevant others assess the state's position (Ward, 2020). Persuasively addressing the question of how comparative knowledge about standing – where states rank relative to others in the minds of relevant observers – is produced, and how it should be evaluated empirically, is one of the key challenges for research regarding status in world politics (see in this volume Müller et al, Chapter 1).

Most authors address this challenge by resorting to proxy measures that they argue (or assume), reflect attributed status. The most common proxy relies on the number of diplomatic representatives present in a country's capital. Because diplomatic exchange is costly, most states cannot maintain embassies in all other countries' capitals. The embassies they choose to maintain should, by assumption, include higher-status countries. Thus status should correlate with an increasing number of embassies hosted (Renshon, 2016; Duque, 2018). Research employing this measure has indeed yielded important findings (Rhamey and Early, 2013; Bezerra et al, 2015; Miller et al, 2015; Renshon, 2016; Duque, 2018; Røren and Beaumont, 2019). Yet doubts remain about whether the measure reliably reflects status. Decisions about diplomatic allocation likely operate differently than justifications assume, and diplomatic networks may reflect the aggregated influence of other factors rather than just status. For example, an increase in the rank of a state's diplomatic representative in another's capital can reflect the sender's judgement that enhanced diplomatic relations have become more important for contextual reasons, rather than because the target's status has increased. This process explains the upgrade of Brazil's representative in Washington in 1904; the upgrade of the United States' representatives in the capitals of a number of states in Europe and Latin America during the Second World War; and a similar upgrade in the rank of Iran's representatives after the outbreak of the Iran–Iraq War (Smith, 1991: 50; Ehteshami, 1995; Leonard and Bratzel, 2007; Sabet-Saeidi, 2008; Rundle, 2008). The justification for using diplomatic exchange as a proxy for status also requires the assumption that the meaning of diplomatic representation and rank is invariant across different temporal and regional settings – an assumption that is empirically questionable and inconsistent with the ontological commitments that underlie much work on status in world politics. For instance, American diplomatic 'ministers' were upgraded to 'ambassadors' beginning in 1893, not because Washington assessed that the host countries merited higher-status representation, but because American political culture had long blocked the use of titles that indicated 'special status', and thus the United States did not use the term 'ambassador' for its first century. This created problems for diplomats serving overseas, who themselves successfully pushed the government to upgrade their status in the early 1890s (Jett, 2014: Chapter 1).

Moreover, research designs employing the diplomatic exchange indicator are not well suited to answer central questions about the production of comparative knowledge about status. For instance, how are different kinds of status markers related to one another? Prior research suggests that behaviours as varied as military aggression and international athletic competition may be treated as substitutable strategies to boost one's standing as measured by the distribution of diplomats across capitals (Rhamey and Early, 2013; Bezerra et al, 2015; Renshon, 2016). It seems likely, however, that this is not a particularly useful way of thinking about status competition in such different contexts. What if, as we will discuss later, status competition takes place in specific fields such that achievement in one context might yield a different form of status than that won on the battlefield? Research designs based on the diplomatic exchange measure would be too blunt to analyse that question.

Another question that research designs based on diplomatic exchange data cannot answer involves whether evaluations of status markers vary by group. Political rhetoric frequently invokes status in ways that attach dramatically different meanings to salient attributes and policies. For instance, Brexit supporters contended that leaving the European Union would allow the UK to bolster its status as leader of the 'Anglosphere' (Beaumont, 2017; Bell and Vucetic, 2018), while opponents argued that the departure harmed the UK's standing in the world (Gifkins et al, 2019). Understanding such varied evaluations of status is key to unravelling questions about how status relates to domestic politics. Yet the current tools available to analysts for evaluating international status do not lend themselves to these investigations.

Status, fields and capital

This chapter introduces a means of exploring international status comparisons by investigating the beliefs of individuals about the relative ranking of states within specific fields of competition. We first explain how we ground our analysis in a framework adapted from Pierre Bourdieu's understanding of social fields and subsequently develop the case for our empirical approach.

As applied to international politics, field theory depicts a world in which states compete for position within fields defined by different 'species of capital that confer status, prestige, and power' (Nexon and Neumann, 2018: 668). In other words, rankings within different fields are determined by production, performances, distinctions, tastes and achievements that matter within those fields as determined by participants and audiences. Status markers that matter within the military field may matter less within the diplomatic field and not at all in the cultural field, for example.

Although related to broader dynamics of class and power, fields operate separately, and in some ways autonomously, from the distribution of those elements; they are not reducible to class relations, for instance. Daniel Nexon and Iver Neumann (2018: 669) emphasize the socially constructed nature of field-specific capital: 'certain species and subspecies of capital – whether cultural, economic, social, military, or whatever – become infused with specifically ideological meaning that renders them particularly valuable'. (Academics may appreciate how the quest for position in their fields may be all-consuming to them yet entails markers of status that are indecipherable to the public, or even scholars in other fields.)

The accumulation of these specific forms of capital determines players' rankings within different fields. Capital may be fungible, and some forms may be more fungible than others. Exchange rates between fields and varieties of capital vary and must be ascertained empirically. Field theory thus provides both a warrant for understanding how different forms of status operate separately and a guide to empirically assessing rankings across those different varieties. Scholars have applied field theory to understand, for example, the choices of actors and the development of hierarchies in Ming China, US and UK imperialism, and the global art market (Go, 2008; Musgrave and Nexon, 2018; MacKay, 2022).

To demonstrate the utility of this approach, we focus on status within the field of international space exploration. This field offers several advantages. Scholars of world politics and status have long claimed that international status competition drives states to engage in space exploration. Lilach Gilady (2018: Chapter 5) argues that human and robotic space missions constitute conspicuous consumption that signals prestige, while Deganit Paikowsky (2017) suggests that possessing space capabilities grants states entrance into a status club. Soviet space 'firsts' spurred the US to invest tremendous sums in a space race to protect its hegemonic position (Musgrave and Nexon, 2018). Prestige-seeking states are more likely to develop civil space agencies, and contemporary Chinese investment in space exploration may be motivated at least in part by status concerns, perhaps especially to influence domestic audiences (Sheehan, 2013; Early, 2014).

Space exploration also constitutes a specialized, bounded field that makes it a good candidate for empirical examination. The field emerged in the late 1950s as an outgrowth of more generalized science and technology competition (Musgrave and Nexon, 2018: 34). Although many space endeavours are linked to economic incentives or military competition, at least parts of the field remain at least partially autonomous from profit and security motivations, especially with regard to human spaceflight and research endeavours (Sheehan, 2013; Musgrave and Nexon, 2018; Hines, 2019). Furthermore, capital in the space field remains highly valued enough that both the US and the People's Republic of China have plans or programmes underway for lunar (and potentially Martian) missions. Advances in peaceful, robotic exploration of the Moon and Mars by the People's Republic of China prompted US National Aeronautics and Space Administrator Bill Nelson to warn of a loss of US leadership in space (Foust, 2021). That a Chinese space 'first' would prompt calls for increased spending supports the idea that competition in this field takes place autonomously of military and economic dimensions, as Beijing's lunar intentions have little immediate consequence for terrestrial great power rivalries (although they might have remote implications for lunar resource control) and its Martian ambitions are even more remote. At the same time, the fact that Sino–American rivalry on Earth makes robotic space science valuable in prestige terms suggests that contests in other fields can lead to the valuing or revaluing of accomplishments within the space exploration field for at least some audiences. What would be interesting to know is the degree to which audiences are receptive to such claims, and under what conditions.

Investment in space competition may seek to influence how different audiences (or combinations of audiences) make status comparisons. One category comprises foreign audiences, as with US missions to the Moon in the 1960s and 1970s, which originated as means of winning the 'hearts and minds of the nonaligned world' (Musgrave and Nexon, 2018: 611; Muir-Harmony, 2020). A second category comprises domestic audiences. Research in other substantive areas demonstrates that at least some domestic audiences care about the status of the state with which they identify, and that governments may thus face incentives to invest in various forms of social capital to shore up support among key groups (Sambanis et al, 2015; Lin and Katada, 2020; Ward, 2022). Concerns about domestic support and regime legitimacy might help explain patterns in China's investment in space exploration (Sheehan, 2013; Hines, 2022).

An experimental approach to status and fields in world politics

While investment in space exploration is likely *motivated* by status concerns, little is known about how different kinds of achievements and characteristics influence assessments of relative standing within that field. One promising avenue for exploring assessments of status in the space field involves survey experiments. Survey experiments enable researchers to randomly assign respondents to different conditions. Random assignment enables cleaner causal inference about what factors produce which outcomes than is possible in case studies or observational designs. Because survey experiments involve the creation of new data, research designs employing this format are not limited to indirect proxy measurements like diplomatic exchange as a measure for prestige. Instead, researchers can contrive more direct operationalizations of the concept.

The application of statistical methods to test hypotheses derived from field theory may seem unusual, given the common association in International Relations scholarship of Pierre Bourdieu with qualitative and critical methods. However, Bourdieu employed statistical and survey methods in his own work (Bourdieu, 1984; Lebaron, 2009; Duval, 2018). He may have favoured different methods (specifically, geometric data analysis and multiple correspondence analysis), but our intentions are similar: contributing to an understanding of what constitutes relevant capital and meta-capital by examining how audiences display tastes for performances in a specific field. In particular, we are interested in understanding how the American public understands the international field of space exploration, recognizing that a study of German, Thai or Nigerian publics might yield different understandings. Nevertheless, mapping how the public of a leading country in most international status indicators views relative position offers an immediate theoretical payoff and points toward further comparative work (across fields and countries) later. Thus, just as Bourdieu's *Distinction* used analysis of data from surveys to explore questions of culture and status in France, so we offer this methodology as a step toward a more rigorous microfoundational approach to the study of international status.

Moreover, conjoint experiments, in which respondents choose between profiles that vary on many attributes, involve the same sort of judgements regarding taste and distinction that, Bourdieu writes, *feel* to those in the fields as if they are natural and automatic but which actually reflect a long process of education and socialization (Bourdieu, 1984: 2). Respondents may not be able to report why they chose one profile over another, but if large numbers of them make similar choices on average over many observations, then we should be confident that this choice reflects some underlying disposition of the field's audience. To be clear: because status is contextual and socially constructed, we do not think that any given accomplishment will always have the same effect under all conditions, but rather that these methods help us uncover the logic of the field as it exists under contemporary conditions for our audience.

In a conjoint experiment, subjects are presented with a task to complete, such as choosing which of two profiles of immigrants to admit to the US (Hainmueller et al, 2014; Hainmueller and Hopkins, 2015). These profiles contain attributes, such as the nationality and education level of the immigrant, which each have different levels, such as Iraqi or French and a high school diploma or a doctorate. Subjects usually complete several such tasks in a given setting. Comparing which choices are made as those levels vary enables researchers to estimate the marginal contribution of each attribute (according to its levels) to outcomes in general. Conjoint methodology allows researchers to simultaneously vary many factors and return useful information even when respondents are asked to complete many tasks or tasks with many different features. Consequently, the approach is increasingly popular in International Relations scholarship (Clary and Siddiqui, 2021; Escribà-Folch et al, 2021; Leal and Musgrave, 2022; 2023; Musgrave and Ward, 2023).

Our experiment presented respondents with a scenario in which they were asked to imagine that the United Nations was creating an international agency for international cooperation in space. Respondents were told that they would review pairs of hypothetical countries applying to host the new agency's headquarters and pick which of the pair would make a better host.

The opening vignette informed them that many people believe that hosting such an agency would be a prestigious honour. Because we were interested in how Americans rank other countries in terms of status, we informed them that the US was ineligible to host this new headquarters because the main UN headquarters was already in the US.

The wager of our scenario is that, all else being equal, audiences would prefer to put an international headquarters in a place that 'feels' as though it is suitable. The wealth, regime type and so on of a potential host country will likely influence respondents, but, if status distinctions matter, so too should salient accomplishments in the most relevant field: space exploration. (Note that the 'null hypothesis' is meaningful: it could be that status distinctions do *not* matter and that general attributes like wealth and cultural similarity dominate field-specific status markers.) There is evidence from previous selection efforts that actors view the location of UN headquarters as markers of prestige. For instance, during a period when it was uncertain whether the International Civil Aviation Organization (ICAO) would remain in Montreal, the Canadian government decided to campaign to remain ICAO's host not only because of the tangible benefits (employment for 300 nationals and saving the cost of Canadian diplomats who would otherwise be posted abroad) but also to bolster 'international recognition and prestige' (MacKenzie, 2010: 142).

To be clear, our ambition is not to explain the siting of the headquarters of intergovernmental organizations. It is, instead, to use the task of deciding the location of a hypothetical headquarters to illuminate how respondents view international status. To that end, variation in field-specific accomplishments should tell us something about the relative importance of those forces for status assessments, both compared to each other and compared to potentially status-laden accomplishments and traits that are unrelated to the field of space exploration. Indeed, in this we make no stronger assumptions than observational studies that employ diplomatic exchange data, some key independent variable (like Olympic medals), and a host of controls like population, GDP, regional controls, military prowess and so on (Bezerra et al, 2015: 263, but the examples could be multiplied). Such models similarly assume that the effect of status-enhancing activities can be measured as a residuum not explained by other factors. Indeed, considering the advantages for causal inference of experimental over observational studies, and the fact that the relationship between our dependent variable and the concept we seek to measure is tighter than that between diplomatic exchange and status, we are likely making much weaker assumptions than current studies.

This scenario was intended to elicit beliefs about what factors contribute to a country's status. To that end, we included attributes from two categories. The first category contained attributes that relate to a state's general level of wealth, military power, cultural similarity, regime type and record regarding human rights; the second category contained attributes related to a country's accomplishments and normative performance with regard to civilian space exploration, both robotic and human-crewed.

Including factors in the first, general category enabled us to provide greater information equivalence across types of status markers (Dafoe et al, 2018). Without information about a country's income per person or type of government being explicitly provided, respondents might have inferred something about those traits from those in the second category. Yet there are many countries that have achieved significant outcomes in space exploration without a high GDP per capita (the Soviet Union or the People's Republic of China) and many countries with a high GDP per capita that lack such accomplishments (Norway, for instance, has not yet placed a single astronaut in space). Our design thus explicitly separated space accomplishments and performance from these latent variables.

This design also facilitates an investigation of whether and how general traits as opposed to endowments and accomplishments in specific fields influence status assessments. Endowments of different forms of capital may help shape the status of countries across a variety of fields. For instance, Nexon and Neumann note that 'there are (at least) as many hierarchies in world politics as there are fields', and that one of the key tasks for understanding 'generalized status' in world politics involves investigating the 'terms of exchange *among* fields'. In other words, status within an 'economic field' or a field defined by ideas about the value of different kinds of political institutions may influence status within ostensibly unrelated fields (like space exploration) (Nexon and Neumann, 2018: 672–3). Including variables directly related to space exploration, as well as variables that have been linked to status but do not involve achievements within the field of space exploration, enables us to take a step toward investigating status exchange rates across fields. A country's population, predominant language or regime type may contribute to how audiences judge status even when these attributes have no plausible link to performance within the relevant field, just as beauty, height and race may affect a wide range of interpersonal status comparisons. Such attributes are difficult to change, and so the status literature has frequently explored how states use other sorts of accomplishments, such as winning Olympic medals or operating aircraft carriers, to influence how other states and audiences view them *despite* their endowments in less manipulable categories (Rhamey and Early, 2013; Gilady, 2018). In other words, researchers have already tacitly acknowledged exchange rates between fields; we set out to develop and demonstrate a means of measuring them systematically.

The survey was programmed on the Qualtrics survey platform. We recruited respondents using the Lucid online service between 16 June and 22 June 2021. Lucid has been found to offer comparable or superior response quality to Mechanical Turk (Coppock and McClellan, 2019). Our respondent pool was specified to be recruited from the US and respondents certified they were US citizens aged 18 or over. A total of 2,016 respondents completed the survey, including seven conjoint tasks, yielding a total N of 14,112. We preregistered our hypotheses and analysis plan with the Open Science Foundation.

Results

Our first attribute category – encompassing general characteristics plausibly related to status but not directly related to achievements in space exploration – included population, average annual income per person, region, type of government, nuclear arsenal, military strength, use of the English language, religion, human rights record and gender equality. We chose population cutoffs to reflect sensible breakpoints in the distribution of countries' populations: roughly the top 100 (7 million), top 50 (22 million), top 30 (47 million), top 20 (72 million), and top 10 (more than 100 million). Because we assumed that respondents were unlikely to know how a dollar figure for GDP per capita related to global distributions, we described average annual income per person categorically, from 'low' to 'very high'. We similarly described regime type on a four-point scale from 'not at all democratic' to 'highly democratic'. Because nuclear arsenals are frequently posited to be sources of prestige, we included an indicator for whether a country has a large, small or no nuclear arsenal (Ritchie, 2014; Haynes, 2020; Egel and Hines, 2021). Similarly, we described a country as having a powerful, moderately powerful or weak military, given the common claim that military strength structures status hierarchies. Given the possibility that in-group biases or prejudices might affect respondents' perceptions of status, we also varied whether the candidate country had a population that could speak English and the description of the country's predominant religious heritage (Hanania and Trager, 2021). Finally, we included information about the quality of human rights and gender equality (operationalized as women's share of top government posts), as both may influence status evaluations in international relations (Towns, 2010).

Figure 5.1 displays results from the conjoint experiment for these general (or non-space-specific) characteristics. Some attributes, like population, do not display substantial or statistically significant variation. Perhaps more surprisingly given the prominence of prestige as an explanation for the acquisition of nuclear weapons, neither does the presence or size of a state's nuclear arsenal. A state's military strength does matter somewhat, though there is only a 2.8 percentage point difference between 'weak' and 'powerful' states in favour of the powerful. Regional variation matters more: Western Europe has a 4.9 percentage point advantage over South Asia, and North and Central America have a 3.4 percentage point advantage. (The US-centric

Figure 5.1: General characteristics

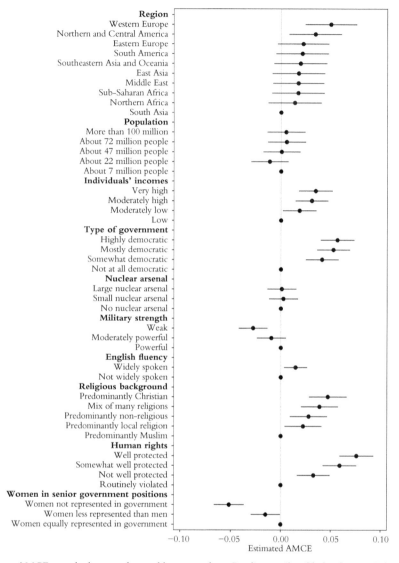

Note: AMCEs standard errors clustered by respondent. Baseline attributable levels set at 0 for ease of interpretation.

audience preferring Western Europe to Northern America may be a consequence of the scenario instructions reminding them that the US was ineligible to host.) No other region was substantively or statistically different from South Asia. English fluency was preferred to non-English fluency by 1.5 percentage points, a comparatively small amount. However, respondents showed a pronounced preference for Christian countries. Notably, the other religion that has spread beyond its original region, Islam, suffers a significant penalty, being 4.7 percentage points less likely to be chosen (equivalent to the pro-Western Europe bonus).

Respondents penalized undemocratic states relative to even partly democratic ones, with 'somewhat democratic' countries rated 4.1 percentage points more favourably and 'highly democratic' countries rated 5.6 percentage points more likely to be chosen. Similarly, countries with very high income per person were 3.5 percentage points more likely to be chosen than countries with low income per person. Gender equality also mattered: countries that did not represent women in government received a penalty of 5.2 percentage points compared to those that represented them equally to men. The most important factor within the general characteristics category pertained to human rights. Countries that protected rights well were favoured by 7.6 percentage points over those that routinely violated human rights.

These results suggest that a generic high-status country would be a rich, democratic Western European country with at least a moderately powerful military, strong protections for human rights and a progressive distribution of high government offices for women. Similarly, a low status country would be a poor, South Asian autocracy with a weak military and highly Muslim population whose government routinely violated human rights and excluded women from public life. On the one hand, those results are probably intuitive. But note that the fact that they are unsurprising validates the conjoint approach, since few if any respondents would have compared exactly those profiles: these findings emerged from thousands of responses to randomly varied traits. Similarly, although the qualitative import of our findings may be unsurprising, the conjoint methodology allows us to state with precision that a combination of political factors (democratic government, respect for human rights and gender equality) and cultural ones (specifically, whether or not a country is predominantly Muslim) account for differences between high and low status profiles, rather than being unable to discern among those traits. It is also worth emphasizing that these factors are – at best – very loosely related to capacity or achievements in the field of space exploration; some (like religion or language) might even be considered by some respondents normatively inappropriate to mention as reasons to favour one country over another as the host of a UN organization aimed at governing space exploration, even if they would factor those traits into their decision. It is striking – and a key benefit of our methodological approach – that we can identify and assess the magnitude of the influence of these factors on the production of comparative knowledge about international status.

The general findings provide context for Figure 5.2, which contains the space-field-specific findings. Two attributes are straightforward: the number of satellites a country has currently orbiting the Earth and the number of its astronauts who have ever been to space. We chose numbers that

Figure 5.2: Space characteristics

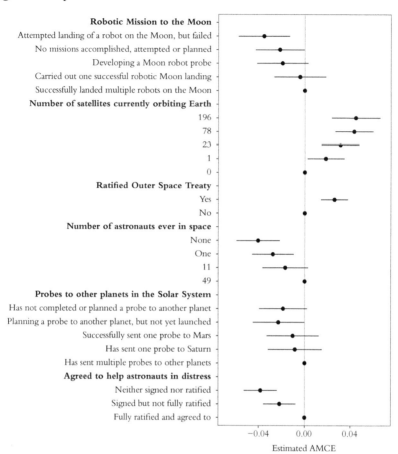

Note: AMCEs standard errors clustered by respondent. Baseline attributable levels set at 0 for ease of interpretation.

ranged from zero to very high (but not equal to Russia/the USSR or the United States, the leaders in these categories), in both cases also including a 'one' to indicate that the threshold had been passed but no more. A third attribute specified the number of interplanetary probes that a country had accomplished (multiple probes, one to Saturn, one to Mars, probes planned but not accomplished, and none planned or accomplished). A fourth attribute sought to measure both achievement and failure by specifying whether a country had successfully completed one or multiple robotic Moon landings, had a mission in development, had not accomplished or attempted any and had none planned, or had attempted *but failed* to land a robot on the Moon.

Finally, two attributes measured normative compliance, which earlier work has suggested could be a basis for status attribution (Miller et al, 2015).

One attribute measured whether states have ratified the Outer Space Treaty, the 'foundation of international space law'; the other measured whether states have ratified, signed but not ratified, or neither signed nor ratified the Rescue Agreement by which states promise to provide assistance to astronauts in distress. These descriptions accurately, if pointedly, reflect their content (Peterson, 2006). Our goal in including them was to give a sense of normative compliance, and we exploited the fact that there is real-world variation in assent to these agreements (112 countries are parties to and a further 23 are signatories to the Outer Space Treaty; 121 countries are parties to or signatories to the Rescue Agreement) in order to do so.

We begin with the striking findings regarding lunar exploration. It is unsurprising that respondents ranked countries that had successfully landed multiple robots on the Moon highest, followed by those who had successfully carried out one such landing. Yet it is notable that they ranked lowest those that attempted to land a robot on the Moon but had failed. The penalty for failing relative to succeeding (once or multiple times) was more than 3.5 percentage points. This suggests that prominent failures, such as the 1960 Mercury-Redstone 'four-inch flight' (a NASA rocket that blew up on the launch pad), the 2023 failed Virgin Orbit launch, and the August 2023 crash of the Russian Luna-25 on the surface of the Moon, may indeed carry substantial status penalties for their sponsors (Reed, 2023).

Successfully placing even one satellite into orbit (akin to, say, Bangladesh) enhances respondents' evaluation of suitability to host the UN space agency by 1.8 percentage points relative to those who have not placed any. There are diminishing marginal returns to more satellites. Placing 23 satellites (roughly the level of South Korea at the time of our experiment) had an effect size of 3.1 percentage points over no satellites, while orbiting 196 satellites (roughly the level of Japan) had an effect size of 4.5 percentage points over a no-satellite condition (the difference between those two high-achieving levels was not significantly different). Similarly, placing 49 astronauts into space (the level achieved by the Russian space programme after the Soviet era) shifted respondents' approval by 4 percentage points relative to having placed none. There are diminishing marginal returns, as this effect size is not statistically distinguishable from having placed 11 astronauts in orbit (the level of Germany).

Interplanetary probes do not appear to register as a source of prestige. In some senses, this is surprising. Interplanetary probes are enormously expensive relative to lunar missions. The Pioneer Venus probe (1978–1992) cost an inflation-adjusted US$1.3 billion for one orbiter and one lander, while the NASA Lunar Prospector mission (1998–1999) cost an inflation-adjusted US$114.1 million (see The Planetary Society, no date). By contrast, Luxembourg's private Manfred Memorial Moon Mission, which successfully conducted a lunar flyby, was much cheaper – reportedly in the region of six figures (Wall, 2014). Our results may be explained at least in part by the fact that this category, unlike lunar robotic missions, does not include a level for trying but failing, the source of the most significant variation for lunar results. At the very least, however, these results invite further study.

By contrast, accession to international agreements does matter. Ratification of the Outer Space Treaty raised support by 2.6 percentage points, roughly the difference between having a 'powerful' and 'weak' military. Accepting the Rescue Agreement raised support by 3.8 percentage points – slightly larger than the difference between a country with 'low' and one with 'very high' individual incomes. Respondents appear to reward compliance with international norms depicted as prosocial.

As noted earlier, audiences may vary in how they perceive performances based on a range of factors, including their different interests, identities and ideas. We test this by segmenting results by demographics and attitudes. Our analysis identified little substantive variation by gender or political party. Respondents' attitudes about the value of space as a field of competition are much more significant. Separate from the conjoint tasks, we asked respondents whether they thought that having a leading position internationally in space exploration would help a country to raise its status relative to other countries a great deal, somewhat or very little. Among those who answered 'a great deal' (compared to those who said space matters only somewhat or very little), attempted but failed lunar landings were penalized more harshly, as were countries that had not yet completed an interplanetary probe. These respondents were also less likely to penalize states that have not acceded to the Rescue Agreement. Figure 5.3 reports these results.

We also asked respondents if they believe it is very important for a country to be a world leader in scientific achievements. Figure 5.4 reports results separately for those who agreed with this statement and for those who did not. Those who believe science leadership is very important were more likely to penalize a country that tried but failed to land a lunar rover; they were also more likely to penalize countries that have never put an astronaut into space. However, these respondents were no more likely to reward countries for accomplishments in interplanetary probes.

Taken together, these results suggest that audiences who are more attuned to scientific and space exploration as zones of competition regard accomplishments in space differently from other audiences. The concept of status – like other forms of comparative knowledge – thus appears to be multiple and contested in ways that are contrary to its typical depiction in the International Relations literature.[2] This is a possibility worthy of

---

2 For similar points about other forms of comparative knowledge, see, in this volume, Krause, Chapter 7; Jakobi and Herbst, Chapter 8.

Figure 5.3: By belief in space as status-enhancing

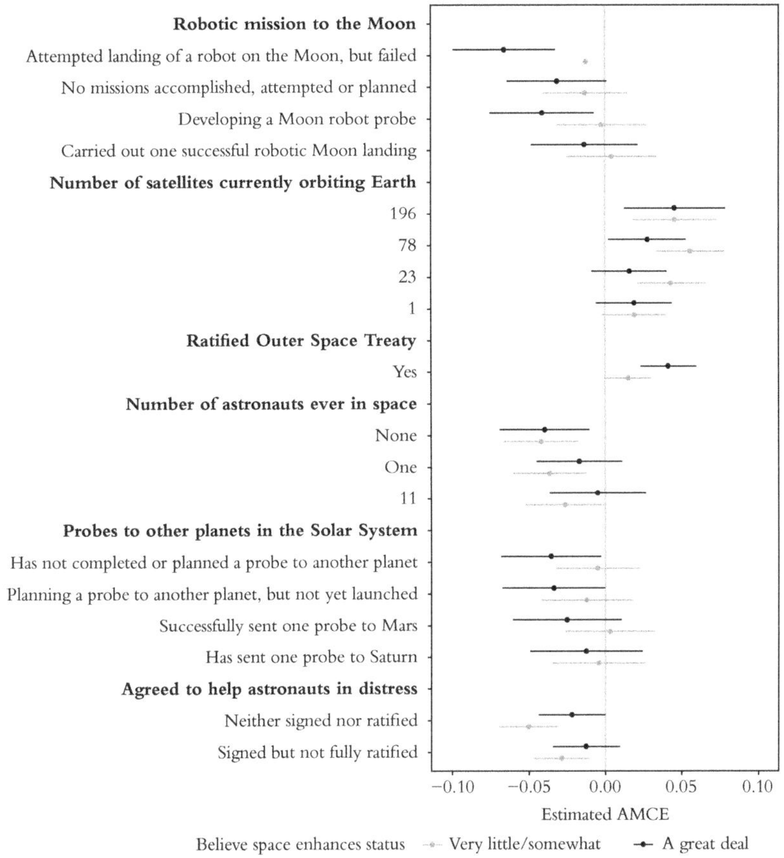

Note: AMCEs standard errors clustered by respondent. Baseline attributable levels set at 0 for ease of interpretation.

further investigation, but beyond the scope of conventional measures of relative standing.

Conclusion

This chapter has developed and illustrated a novel means of empirically assessing observers' view of international status, conceived of in terms of field theory. We demonstrate that, within the field of international space competition, both general and field-specific factors influence an audience's evaluation of international status. Status-seeking actors in world politics thus may indeed be able to gain status in a given field through their accomplishments despite unfavourable traits. Substantively, some types of accomplishment matter more than others, with lunar and near-Earth

Figure 5.4: Differences by belief in science leadership

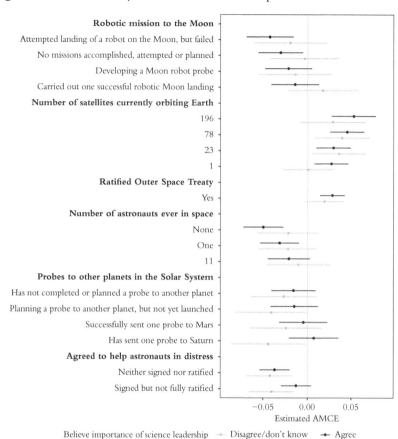

Note: AMCEs standard errors clustered by respondent. Baseline attributable levels set at 0 for ease of interpretation.

activities (including human space travel) more valued than interplanetary robotic exploration, despite the latter missions' sophistication and expense. Compliance with international norms, as measured by signing relevant agreements, matters as well.

It is striking, though, that we do not find evidence that factors related to traditional conceptions of security (like the possession of nuclear weapons, or the balance of military capabilities) strongly influence evaluations of status in the field of international space competition. This is surprising given the fact that development and achievements in the field of space exploration have plausible links to security concerns and capabilities, and the common assumption throughout the literature on status that indicators and demonstrations of military power are among the most significant status symbols in world politics. Our study thus suggests a need to interrogate this latter assumption empirically – and a means of doing so.

Our approach also points to a need for other refinements to theory and practice in the study of international status. Relying on observational data through proxies has been generative but future work should more carefully consider how to measure status in a theoretically appropriate manner. This complements a turn toward studying individual and group attitudes rather than state-level observations. As Bourdieu emphasized, 'symbolic capital' is only valuable to the extent that 'agents [are] socialized in such a way as to be familiar with and acknowledge' it (Nexon and Neumann, 2018: 669). This means, of course, that agents not socialized 'to be familiar with and acknowledge' certain forms of capital will not recognize them in the same manner. Applied work – using methods like those we demonstrate in this chapter – could thus map variation in status assessments across social groups and countries. Perhaps elite audiences would differ in their assessments – and perhaps their tastes would be more influential in setting the terms of competition within the field. However, political scientists may overstate the degree to which elite and mass opinion differs (Kertzer, 2020).

Our study also points toward promising avenues for the broader study of comparisons in world politics. The most obvious is to suggest a novel means of understanding the factors that may contribute to particular kinds of comparative knowledge, but may not be apparent from studies that rely on narrative-based evidence (see in this volume Müller et al, Chapter 1). For instance, we find that Americans' ranking of other countries in the field of space competition depends significantly on those countries' religious and linguistic similarity – two factors that may, for a variety of reasons, not frequently be explicitly cited as the basis for ranking countries in this area. One of the strengths of our approach is that we are nonetheless able to identify and measure the influence of these factors on comparative practices. While not the focus of this chapter, the method we demonstrated earlier may also prove useful for understanding the processes by which comparative practices become politically relevant. One straightforward extension of our experimental design could investigate the effect of variation in the salience of different kinds of comparisons on support for different kinds of related policies (see in this volume Müller et al, Chapter 1).

References

Barnhart, J. (2016) 'Status competition and territorial aggression: evidence from the scramble for Africa', *Security Studies*, 25(3): 385–419.

Barnhart, J. (2020) *The Consequences of Humiliation: Anger and Status in World Politics*, Ithaca, NY: Cornell University Press.

Beaumont, P. (2017) 'Brexit, retrotopia and the perils of post-colonial delusions', *Global Affairs*, 3(4–5): 379–90.

Beckley, M. (2018) 'The power of nations: measuring what matters', *International Security*, 43(2): 7–44.

Bell, D. and Vucetic, S. (2018) 'Brexit, CANZUK, and the legacy of empire', *The British Journal of Politics and International Relations*, 21(2): 367–82.

Bezerra, P., Cramer, J., Hauser, M., Miller, J.L. and Volgy, T.J. (2015) 'Going for the gold versus distributing the green: foreign policy substitutability and complementarity in status enhancement strategies', *Foreign Policy Analysis*, 11(3): 253–72.

Bourdieu, P. (1984) *Distinction: A Social Critique of the Judgement of Taste*, Translated by Richard Nice, Cambridge, MA: Harvard University Press.

Butt, A.I. (2019) 'Why did the United States invade Iraq in 2003?', *Security Studies*, 28(2): 250–85.

Clary, C. and Siddiqui, N. (2021) 'Voters and foreign policy: evidence from a conjoint experiment in Pakistan', *Foreign Policy Analysis*, 17(2): orab001.

Coppock, A. and McClellan, O.A. (2019) 'Validating the demographic, political, psychological, and experimental results obtained from a new source of online survey respondents', *Research & Politics*, 6(1): 1–14.

Dafoe, A., Renshon, J. and Huth, P. (2014) 'Reputation and status as motives for war', *Annual Review of Political Science*, 17: 371–93.

Dafoe, A., Zhang, B. and Caughey, D. (2018) 'Information equivalence in survey experiments', *Political Analysis*, 26(4): 399–416.

Duque, M.G. (2018) 'Recognizing international status: a relational approach', *International Studies Quarterly*, 62(3): 577–92.

Duval, J. (2018) 'Correspondence analysis and Bourdieu's approach to statistics', in T. Medvetz and J.J. Sallaz (eds) *The Oxford Handbook of Pierre Bourdieu*, New York, NY: Oxford University Press, pp 512–27.

Early, B.R. (2014) 'Exploring the final frontier: an empirical analysis of global space proliferation', *International Studies Quarterly*, 58(1): 55–67.

Egel, N. and Hines, R. L. (2021) 'Chinese views on nuclear weapons: evidence from an online survey', *Research & Politics*, 16 July, https://doi.org/10.1177/20531680211032840 [Accessed 16 January 2023].

Ehteshami, A. (1995) *After Khomeini: The Iranian Second Republic*, London, New York, NY: Routledge.

Escribà-Folch, A., Muradova, L.H. and Rodon, T. (2021) 'The effects of autocratic characteristics on public opinion toward democracy promotion policies: a conjoint analysis', *Foreign Policy Analysis*, 17(1): oraa016.

Fettweis, C. (2018) *Psychology of a Superpower: Security and Dominance in US Foreign Policy*, New York, NY: Columbia University Press.

Foust, J. (2021) 'Nelson uses Chinese Mars landing as a warning to congress', *SpaceNews*, 20 May, https://spacenews.com/nelson-uses-chinese-mars-land ing-as-a-warning-to-congress/ [Accessed 16 January 2023].

Gifkins, J., Jarvis, S. and Ralph, J. (2019) 'Brexit and the UN Security Council: declining British influence', *International Affairs*, 95(6): 1349–68.

Gilady, L. (2018) *The Price of Prestige*, Chicago, IL: University of Chicago Press.

Go, J. (2008) 'Global fields and imperial forms: field theory and the British and American empires', *Sociological Theory*, 26(3): 201–29.

Götz, E. (2021) 'Status matters in world politics', *International Studies Review*, 23(1): 228–47.

Hainmueller, J. and Hopkins, D.J. (2015) 'The hidden American immigration consensus: a conjoint analysis of attitudes toward immigrants', *American Journal of Political Science*, 59(3): 529–48.

Hainmueller, J., Hopkins, D.J. and Yamamoto, T. (2014) 'Causal inference in conjoint analysis: understanding multidimensional choices via stated preference experiments', *Political Analysis*, 22(1): 1–30.

Hanania, R. and Trager, R. (2021) 'The prejudice first model and foreign policy values: racial and religious bias among conservatives and liberals', *European Journal of International Relations*, 27(1): 204–31.

Haynes, S.T. (2020) 'The power of prestige: explaining China's nuclear weapons decisions', *Asian Security*, 16(1): 35–52.

Hines, R.L. (2019) 'Is China catching up to the United States in space?', *Washington Post*, 24 April, www.washingtonpost.com/politics/2019/04/24/is-china-catching-up-united-states-space/ [Accessed 16 January 2023].

Hines, R.L. (2022) 'Heavenly mandate: public opinion and China's space activities', *Space Policy*, 60: 101460.

Hogg, M. and Abrams, D. (1988) *Social Identification: A Social Psychology of Intergroup Relations and Group Processes*, London, New York, NY: Routledge.

Jerven, M. (2013) *Poor Numbers*, Ithaca, NY: Cornell University Press.

Jett, D. (2014) *American Ambassadors: The Past, Present, and Future of America's Diplomats*, New York, NY: Palgrave Macmillan.

Kertzer, J.D. (2020) 'Reassessing elite–public gaps in political behavior', *American Journal of Political Science*, 66(3): 539–53.

Larson, D.W. and Shevchenko, A. (2010) 'Status seekers: Chinese and Russian responses to US primacy', *International Security*, 34(4): 63–95.

Larson, D.W. and Shevchenko, A. (2019) *Quest for Status: Chinese and Russian Foreign Policy*, New Haven, CT: Yale University Press.

Leal, M.M. and Musgrave, P. (2022) 'Cheerleading in cyberspace: how the American public judges attribution claims for cyberattacks', *Foreign Policy Analysis*, 18(2): orac003.

Leal, M.M. and Musgrave, P. (2023) 'Hitting back or holding back in cyberspace: experimental evidence regarding Americans' responses to cyberattacks', *Conflict Management and Peace Science*, 40(1): 42–64.

Lebaron, F. (2009) 'How Bourdieu "quantified" Bourdieu: the geometric modelling of data', in K. Robson and C. Sanders (eds) *Quantifying Theory: Pierre Bourdieu*, Heidelberg: Springer Dordrecht, pp 11–29.

Leonard, T. and Bratzel, J. (eds) (2007) *Latin America during World War II*, Washington, DC: Rowman & Littlefield.

Lin, A.Y. and Katada, S.N. (2020) 'Striving for greatness: status aspirations, rhetorical entrapment, and domestic reforms', *Review of International Political Economy*, 29(1): 1–38.

MacDonald, P.K. and Parent, J.M. (2021) 'The status of status in world politics', *World Politics*, 73(2): 358–91.

MacKay, J. (2022) 'Art world fields and global hegemonies', *International Studies Quarterly*, 66(3): sqac029.

MacKenzie, D. (2010) *ICAO: A History of the International Civil Aviation Organization*, Toronto, ON: University of Toronto Press.

Miller, J.L., Cramer, J., Volgy, T.J., Bezerra, P., Hauser, M. and Sciabarra, C. (2015) 'Norms, behavioral compliance, and status attribution in international politics', *International Interactions*, 41(5): 779–804.

Muir-Harmony, T. (2020) *Operation Moonglow: A Political History of Project Apollo*, New York, NY: Basic Books.

Murray, M. (2018) *The Struggle for Recognition in International Relations: Status, Revisionism, and Rising Powers*, New York, NY: Oxford University Press.

Musgrave, P. and Nexon, D.H. (2018) 'Defending hierarchy from the moon to the Indian Ocean: symbolic capital and political dominance in early modern China and the Cold War', *International Organization*, 72(3): 591–626.

Musgrave, P. and Ward, S. (2023) 'The tripwire effect: experimental evidence regarding U.S. public opinion', *Foreign Policy Analysis*, 19(4): orad017.

Nexon, D.H. and Neumann, I.B. (2018) 'Hegemonic-order theory: a field-theoretic account', *European Journal of International Relations*, 24(3): 662–86.

Onea, T.A. (2014) 'Between dominance and decline: status anxiety and great power rivalry', *Review of International Studies*, 40(1): 125–52.

Paikowsky, D. (2017) *The Power of the Space Club*, New York, NY: Cambridge University Press.

Paul, T.V. (2016) 'The accommodation of rising powers in world politics', in T.V. Paul (ed) *Accommodating Rising Powers: Past, Present, and Future*, New York, NY: Cambridge University Press, pp 3–32.

Paul, T.V., Larson, D. and Wohlforth, W.C. (eds) (2014) *Status in World Politics*, New York, NY: Cambridge University Press.

Peterson, M.J. (2006) *International Regimes for the Final Frontier*, Albany, NY: State University of New York Press.

Reed, S. (2023) 'Failure of Britain's first space launch is a setback to emerging industry', *New York Times*, 10 January, www.nytimes.com/2023/01/10/business/uk-satellite-virgin-orbit.html [Accessed 16 January 2023].

Renshon, J. (2015) 'Losing face and sinking costs: experimental evidence on the judgment of political and military leaders', *International Organization*, 69(3): 659–95.

Renshon, J. (2016) 'Status deficits and war', *International Organization*, 70(3): 513–50.

Renshon, J. (2017) *Fighting for Status. Hierarchy and Conflict in World Politics*, Princeton, NJ: Princeton University Press.

Rhamey, J.P., Jr and Early, B.R. (2013) 'Going for the gold: status-seeking behavior and Olympic performance', *International Area Studies Review*, 16(3): 244–61.

Ritchie, N. (2014) 'Waiting for Kant: devaluing and delegitimizing nuclear weapons', *International Affairs*, 90(3): 601–23.

Røren, P. and Beaumont, P. (2019) 'Grading greatness: evaluating the status performance of the BRICS', *Third World Quarterly*, 40(3): 429–50.

Rundle, C. (2008) 'Iran–United Kingdom relations since the revolution: opening doors', in A. Etheshami and M. Zweiri (eds) *Iran's Foreign Policy: From Khatami to Ahmadinejad*, Reading: Ithaca Press, pp 89–104.

Sabet-Saeidi, S. (2008) 'Iranian–European relations: a strategic partnership?', in A. Etheshami and M. Zweiri (eds) *Iran's Foreign Policy: From Khatami to Ahmadinejad*, Reading: Ithaca Press, pp 55–72.

Sambanis, N., Skaperdas, S. and Wohlforth, W.C. (2015) 'Nation-building through war', *American Political Science Review*, 109(2): 279–96.

Sheehan, M. (2013) '"Did you see that, grandpa Mao?" The prestige and propaganda rationales of the Chinese space program', *Space Policy*, 29: 107–12.

Smith, J. (1991) *Unequal Giants: Diplomatic Relations between the United States and Brazil, 1889–1930*, Pittsburgh, PA: University of Pittsburgh Press.

Tajfel, H. (1978) *Differentiation between Social Groups: Studies in the Social Psychology of Intergroup Relations*, New York, NY: Academic Press.

The Planetary Society (no date) *Planetary Exploration Budget Dataset*, compiled by Casey Dreier for The Planetary Society, https://rb.gy/fj14dy [Accessed 8 August 2022].

Towns, A.E. (2010) *Women and States: Norms and Hierarchies in International Society*, New York, NY: Cambridge University Press.

Wall, M. (2014) 'First private moon mission to launch on Chinese rocket today', *space.com*, 23 October, www.space.com/27518-private-moon-miss ion-4m-luxspace.html [Accessed 16 January 2023].

Ward, S. (2017) *Status and the Challenge of Rising Powers*, New York, NY: Cambridge University Press.

Ward, S. (2019) 'Logics of stratified identity management in world politics', *International Theory*, 11(2): 211–38.

Ward, S. (2020) 'Status, stratified rights, and accommodation in international relations', *Journal of Global Security Studies*, 5(1): 160–78.

Ward, S. (2022) 'Decline and disintegration: national status loss and domestic conflict in post-disaster Spain', *International Security*, 46(4): 91–129.

Wohlforth, W.C., De Carvalho, B., Leira, H. and Neumann, I.B. (2018) 'Moral authority and status in international relations: good states and the social dimension of status seeking', *Review of International Studies*, 44(3): 526–46.

PART II

How Comparisons Constitute Governance Objects

6

Not Yet Comparable? Maritime Security Knowledge and the Messiness of Epistemic Infrastructures

Christian Bueger

Introduction

In September 2021, the UN Security Council held an open debate titled 'Enhancing maritime security: A case for international cooperation'. It was the first time that the Council had held an explicit debate on 'maritime security', but it was also special given the level of speakers. The president of India, Narendra Modi, chaired the meeting. He was joined by Russian President Vladimir Putin, US Secretary of State Antony Blinken and Kenyan President Uhuru Kenyatta, among other high-level representatives. The Council members agreed that the international community should make more efforts to address maritime security. In their speeches it was primarily non-military issues that were of concern. Piracy, illegal fishing, human and narcotic smuggling, but also the damage caused by shipping were the issues the Council members highlighted (Bueger, 2021).

In this chapter I investigate how non-state and non-military oceanic activities of this kind became an object of global security politics and a priority concern of the world's leaders. It is a development at the heart of the evolution of maritime security thinking (Bueger and Edmunds, 2024), in which threats are seen as emerging primarily not from state-sponsored military activities, but from other entities, in particular criminal groups running pirate, smuggling or illegal fishing operations.

Maritime security evolved from the 1990s and to some degree reflects the arrival of the widened and enlarged security agenda at sea (Bueger and

Edmunds, 2017; Percy, 2018). It is noteworthy since it renders any kind of oceanic activity a potential threat, insofar as any seagoing vessel could, in principle, be part of a terrorist or criminal operation (Bueger and Edmunds, 2024). While military and state-run operations are increasingly included in the concept of maritime security, I shall bracket this dimension of insecurity at sea here, not least since naval power and military operations at sea are certainly not recent phenomena (see Chapter 10 by Kerrin Langer, this volume), although they have significantly evolved and the rise of grey zone tactics is complicating the picture.[1]

How have shipping, fishing, sailing – civic and commercial oceanic activities – become an object of attention in global security politics? While one line of reasoning would point to public speech acts, decision making in state capitals and ministries or emphasize the economic interests at stake, I shall put forward an alternative interpretation here and argue that this story is closely tied to the emergence and making of epistemic infrastructures. It is these infrastructures that make oceanic activity visible and known, and provide the data and knowledge that informs security politics up to the level of the UN Security Council.

The epistemic infrastructures provide the preconditions for securitization processes, that is, the construction of global security objects. They do so by recording and classifying suspicious, dangerous and non-dangerous oceanic activity and turning them into data. Once these become data, they enable and become part of comparative practices across time, regions and 'issues'. They thus provide the basis for political claims regarding what kind of trends are observable or of concern, and how urgently they need to be dealt with by political actors. Epistemic infrastructures hence are a basic unit of analysis that *enables the comparative practices* that decision makers draw on to problematize issues and prioritize security interventions.

Similar to global crime (see Chapter 8 by Anja Jakobi and Lena Herbst, this volume), state fragility (Chapter 7 by Keith Krause) and cybersecurity (Chapter 9 by Madeleine Myatt and Thomas Müller), maritime security is characterized by a plurality of epistemic infrastructures, which has given rise to problems of comparability and ambiguous comparative knowledge. The epistemic infrastructures of maritime security do not form a unified or hierarchical system. As I shall show, drawing on data from a multi-year project,[2] we are looking at a messy picture which can be described as a

---

[1] The rise of grey zone tactics has been increasingly observed and related to the foreign policies of revisionist states and ongoing interstate rivalries and disputes. See Bueger and Stockbruegger (2022) and Bueger and Edmunds (2023).

[2] The Transnational Organized Crime at Sea in the Indo-Pacific project ran from 2019 to 2022, and was funded by the Research Council UK, and led by Timothy Edmunds, University of Bristol. See www.safeseas.net for further information.

fragmented, diverse and rhizomatic assemblage through which infrastructures relate in various ways. Over time there has been a substantial growth in such infrastructures at the regional and global level that tend to advance their own methodologies and classifications. There is, consequently, a variety of infrastructures in terms of focus and methodology, with little sign that they are merging, consolidating or being harmonized with respect to standards and classifications.

While this can be partially explained by the relative novelty and complexity of the maritime security agenda, it is also a reflection of related security politics. The majority of infrastructures are formed with two goals in mind: to improve operational responses at sea in specific regions and to raise awareness of maritime security among security policy makers. Yet, there are also substantial struggles between the operators of the infrastructures. These reflect regional priorities on the one hand; on the other, they also relate to larger political questions, such as different positions as to whether ocean security should be seen as a regional or a global problem, and which issues should be considered as forming part of the maritime security agenda. For example, incidents of piracy are recorded both through international platforms and a variety of regional infrastructures, which reflects different positions in regard to whether piracy primarily demands local and regional measures or international action.

I shall start by briefly revisiting the core arguments and concepts of the theory of epistemic infrastructures. I shall then give an overview of different types of international infrastructures that deal with maritime insecurity. Since the number of these is extensive, I shall only give a brief high-level overview to provide some orientation.

I then proceed to investigate two examples in greater depth: (1) the evolution of epistemic infrastructures dealing with the quantification of the issue of piracy, and (2) the rise of so-called maritime domain awareness centres, which are initiatives to develop shared understandings and operational pictures of maritime activities at sea and to share information on incidents and suspicious activities across the spectrum of maritime security issues. This gives us an idea of the variety of structures and their effects.

Security knowledge and epistemic infrastructures

Within theory-driven European Security Studies there is an established consensus that knowledge production is vital for understanding security politics. There is, however, quite some variety of claims regarding why and how knowledge matters. In classical securitization theory, for instance, knowledge is a resource in speech acts through which issues are turned into security objects (Berling, 2011). Those who draw on versions of Bourdieusian field theory, by contrast, highlight that it is the everyday knowledge production activities of analysts and bureaucrats (conceptualized as security professionals) that produce what count as security objects (see Bigo, 2014). Arguments based on discourse theory focus on a more diffuse knowledge setup expressed in vocabularies and language choice that is constitutive of security politics (Hansen, 2006), paying less attention to how such knowledge is made or produced. Others advance concepts of expertise, that is, the processes through which knowledge is rendered authoritative (Berling and Bueger, 2015).

The theory of epistemic infrastructures draws on and extends these insights by offering a genuine conceptual alternative. The core claim of the theory is that there are particular socio-material structures in place through which knowledge is produced that both constitutes security politics and is also used as a resource in security controversies and decision making.

The core objective of the theory of epistemic infrastructures is to provide a conceptual framework for the practical production of knowledge in epistemic practices on an international level in order to understand how issues become known and are turned into objects of concern and governance. Building on premises from science and technology studies and international practice theory, the framework shares ideas with the epistemic community framework, in particular its practice theory version (Adler and Faubert, 2022).

Contrary to the notion of epistemic communities, the concept of infrastructures moves away from the idea that there are clearly identifiable groups of people who share norms, values or practices (for example validatory standards). It also aims at integrating the importance of material, technological and digital dimensions that are increasingly vital in contemporary knowledge production in the digital age (for example the computer processing of large amounts of data, or the use of spreadsheets to collate data). Moreover, the framework pays more attention to the importance of practices of maintaining the flow of knowledge through mundane tasks such as reporting, filling out forms, classifying and compiling statistics. The notion of 'infrastructure' helps to avoid the humanist and normative bias of the community concept, and brings maintenance activities to the fore.

In an earlier article, I outlined a basic framework for the study of epistemic infrastructures drawing on the work of Karin Knorr Cetina and other practice theorists (Bueger, 2015a). I placed the notions of *epistemic practice* and *laboratories* in the foreground to study epistemic infrastructures and defined the relations between these concepts as follows:

> The concepts of epistemic infrastructures as well as epistemic practices aim at grasping orders of meaning and the instruments that maintain it. While the notion of epistemic infrastructures refers to the larger formations that connect practices and sites to each other, the notion of epistemic practices conceptualizes the practical patterns of actions

that keep the structure running through assembling, translating, and representing. The concept of laboratories points us to those sites which are the crucial nodal points in keeping an epistemic infrastructure running and which are the major hosts of epistemic practices. (Bueger, 2015a: 8)

In the article, I drew on an exploratory case study of knowledge production relevant for the UN Security Council's understanding of maritime piracy. My intention was to identify and analyse some of the core epistemic practices and laboratories that maintain the epistemic infrastructure of piracy. I showed how three different prototype laboratories offer representations of piracy on which the UN Security Council bases its decisions. The study allowed for a primer to advance the conceptualization of epistemic infrastructures and the research strategies that follow from it.

Rather than further advancing the conceptual apparatus (which is done elsewhere, see Bueger and Stockbruegger, 2024), my aim in what follows is to draw on the framework to zoom out and conduct a macroscopic analysis of the epistemic infrastructures that turn civic oceanic activities into objects of global security politics. This gives us an initial understanding of what these infrastructures are, but also an idea of how an overall (maritime security) system has evolved. I will show that the overall system of infrastructures is incoherent and fragmented. The system is, hence, better understood as a moving and messy assemblage rather than a well-ordered structure.

Epistemic infrastructures and oceanic insecurity

Maritime security continues to be a field or problematic that is seen as novel and in which no clear global centre or authority has evolved (Bueger and Edmunds, 2024). This might be partially because of a lack of urgency (compared, for instance, to the field of terrorism), its uncertainty and complexity (considering the broad range of issues and actors involved), or the general terra-centrism of global politics which, historically, has paid scant attention to what happens at sea – at least since the conclusion of the UN Convention on the Law of the Sea negotiations in the 1980s (Bueger and Edmunds, 2017).

Maritime security as an independent issue has substantially captured the imagination of security discourses, leading to policies and strategies at different levels. Yet, it has escaped a global definition in law, practice or academia. It continues to be a substantially contested concept with undefined boundaries to security on land, or other oceanic security concepts preceding it, such as 'sea power' or 'marine safety'.

Like with any other contested concept, however, a conceptual core can be identified, in that maritime security is related to particular problems and responses (Bueger and Edmunds, 2024). One element of that core is the problematic of transnational organized crime, also conceptualized as 'maritime crime' or 'blue crime'. Among the activities that make up this kind of crime, piracy is often considered the most important issue that forms part of the maritime security agenda. This reflects the fact that the rise of maritime security as a prominent agenda has been closely linked to the urgency given to piracy. An important part of the evolution of maritime security practices are initiatives known by the term 'maritime domain awareness' or MDA. It stands for attempts by security actors to produce knowledge about insecurity at sea through surveillance, data collection and information sharing.

In what follows, I unpack the epistemic infrastructures through which oceanic activities are rendered as security objects from these three directions. Maritime crime, piracy and MDA provide me with three different entrance points to a reconstruction of the complexity of maritime security knowledge production. Each of the following three episodes provides a different insight into this fractured whole. The first draws on quantitative data and shows the diversity of the laboratories and indeed infrastructures involved and the degree of fragmentation between them. The second, on piracy, adds to that picture by providing an account of the growth of laboratories. It also documents their entanglement with politics, and the level of contestation between them. The third leads us to a picture of further expansion across maritime security issues, but also shows how laboratories cooperate and compete.

The epistemic infrastructures of maritime crime

The maritime domain is rendered knowledgeable through a rich set of epistemic infrastructures. This initially includes infrastructures that monitor oceanic activity more generally without an explicit relation to security concerns, an important example being systems for tracking ship movements such as the automatic identification system (AIS) that is compulsory for larger vessels under the regulations of the International Maritime Organization (IMO). These systems were installed for the purpose of safety of navigation (to prevent accidents and collisions) and are also used by companies for route planning, navigation and monitoring. Other examples include epistemic infrastructures that collect data and produce knowledge about the maritime environment. UNESCO's Intergovernmental Oceanographic Commission or Regional Fishery Monitoring Organizations under the auspices of the Food and Agricultural Organization compile data on waves, biodiversity and fish stocks. While mainly meant to monitor nature, they also provide clues on human activity at sea, in particular with regard to fishing. General maritime infrastructures of this nature often form the backbone of infrastructures with explicit security concerns.

Infrastructures that produce data on security-related concerns are in many ways the domain of sovereign states. For centuries states have been collecting intelligence for military and defence purposes. From the 1980s, however, a growing range of international infrastructures were developed that are concerned with security incidents at sea. These predominantly monitor and collect data on various illicit maritime activities. They, for instance, collate data on incidents and arrests in order to provide statistics on the state of maritime security.

In a mapping conducted in 2020 and 2021 we attempted to identify all international epistemic infrastructures that deal with instances of crime at sea.[3] Distinguishing between three types of blue crime – piracy, smuggling and environmental abuse – the objective was to identify those processes that produce publicly accessible data and related reports. This mapping identified 65 entities and processes that collect and process international data on maritime crime.

International organizations, in particular United Nations (UN) bodies such as the IMO, the UN Office on Drugs and Crime, the International Organization for Migration, as well as the World Customs Organization and International Police Organization are the core sites that provide the laboratories for the infrastructures. The vast majority of these are issue-specific, that is infrastructures that produce representations on an often isolated issue, such as piracy or the smuggling of narcotics or wildlife. Even if international organizations run processes on more than one issue, they do so through separate procedures and laboratories. These procedures are characterized by knowledge production carried out through state apparatuses and data collection is organized either by sending surveys to governments, or by verifying national level data through governments. Examples include the UN Office on Drugs and Crime's annual Crime Trends Survey and the World Customs Organization's seizure report. Both of these are indicators that such processes often do not clearly distinguish between crime on land and at sea. About 25 per cent of identified epistemic entities belong in this category.

Infrastructures that go beyond a single-issue focus and aim at providing more combined and integrated knowledge production processes on maritime

---

[3] The mapping was organized in three reports that focus on piracy, smuggling and environmental crime. They identify international infrastructures that provide publicly available representations and are, in one way or the other, linked to governmental or regulatory activity; expert bodies, commissions, and think tanks are included where relevant, but academic and university-based studies are excluded. See Joubert (2020), Joubert et al (2021) and Lycan et al (2021).

crime, predominantly operate at the regional level. They are either sited in and established by formal regional organizations, such as the European Union, or work through a separate multilateral agreement on information sharing and data collection, as do the MDA centres discussed later. Compared to international organizations, such entities tend to run data collection more independently and only partially rely on governmental reports or verification. About 30 per cent of epistemic entities have a regional focus and are organized in such ways. Examples include the Information Fusion Centre of the Singapore navy that produces weekly, monthly and annual reports on regional maritime security incidents, or the Information Fusion Centre – Indian Ocean Region operated by the Indian navy which provides similar services.

Finally, non-governmental and civil society actors are playing an evolving role in producing knowledge on maritime crime, with about 40 per cent of epistemic entities organized in this way. The vast majority of non-governmental infrastructures are in the field of environmental crimes, monitoring issues such as illegal fishing or pollution (28 per cent – 18 in total). An example is the IUU (Illegal, Unreported and Unregulated) Fishing Index run by the Geneva-based Global Initiative Against Transnational Organized Crime which provides country scores and a ranking on how well fishing states are dealing with the crime.[4] Entities led by non-governmental organizations (NGOs) tend to be issue-specific – with one exception. The US non-profit association Stable Seas is the first to engage in the process of constructing a global maritime security index that aims at providing country-level data on how states are affected by maritime insecurity and what capacities they have in place to respond to them (see Stable Seas, 2021).

This gives us an initial understanding of the wealth of laboratories engaged in the production of knowledge on maritime crimes and their variety. As indicated, the majority of the mapped entities produce knowledge on a particular issue, such as piracy, narcotics smuggling or illicit fishing. While relating their work to the concept of maritime security, they do not intend to provide overall views of maritime crime. Yet, a number of entities, including MDA centres and the Stable Seas initiative, aggregate data in order to provide a more comprehensive understanding of crimes at sea.

Some of the processes, such as the piracy data set of the IMO, go back to the 1980s, but the majority are of more recent origin. MDA initiatives, for instance, were launched from the mid-2000s and their growth intensified in the late 2010s with, for instance, the Singapore centre being inaugurated in 2009 and the India centre in 2018. NGO processes such as the IUU Fishing

---

[4] See the IUU Fishing Index (Poseidon Aquatic Resource Management Ltd and Global Initiative against Transnational Organized Crime, no date).

Index and Maritime Security Index were also launched in the late 2010s. This reflects and corresponds to the evolution of maritime security as an agenda of security politics, in which holistic understandings of maritime security have been settling since the early 2010s (see Bueger and Edmunds, 2024).

With some minor exceptions, all of the mapped epistemic processes operate with independent data collection methods, bespoke metrics and categorizations. The data quality of international organizations is often dependent on the methods used by the governments on which they rely. Non-governmental processes sometimes rely on direct reporting but often on public resources. Moves towards the aggregation of data, as represented by the IUU Fishing Index and Maritime Security Index are relatively recent, but even they rely on proprietary classifications and methods. As will be explored later, some of the MDA initiatives are moving towards the use of global systems and harmonization, yet the systems, metrics and classifications of reports remain bespoke. This implies that, with the exception of the still nascent Maritime Security Index – which does not rank countries – there are no all-embracing data on maritime crime, which would allow insecurity or trends across issues, countries and regions to be compared.

This macroscopic overview of epistemic processes relating to maritime crime, therefore, gives us first of all an idea of the substantial growth of laboratories and epistemic practices that temporarily corresponds to the development of the maritime security agenda overall. As of 2024 no coherent body of knowledge or organized data has been produced, and processes are dispersed. It thus makes sense to speak about epistemic infrastructures in the plural. While security objects, such as piracy or illicit fishing, are produced in formations of closely connected laboratories that relate directly to each other, a more overarching formation that produces explicit maritime security knowledge has not yet emerged.

Quantifying piracy

A focus on piracy – one of the core issues on the maritime security agenda, where knowledge production is expansive – adds further evidence for the general growth of epistemic practice, but also demonstrates the contestations that persist within a more or less matured epistemic infrastructure. As I shall demonstrate, many of these disputes are linked to the political motives driving knowledge production, with the main controversies produced by diverging classifications.

Piracy became a matter of concern on an international level when, in the early 1980s, the international transport industry called for political attention to the problem. To raise awareness and assist its members, the industry created an international body and requested that the International Chamber of Commerce open an International Maritime Bureau (IMB), tasked with reducing the risk of piracy (see Bueger, 2015b). The IMB started to systematically record incidents, inform law enforcement officials, issue alerts for the industry and produce annual reports – a service that it has continued to provide until today with increasingly greater sophistication (such as a 24 hour watch and reporting centre, a website, live updates and piracy maps).

The key international organization in charge of the regulation of the shipping industry and ensuring maritime safety, the IMO, started to address the matter after pressure from industry in its safety committee. In turn, the IMO likewise started to record incidents and compile reports (see Bueger, 2015a). In contrast to the IMB, which relied on reports from the shipping industry, the IMO requested verified reports from its member states (though often drawing on IMB data in its requests). The incidents recorded in both databases differ as a result, since not all incidents reported by the industry are officially verified by governments. Moreover, the IMB adopted a technical and highly pragmatic understanding of piracy. Contrary to the then established legal consensus that piracy is an activity that takes place on the high seas, the IMB also included robbery in ports or coastal territorial waters in its definition of piracy. We are consequently faced with two closely related laboratories, one industry-operated one, and one maintained by a UN body which formed the epistemic infrastructure of piracy in the 1980s and 1990s.

From the late 1990s onwards, the story becomes much more complex, since a substantial number of regional infrastructures were constructed (see the summary of infrastructures in Joubert, 2020). The regional constructs reflect the fact that incidents of piracy occur in particular hotspots, with the Strait of Malacca and Singapore and the Sulu and Celeb Seas in Southeast Asia, the Western Indian Ocean and the area 'off the coast of Somalia', as well as the Gulf of Guinea in Western Africa recognized as the primary hotspots (see also Bueger and Edmunds, 2024: Chapter 5). The intensification of epistemic practices and the construction of laboratories largely goes along with a rise in numbers of incidents and the international attention given to these regions. The construction started out in Southeast Asia, continued in the Western Indian Ocean and then intensified in the Gulf of Guinea, with the planning and design of regional laboratories heavily influencing each other from region to region.

Under pressure from international actors, in particular the US and Japan, Southeast Asia saw the creation of a piracy reporting centre based on an international treaty (the 'Regional Cooperation Agreement on Combating Piracy and Armed Robbery against Ships in Asia'; see Ho, 2009 and Bueger, 2015b). This mechanism was replicated in the Western Indian Ocean and later in the Gulf of Guinea (see Menzel, 2018; Yücel, 2021). Each of these is organized slightly differently, yet the basic underlying principle of the three laboratories is the same: to collect and share information on piracy incidents, record them and publish alerts, statistics and reports. They are entities that intend to ensure that awareness of piracy among regional states remains high, but the reports also are important for the lobbying activities of the shipping industry.

For piracy in the Western Indian Ocean another type of regional laboratory became vital: epistemic entities that aim at supporting maritime security operations at sea. In support of the naval missions with a counterpiracy mandate operating in the region, the US, the UK, NATO and the EU created reporting centres. These were tools to engage with the transiting shipping industry and to issue warnings and alerts, but also aimed at producing statistics to measure the severity of the problem as well as operational success. These are more pragmatic and temporary: they draw on restricted military mandates that require renewal, primarily aim at supporting naval counterpiracy missions, and intend to inform the political decision-making process providing the mandates for the operations. The reports from these initiatives provide key resources for briefing policy makers and diplomats about trends in piracy and the need for continued operations.

Somali piracy also led to significant efforts by non-state actors beyond the IMB. Most influentially, from 2010 to 2018 a US foundation decided to devote resources to the problem of piracy and created the advocacy organization Oceans Beyond Piracy – the predecessor to Stable Seas, which developed the maritime security index discussed earlier. As the primary NGO engaging with the issue, its main activity became to produce an annual report that focused on calculating the costs linked to piracy. The first series of reports aimed at estimating the economic costs of piracy off the coast of Somalia. This was then gradually extended to also include the so-called 'human costs', and to cover other regions.

These reports documenting the (human and economic) costs were important resources for two actors in particular. For the main victims of piracy – the shipping industry and its employees – the reports provided evidence to call for the engagement by states to be expanded, in particular through military operations at sea in order to reduce the financial burden on the industry imposed by private protection or rerouting. The reports by Oceans Beyond Piracy were partially funded by the UN Office on Drugs and Crime. For the UN agency, which was expanding its capacity-building programmes for maritime security, the reports were a useful resource in raising funds for their projects. With the decline of attention to Somali piracy, the entity was closed, and a new organization called Stable Seas was formed. It continued the production of the annual costs of piracy reports, but also branched out to address other maritime security issues and produce reports, in particular for the UN Office on Drugs and Crime.

This short account of the evolution of the epistemic infrastructure of counterpiracy gives us an idea of how epistemic practices have multiplied in the face of the escalation of a problem, but also with straightforward objectives, ranging from the lobbying activities of the industry calling for more activities by states, through fund raising ambitions, to the operational needs of counterpiracy missions and international pressure on regional states to secure their waters.

The laboratories described above differ in terms of how they define piracy and what related classifications they use in regards to the nature and severity of incidents, as well as in whether and how they count suspicious activities. This leads to incongruent data and may imply diverging interpretations of trends.

Industry-led infrastructures such as the IMB do not draw on the international legal definition, and also classify incidents as piracy if they take place within territorial waters. State-operated infrastructures rely on the international legal definition, but then face the problem of how to categorize incidents in territorial waters. To deal with this problem, for instance, one entity has developed the category 'Theft, Robbery and Piracy at Sea' and records incidents under the acronym TRAPS. A related issue arises with regard to whether and how to count incidents of petty theft, such as when a watch is stolen from a ship in port.

How contentious the different analytical categories can become is well documented by a controversy in Singapore in 2015, which one commentator described as 'piracy monitoring wars' (Bateman, 2015). The controversy was sparked by a piracy report from one of the three Southeast Asian monitoring centres – the reporting centre of the Regional Cooperation Agreement on Combating Piracy and Armed Robbery against Ships in Asia (ReCAAP). Following the release of the report, the centre was accused of downplaying the piracy threat in the region given that the IMB's piracy reporting centre (PRC) had higher numbers. As an observer explained,

> [part] of the problem arises because [one reporting centre] classifies each incident of piracy and sea robbery according to the level of violence used and economic loss involved. [While the other centre] does not classify incidents and counts an incident of petty theft from a ship at anchor or in port as equivalent to a major incident of ship hijacking. (Bateman, 2015: 1)

The observer continues,

> [with] the vast majority of incidents in the region being ones of petty theft, the PRC's reports can give a distorted picture of the true threat of piracy in the region that may lead to incorrect policy recommendations for governments. The media also often prefers to use the absolute figures presented by the PRC, which can give an exaggerated view

of the threat, rather than the more nuanced reports from ReCAAP.
(Bateman, 2015: 1)

Since the majority of laboratories rely on reports made by the shipping
industry, a related issue is the problem of under- and overreporting. Industry
might have various reasons for whether they report an incident or not.
Underreporting may be linked to the industry avoiding the efforts required to
submit reports, or to fears of public exposure or negative commercial impact
and insurance rates. Overreporting might be due to attempted insurance
fraud. It may also be the result of the business interests of private security
providers, who might want to report an incident as suspicious or attempted
piracy to ensure their ongoing employment. The latter is a noted problem
in the Western Indian Ocean region, where many private security providers
offer lucrative on-board protection services. In that region no successful
piracy incident had been recorded between 2012 and 2023, but suspicious
activities had frequently occured.

The issue has been noted and recognized as problematic, and in particular
representatives of the shipping industry have called for harmonization both
in data collection and trend reports. In consequence, several new working
groups, including one at the IMO, have been created to investigate the
question. Yet regional mechanisms tend to argue that classifications are
either mission-specific or need to be tailored to the particularities of piracy
in the given region. Hence, no common standard or classification system
has been agreed upon yet. The result is a messy and incongruent picture
of whether piracy is on the rise or in decline in regions such as the Gulf of
Guinea and Southeast Asia, and whether it continues to be a threat at all in
the Western Indian Ocean sufficient to justify ongoing military operations.
This blurry picture can be linked to different motivations, for the industry
and states engaged in capacity building documenting a persistent threat is
beneficial – likewise for legitimizing military operations (which might be
carried out for other reasons than immediate counterpiracy).

Maritime domain awareness

The case of piracy provides us with insights into how an infrastructure
evolves along with a particular issue, and how the political motives underlying
knowledge production prevent a close integration of it through shared
standards and classifications. The case of MDA provides us with another
window into the rise of epistemic infrastructures and the tensions within and
between them. Contrary to the discussion of the overall state of knowledge
production on maritime crime, and the issue of piracy, the evolution of MDA
stands for a type of knowledge production that aims at generic, cross-issue
maritime security knowledge. As already indicated, the MDA laboratories

are primarily regional in outlook. Key tensions that arise are linked to how to carve out the borders between regions, but also whether and how a globally integrated infrastructure is a possibility.

The concept of MDA originated in US strategic discourse of the early 2000s.[5] Launched in part as an element in the global war on terror, the concept argues that maritime security – back then the prevention of terrorist activities at sea – requires the sharing of information between agencies and states in order to arrive at a shared common picture of dangers, risks and threats that could enable common priorities and strategies as well as interoperability between seagoing forces. Since being outlined by the US government, MDA has been widely adopted by international organizations such as the IMO, the EU and states worldwide as a guiding vision and operational tool to enhance effectivity.

The underlying idea of MDA is to monitor in real time all maritime activity, including the collection of historical data on the movement of ships, goods and people, as well as on flag states, ownership and customs procedures. The idea is that fusing such data would allow suspicious activities and vessels to be identified and interrupted, response times to incidents to be shortened, areas identified as hot spots to be more effectively policed, and broader trend analyses to be provided. The technical backbone of MDA is the data provided by AIS, which contains ship data, allowing vessel movements to be tracked in real time and the compilation of geo-located incident databases.

On the basis of this idea, an interconnected global network of centres that monitor a particular oceanic region is emerging. These centres take an overall view of maritime security and focus on a particular maritime space, defined as their 'area of interest'. While anchored in a particular political region, these areas can be substantially larger. For instance, the centre in Southeast Asia has an area of interest which stretches both into the Western Indian Ocean in the west, and to the Pacific in the east. These centres are based on informal memoranda of understanding for information sharing and cooperation, and tend to imply that participating countries send staff to be physically present as liaison officers. These liaison officers, together with the visualizations, databases and algorithmic analysis tools, form the core of these laboratories. As centres and initiatives have become quite numerous in the meantime, I flag a number of influential examples below.

The Mediterranean Sea region is one of the major origins of regional MDA. The Italian navy started a pilot project to exchange data between 20 countries there. In 2006 the Virtual Regional Maritime Traffic Centre (V-RMTC) was launched with a data fusion centre close to Rome. The

---

[5] For a discussion of the origins of MDA, see Boraz (2009) and Dittmer (2021). The following section draws on Bueger (2020).

centre was initially created to exchange shipping data between countries in the Mediterranean – an important resource, before satellite-based AIS made such data more readily available. Through the network, incident data was also shared and compiled into reports made available to the network members. As a core feature, the V-RMTC enabled a range of new communication channels on the basis of secured real-time transmission of text messages from sender to receiver (chat) and encrypted email. This provided the capacity to work in different informal configurations. The centre shares data in what are called 'communities', which include different countries and classification standards.

In 2009 an Information Fusion Centre (IFC) was launched in Singapore operated by the Singapore navy (Bueger, 2015b). Drawing on the Italian model to provide a similar structure for Southeast Asia, the centre was also innovative, since it introduced the idea of complementing virtual data exchange with the physical presence of international liaison officers. These officers provide an additional resource, both for the exchange of information, and for interpreting maritime incidents though national lenses and providing direct communication links to government authorities. The Singaporean regional model became the standard setting, and its basic structures have been replicated in several other regions.

In the East Africa and the Western Indian Ocean regions, regional MDA structures were developed as part of the capacity-building response to the rise of piracy off the coast of Somalia from 2005. The Regional Maritime Fusion Centre in Madagascar became operational in 2018. In its structure it adopts the model of the Singaporean IFC. The area of interest was designed in such a way that it borders that of the IFC stretching to the Maldives in the East. In 2018 the government of India inaugurated a regional centre, the Information Fusion Centre-Indian Ocean Region (IFC-IOR) to enhance information sharing among the members of the Indian Ocean Naval Symposium. With an area of interest that stretches from Western Africa to Japan and Australia, the geographical focus overlaps with both the centre in Madagascar and the IFC. India extended an invitation to countries to send international liaison officers and hence also followed the IFC template.

There are further regional structures and centres either established or under development. They include a centre developed in Peru with a prospective area of interest in the South Atlantic, and a Fusion Centre launched by the Pacific Islands Forum for the South Pacific region. Both these platforms draw significantly on the experience of the IFC in Singapore and further expand the global network of regional centres. Within Europe it is the European Union's Common Information Sharing Environment (CISE), developed by the European Maritime Safety Agency (EMSA) and the Maritime Surveillance (MARSUR) project of the European Defence Agency (EDA). Both CISE and MARSUR rely on an area of interest defined by the EU's commercial and foreign and security policies, which stretches far beyond Europe and includes the Atlantic and Western Indian Ocean.

The rise of MDA shows first of all how a transnational and transregional global network of epistemic structures is emerging. These centres, each different in their detailed institutionalizations, all pursue a similar style of epistemic practices based on real-time surveillance, information sharing, data fusion, anomaly detection and trend analysis. They are geared to operational support, but also aim at informing policy making. As the core emerging epistemic infrastructure for maritime security, the laboratories face, on the one hand, similar challenges to the piracy centres. While AIS data is the shared backbone, and there is an exchange of data between centres, for instance on suspicious vessels, they rely on bespoke metrics and classifications to provide statistics for incidents and trends. The spatial concept of areas of interest reveals an important struggle between centres in that their work overlaps. They might even compete over the authority to make insecurity claims, as is the case in the Western Indian Ocean region, where several IFCs collate incident data and also compete with entities exclusively devoted to piracy.

Conclusion

The quantitative overview of epistemic entities that deal with maritime crime, together with the two examples – piracy and the evolution of MDA – demonstrate how the epistemic activities that inform maritime security policy have accelerated since the 2000s. In particular, over the last five to ten years, practices and infrastructures have multiplied considerably. While there is some degree of cooperation between these different laboratories and infrastructures, they remain loosely coupled with no overarching mechanisms coordinating or steering data collection and maritime security knowledge production. Indeed, we are looking at a messy patchwork of various data collection mechanisms, centres and reports, among which some are, however, striving to cooperate more closely, harmonize their work or develop standards for maritime security reporting. The overall system is far from homogeneous. This means that the production of accurate statements concerning the state of maritime security on a regional or global level is intricate and the basis for systematic comparison not given.

In many ways these infrastructures are perceived as technical and operate in the background. They were developed to enhance law enforcement at sea and interoperability, to prevent incidents or improve the responses to them. Yet, they are key in shaping political awareness of the security implications of oceanic activity. Indeed, the products that are the outcome of infrastructures, such as annual incident reports, are the key knowledge that security policy makers and diplomats draw on in their evaluations of the significance of issues such as piracy or maritime security overall. Sometimes, as we have seen in the case of piracy reporting, political awareness can be the key ambition motivating knowledge production in the first place, and this might be directly linked to commercial interest or fundraising.

Objects of security politics and epistemic infrastructures are closely intertwined. In order to govern a problem, it must be made known and represented in particular ways. In this chapter, I have shown the richness of epistemic infrastructures that make oceanic activity known. These provide the precondition for the global maritime security agenda. It is this global machinery that allows us to make claims about what is dangerous and what not, but it is also these systems and their evolution that provide material for the notion that the oceans can be secured.

Considered as a whole, the evolution of infrastructures suggests a growing awareness of (the dangers of) the sea. Yet, the messy character of the overall structure, tells us a story that is far from unidirectional but indicative of a contestation process regarding how the oceans should be governed and whose security interests should be prioritized.

References

Adler, E. and Faubert, M. (2022) 'Epistemic communities of practice', in A. Drieschova, C. Bueger and T. Hopf (eds) *Conceptualizing International Practices: Directions for the Practice Turn in International Relations*, Cambridge: Cambridge University Press, pp 47–76.

Bateman, S. (2015) *Piracy Monitoring Wars: Responsibilities for Countering Piracy*, RSIS Commentary No. 115, 13 May, www.files.ethz.ch/isn/191045/CO15115.pdf [Accessed 9 February 2023].

Berling, T.V. (2011) 'Science and securitization: objectivation, the authority of the speaker and mobilization of scientific facts', *Security Dialogue*, 42(4–5): 385–97.

Berling, T.V. and Bueger, C. (eds) (2015) *Security Expertise: Practices, Power and Responsibility*, London: Routledge.

Bigo, D. (2014) 'The (in)securitization practices of the three universes of EU border control: military/navy – border guards/police – database analysts', *Security Dialogue*, 45(3): 209–25.

Boraz, S.C. (2009) 'Maritime domain awareness. Myths and realities', *Naval War College Review*, 62(3): 137–46.

Bueger, C. (2015a) 'Making things known: epistemic practice, the United Nations and the translation of piracy', *International Political Sociology*, 9(1): 1–19.

Bueger, C. (2015b) 'From dusk to dawn? Maritime domain awareness in Southeast Asia', *Contemporary Southeast Asia: A Journal of International & Strategic Affairs*, 37(2): 157–82.

Bueger, C. (2020) 'A glue that withstands heat? The promise and perils of maritime domain awareness', in E.R. Lucas, S. Rivera-Paez, T. Crosbie and F.F. Jensen (eds) *Maritime Security: Counter-Terrorism Lessons from Maritime Piracy and Narcotics Interdiction*, Amsterdam: IOS Press, pp 235–45.

Bueger, C. (2021) 'Does maritime security require a new United Nations structure?', *Global Observatory*, 26 August, https://theglobalobservatory. org/2021/08/does-maritime-security-require-a-new-united-nations-structure/ [Accessed 9 February 2023].

Bueger, C. and Edmunds, T. (2017) 'Beyond seablindness: a new agenda for maritime security studies', *International Affairs*, 93(6): 1293–311.

Bueger, C. and Edmunds, T. (2023) 'The European Union's quest to become a global maritime security provider', *Naval War College Review*, 76(2): 67–86.

Bueger, C. and Edmunds, T. (2024) *Understanding Maritime Security*, New York, NY, Oxford: Oxford University Press.

Bueger, C. and Stockbruegger, J. (2022) 'Maritime security and the western Indian Ocean's militarisation dilemma', *African Security Review*, 31(2): 195–210.

Bueger, C. and Stockbruegger, J. (2024) 'Oceans, Objects, Infrastructures: Making Modern Piracy' [unpublished manuscript].

Dittmer, J. (2021) 'The state, all at sea: interoperability and the global network of navies', *Environment and Planning C: Politics and Space*, 9(7): 1389–406.

Hansen, L. (2006) *Security as Practice. Discourse Analysis and the Bosnian War*, London: Routledge.

Ho, J. (2009) 'Combating piracy and armed robbery in Asia: the ReCAAP Information Sharing Centre (ISC)', *Marine Policy*, 33(2): 432–34.

Joubert, L. (2020) *What We Know about Piracy. Report by the Transnational Organized Crime at Seas (TOCAS) Project, Stable Seas & Safe Seas*, 18 May, www.safeseas.net/wp-content/uploads/2020/05/What-We-Know-About-Piracy.pdf [Accessed 9 February 2023].

Joubert, L., Edmunds, T. and Edwards, S. (2021) *What We Know about Maritime Illicit Trades. Report by the Transnational Organized Crime at Seas (TOCAS) Project, Stable Seas & Safe Seas*, 7 June, www.safeseas.net/wp-content/uploads/2021/04/what_we_know_about_maritime_illicit_trades.pdf [Accessed 9 February 2023].

Lycan, T., Van Buskirk, L., Bueger, C., Edmunds, T., Edwards, S. and Seyle, C. (2021) *What We Know About Maritime Environmental Crime. Report by the Transnational Organized Crime at Seas (TOCAS) Project, Stable Seas & Safe Seas*, 6 September, www.safeseas.net/wp-content/uploads/2021/09/What_We_Know_About_Maritime_Environmental_Crime.pdf [Accessed 9 February 2023].

Menzel, A. (2018) 'Institutional adoption and maritime crime governance: the Djibouti code of conduct', *Journal of the Indian Ocean Region*, 14(2): 152–69.

Percy, S. (2018) 'Maritime security', in A. Gheciu and W.C. Wohlforth (eds) *The Oxford Handbook of International Security*, Oxford: Oxford University Press, pp 607–21.

Poseidon Aquatic Resource Management Ltd. and Global Initiative against Transnational Organized Crime (no date) 'About the IUU Fishing Index', https://iuufishingindex.net/about [Accessed 18 September 2023].

Stable Seas (2021) Maritime Security Index, www.stableseas.org/services [Accessed 18 September 2023].

Yücel, H. (2021) 'Sovereignty and transnational cooperation in the Gulf of Guinea: how a network approach can strengthen the Yaoundé architecture', *Scandinavian Journal of Military Studies*, 4(1): 146–57.

7

Framing (State) Fragility: The Construction of Imaginary Global Spaces

Keith Krause

The concept of 'state fragility' has become, over the past two decades, near ubiquitous in practitioners' and policy makers' discourses around development policy and external interventions in the socio-political and economic life of subordinate states in the international system. A Google search for the terms 'fragile states' and 'state fragility' generates almost 2 million hits; the Fragile States Index of the Fund for Peace gets more than 360,000 hits, and the Index itself has around 4,000 citations in Google Scholar. Yet the concept of state fragility is both relatively recent, and quintessentially a knowledge practice, a construct – not just a description of a state of affairs, but constitutive of the phenomenon it purports to describe. State fragility does not exist outside of the label and the relationships that it creates. 'Fragility' is not an objective feature of particular states or polities; just like prior or related concepts such as 'states in transition' or 'less-developed countries' or 'areas of limited statehood', it is a category created by someone for some purpose. This chapter will reveal some of its creators – mainly international institutions – and discuss the ways in which the idea of state fragility has infused international practices as both a justification and a guide to action.

In broad terms, I will argue that the fragile state discourse is presented as a form of expert knowledge about the world that makes certain states and regions 'legible' for policy makers without requiring any additional thought or knowledge. It performs four interrelated functions in world politics. It has:

- reoriented development assistance to different destination countries – moving away from providing for basic (human) needs and poverty reduction, towards more politically controversial interventions in forms of governance;
- changed – at least to some extent – the way in which development assistance is delivered, in both positive and negative ways;
- facilitated the fusion of traditional development concerns with global security concerns ('the securitization of development assistance'); and
- prioritized neoliberal economic interventions and forms of governance (liberal state building), within a neoimperial tradition that goes back as far as the League of Nations.

Not all of these effects are deleterious to human development, and indeed the logic of fragility has potentially reduced insecurity and deprivation in some cases, especially by drawing attention to situations in which overt violence and conflict have not (yet) broken out, or to complex post-conflict environments in which the states do not or cannot provide basic public goods. But this is an empirical question that has not been subject to systematic analysis and cannot be fully developed here. Rather, I will explore four different permutations of fragility comparisons, focusing, in particular, on (a) the Fragile States Index, (b) the OECD *States of Fragility* reports and indicators, (c) the World Bank's Fragile States List (now called the List of Fragile and Conflict-Affected Situations), and (d) the G7+ 'fragility spectrum'. These four have been selected for their public prominence (the Fragile States Index; hereafter FSI), their direct implication in policy making and aid or assistance allocations (World Bank and OECD), and their co-constituted nature involving the participation of so-called 'fragile states' (the G7+) in both the practical definition of 'fragility' and the measures taken to address it. While not all are directly security-related (in the narrow sense), they all partake in the securitization of development assistance (in the broad sense) by orienting global policies and programmes around a constructed and sometimes shared understanding of the threat that state fragility may pose to local, regional and global security (Duffield, 2001; Chandler, 2007). Perhaps more importantly, any measurement of fragility is also a theory of, and argument about, what a state should look like and the form its state–society relations should take, and thus the concept of fragility is a window onto the politics of 21st-century state building. It is also – as the different sources will highlight – fraught with ambiguity and often contested judgements, echoing the analysis by Jakobi and Herbst (Chapter 8 of this volume) and Bueger (Chapter 6), respectively, on comparisons in international crime statistics and maritime security.

In the first section I will situate the emergence of the discourse of state fragility in both contemporary and historical contexts, and offer some reflections on the nature of concept formation, oriented around the question of how fragility has become a governance object. I will then unpack how state fragility rankings are produced, and dive more deeply into the evolution of four different state fragility indices and indicators, highlighting what is 'in' or 'out of' them by way of comparison, and probing the potential sources of some of these differences in orientation. The objective here is to explore how comparative knowledge about state fragility is produced. The third section will address how state fragility is made politically relevant, and how different comparative practices of fragility monitoring shape global interventions and security politics, in particular by generating political support for certain kinds of policies for dealing with state fragility and by having an impact on the flows of development aid.

Constructing the obscure object of a 'fragile state'

The discourse on state fragility emerged in the early 1990s, and Gerald Helman and Steven Ratner's article 'Saving failed states' is a conventional starting point (Helman and Ratner, 1992; see also Jackson, 1991). Their language is of 'failure' not fragility, and they paint a gloomy picture of near anarchy in places such as the former Yugoslavia, Somalia, Sudan, Haiti and Cambodia, characterized by warfare, violence and civil strife, economic breakdown, human rights violations and cross-border refugee flows. Others focused on 'state collapse' – conceptualized as a near total breakdown of state institutions, and included cases such as war-torn Liberia, Zaire/Democratic Republic of the Congo and Chad (Zartman, 1995).

Stepping back a bit, one can easily argue that the language of fragile states is only the most recent in a long line of Western ideas about how to govern the globe – from the imperial *mission civilisatrice*, to the description of the Ottoman empire as the 'sick man of Europe' propped up by other great powers, to the League of Nations mandates system (Roberts, 2015). For example, the Covenant of the League of Nations explicitly described the mandate system as applicable to:

> [T]hose colonies and territories … which are inhabited by peoples not yet able to stand by themselves under the strenuous conditions of the modern world, there should be applied the principle that the … tutelage of such peoples should be entrusted to advanced nations who by reason of their resources, their experience or their geographical position can best undertake this responsibility, and who are willing to accept it. (League of Nations, 1920, article 22)

Such language provided a shared framework to facilitate collective action, and were part and parcel of great power (and imperial) global governance mechanisms and ordering principles (Müller et al, 2022). This is clearly the case for the language of state fragility, and highlights that there is little new in such global ordering practices; as noted by Branwen Gruffydd Jones (2013: 49), 'the discourse must be recognized as a contemporary successor to a much longer genealogy of imperial discourse about Africa and other non-European societies'.

Hence the crux of Helman and Ratner's argument was not purely descriptive – both were former US State Department officials – and they were making a direct plea for active engagement and intervention to 'save' these states (and presumably their populations) from anarchy and its associated ills, via 'conservatorship' – a 'form of guardianship or trusteeship' (Helman and Ratner, 1992: 12). They also linked state failure to the emerging concept (in the UN Secretary-General's *Agenda for Peace*) of post-conflict peacebuilding – a linkage that proved fruitful for a variety of actors promoting a new interventionist role for the international community. Helman and Ratner should not be seen as catalysts though, but rather as having captured the post-Cold War liberal zeitgeist, exemplified by several other geopolitical interventions: President George H.W. Bush's 'new world order', pronounced after the liberation of Kuwait from the 1991 Iraqi invasion by a broad international coalition, and more sombrely, Robert Kaplan's 'The Coming Anarchy' or Susan Woodward's (1995) *Balkan Tragedy*. By Kaplan's account, the world was facing the 'withering away of the central governments of modern states in favour of tribal domains, "city-states, shanty-states, [and] nebulous and anarchic regionalisms"' (Kaplan, 1994: 24, cited in Milliken and Krause, 2002: 753), all subsequent (if overdramatized) characterizations of fragile and failed states.

Analysing state failure very quickly moved beyond a purely intellectual or conceptual exercise. In 1994 the CIA, at the behest of the White House (in particular Vice President Al Gore), sponsored a large-scale open-source research project called the 'State Failure Task Force', intended to uncover the correlates of state failure and – more significantly – 'to develop a methodology that would identify key factors and critical thresholds signalling a high risk of crisis in countries some two years in advance' (Etsy et al, 1995: iii). Hence the discourse of state fragility was in essence policy-driven, with the objective of facilitating American decision makers' preparations for different forms of intervention in the post-Cold War world. In the aftermath of the wars in the former Yugoslavia and the Rwanda genocide, the goal was also to potentially provide some early warning of such things as mass killings and ethnic cleansing.[1] There is little doubt that the investments in data collection

---

[1]   'Four separate kinds of state failure ... were examined: (1) revolutionary wars, (2) ethnic wars, (3) mass killings (genocides or "politicides" in which large numbers of people are killed for their political views and activities), and (4) adverse or disruptive regime changes ... causing an extended period of disorder' (Etsy et al, 1995: vii). Tellingly, the Task Force

and analysis were policy-driven, emerging in a world in which large-scale data collection efforts and analysis were becoming more prominent and easier.[2] The American government was also not alone, however, and, as noted by Susan Woodward, by the mid-1990s 'the concept had, in fact, become a dominant conceptual framework for foreign economic and security policies in much of the North', including for the OECD Development Assistance Committee (DAC), UN agencies, the World Bank and USAID (Woodward, 2017: 2).

By her account, the concept of a failed state is an *ideology*; a set of beliefs that 'provides shared meaning and enables social action' (Woodward, 2017: 3). Or, as succinctly noted by Sonja Grimm and colleagues (2014), fragile states are a political invention. That the concept of fragile states is an ideology and political construct can be taken as a given. What is more important, however, is *how it works* as an ideology or conceptual construct with claims to authoritative knowledge on which decision makers should act. As will be discussed later, it largely places responsibility for 'failure' on local governments and national elites, ignores broader structural and historical forces, justifies external intervention, and partakes of a 'colonialist nostalgia' expressed in calls for international administration (such as was implemented in Kosovo and Timor Leste) (Richardson, 1996; Richmond and Franks, 2008).

What this chapter is interested in, echoing Bueger (Chapter 6, this volume) are the *ways* in which the concept may contribute to the construction and framing of complex geopolitical problems, how its construction *differs* among powerful international actors, and the way in which different constructions of fragility, while sharing a common language, facilitate and make possible certain forms of action (and render other forms impossible). The focus is not so much on the justificatory framework that state fragility offers for forms of radical (military) intervention by major powers in places such as Afghanistan, but rather the attempt to formalize and structure the more mundane 'everyday practices' of intervention such as foreign assistance and lending, development, and security programming in such areas as public management, reform and governance of the security sector, democracy promotion and human rights and rule of law.

The most generic definition of fragility would be 'States that are failing, or at risk of failing, with respect to authority, comprehensive basic service provision, or legitimacy' (Stewart and Brown, 2010: 9). But before unpacking this, one should ask: what, conceptually, does *fragility* mean and what are

---

was in 2003 renamed the 'Political Instability Task Force' and funding for the project apparently ended in 2020.

[2]   One can contrast this with the simplicity of the Human Development Index, founded in 1990 and based on then-available indicators of life expectancy at birth, literacy and educational attainment, and GDP per capita.

its entailments? What 'causes' fragility, what are its characteristics, and what are the consequences of being in a state of fragility? Although Woodward concludes that the concept is essentially meaningless empirically, conceptually and practically, the term *means something* to those who use it, and such meaning often reflects a concept's use in other domains. Much like notions such as 'resilience' or 'proliferation', fragility is a concept imported from another domain, not an intrinsic property of a social system or a state, and this importation comes with 'everyday resonances' for people who use the term. In particular, it applies to everyday objects (glass, especially, which is easily subject to breakage as a result of an external shock), as well as to such things as ecosystems, medical conditions, financial systems, and so on. In everyday use an object can be intrinsically fragile, without one having to question how such fragility came about, and the consequences are fairly self-evident.

In environmental studies, by contrast, ecological fragility (which is a feature of all ecosystems), is understood as 'the degree of sensitivity of habitats, communities and species to environmental change ... involv[ing] a combination of intrinsic and extrinsic factors' (Nilsson and Grelsson, 1995: 678). Noteworthy here are two things: first, *external disturbances* are considered co-equal to internal ones and second, fragility is not just a descriptive characteristic, but also the result of an often complex causal chain. In medicine, fragility involves 'a chronic physical condition which results in a prolonged dependency on medical care' (Law Insider, 2023), connoting both an enduring (chronic) condition that is unlikely to change, and reliance on outside intervention to sustain quality of life. In both of these cases, fragility is not a condition that is easily addressed or 'cured', and it may in fact lead either to total collapse or to a sustained situation of dependence. As will be noted later, the application of the concept of fragility to states draws upon some of these entailments while occluding others, in its ahistorical focus on internal state–society relations (legitimacy, authority, security) and descriptive statistics (indices or checklists) rather than an analysis of historical conditions and causal relationships that might create fragility, underpin it or render it intractable. Likewise, the consequences of fragility are seldom spelled out − or rather are part of the description of the phenomenon itself.

Like many terms with metaphoric entailments, the concept of fragility transmutes somewhat as it is translated, while retaining a shared conceptual core. In French, it appears to describe two very different situations: '[S]oit l'État fragile est en situation de crise politico-sécuritaire (anarchie, guerre civile, absence totale de contrôle de l'État), soit l'État fragile a une faible gouvernance' (Castellanet et al, 2010).[3] A politico-security crisis is a rather occasional event and does not necessarily entail the effacement of stateness or government (perhaps on part of a territory); while weak governance is

---

[3]   Translation: 'either the fragile state is in a situation of politico-security crisis (anarchy, civil war, total lack of state control), or the fragile state has weak governance'.

more of a chronic condition as noted earlier. In German, the predominant usage was influenced both by the prevailing Anglophone discourse, and by a large-scale academic project on 'Governance in Räumen begrenzter Staatlichkeit' (governance in areas of limited statehood), which focused on the functional dimension of state fragility, including public goods or service delivery issues such as security, health, human rights and education (see Lindemann, 2014; Draude et al, 2018).

Similarly, fragility does not exist without its opposite, which in contemporary international development circles is often labelled 'resilience'. Here too, the metaphorical entailments are important: resilience is an *internal* quality of resistance in an object or individual against external shocks, and the objective of strengthening resilience takes for granted that the conditions creating fragility or vulnerability are exogenous and immutable. A focus on building individuals' resilience tends to occlude the root causes or forces that cause vulnerability (such as violence, inequality, lack of opportunity, poverty, exclusion) (Jütersonke and Kartas, 2012; Neocleous, 2013). Both cases require each other to exist, and resonate with more widely held everyday understandings and, one can argue, individualist ontologies of action and agency.

Creating the object

This section will explore the 'similarities and differences between objects' in an effort to unpack how knowledge of fragility is produced in the four different sites outlined earlier, in order to tease out the logic of statecraft and governance that it reflects or instantiates. It will first examine the data-production process (insofar as this is publicly accessible) to highlight the different ways in which such indices construct fragility. Later it will compare and contrast the four fragility frameworks to tease out their differences, and the possible implications of these. As a foretaste: the general orientation of all indices of state fragility is anchored in a liberal governmentality, with some variations as regards the nature of the state, state–society relations, and political economy, depending on the primary actor involved. What is perhaps more puzzling, however, is the shifting nature of the ordering involved in defining and identifying fragile states – which either implies a radical uncertainty about the category and concept, or (more positively) a progressive 'refinement' in order to maximize its political and practical utility. Finally, states subject to being classified as fragile seem (not surprisingly) often reluctant to embrace the label, even if it may bring some financial or economic benefits.

Failed/Fragile States Index

The first FSI did not actually appear until 2005, well after the term 'failed states' had passed into common usage, and a geopolitical universe away from the interventionist optimism of the early 1990s (after the September 2001 attacks and the invasions of Iraq and Afghanistan). As the presentation of the first FSI noted,

> failed states have made a remarkable odyssey from the periphery to the very center of global politics. ... In the 1990s, 'failed states' fell largely into the province of humanitarians and human rights activists. ... For so-called foreign-policy realists, however, these states and the problems they posed were a distraction from weightier issues of geopolitics. (Amburn, 2005)

What then, was the overall purpose and orientation of the FSI (renamed from 'failed' to 'fragile' in 2014)? Its annual public presentation in the American review *Foreign Policy* (until 2018), with a multicoloured global map highlighting states' degree of fragility, guaranteed a large audience for its findings and subsequent analysis.

No map speaks by itself (see Schlag, Chapter 4, this volume), but the various rankings are hardly surprising to political observers – although perhaps Hungarian or Bulgarian observers would be somewhat surprised to find themselves ranked just below Oman and Argentina! The index itself is based on the measurement of 12 indicators in four 'baskets', with more precise indicators in each basket.

They are:

- Cohesion: security apparatus, group grievances, factionalized elites.
- Economic: economic decline, uneven economic development, brain drain.
- Political: state legitimacy, public service delivery, human rights and rule of law.
- Social: demographic pressures, refugees and internally displaced persons (IDPs), external intervention.

Aside from the highly qualitative nature of many of these indicators, within each indicator a whole host of possible factors contributing to fragility are deployed. For example, the indicator for *state legitimacy* includes such elements as confidence in government, peaceful demonstrations or riots, corruption, political assassinations, leadership transitions, and so forth. But are these *causes, symptoms* or *consequences* of being in a fragile state? How, in addition, is the actual indicator or even the entire index constructed? In short: non-transparently. Each indicator in each basket is weighted equally 0 to 10, with an aggregate score of 120. No details are given about weightings within an indicator, and the data collection and analysis processes are based on 'pre-existing quantitative data sets, content analysis, and qualitative expert analysis ... triangulated and subjected to critical review to obtain final scores for the Index' (FSI, no date; see also Bhuta, 2015). The methodological shortcomings are many, and do not concern us here – suffice it to note that most of the indicators are almost certainly correlated with each other, thus reinforcing lower scores across the spectrum and providing no guidance to assess the underlying causes of fragility. These issues are not confined to the FSI, and in fact most indices suffer from a 'lack of solid theoretical foundations, which leads to confusion between causes, symptoms and outcomes of state fragility' (Ferreira, 2017: 1291).

Since the FSI is not directly connected to a policy framework, its impact on shaping security, humanitarian or development practices can only be indirect. It is rather more emblematic of a particular worldview, one that places strong descriptive emphasis (via equal indicator weighting) on liberal forms of governance (representative leadership, strong national identity, public service delivery including such things as job training or public health provision, avoidance of brain drain, low or stable population growth, and so on), as implicit ways of eliminating or mitigating fragility as measured by particular indicators. The remaining three ways of thinking about fragility, however, have had a much more direct impact on global policy and practices and, in particular, are intended to direct programmes towards reducing the fragility of a state/society through specific interventions and forms of assistance.

'Banking on fragility': the World Bank's adoption of fragility language

The World Bank's approach to fragility, driven by more traditional development logics, began with its Country Policy and Institutional Assessments (CPIA), developed in the late 1970s to shape the Bank's lending policies. The CPIA originally focused on four baskets of issues – macroeconomic policy, sustainable and equitable growth strategies, reducing inequality and public sector management – all fitting comfortably into a traditional development orientation for the allocation of development assistance, and generally disregarding political factors (broadly defined) (World Bank Independent Evaluation Group, 2010: 5–6). The CPIA and its successors have been 'used to allocate International Development Association (IDA) resources to eligible client countries' (World Bank Independent Evaluation Group, 2010: xi), so appearing on its lists was not anodyne.

By the early 2000s, however, the Bank had shifted to using its CPIA scores together with other more governance-related indicators to compile its first list of what became 'fragile states': the Low Income Countries under Stress (LICUS). Status on this list was determined by low CPIA scores and possibly also included governance indicators such as 'Voice and Accountability, Political Stability and Absence of Violence/Terrorism, Government Effectiveness, Regulatory Quality, Rule of Law, and Control of Corruption'

(Kaufmann et al, 2010: 2).[4] The LICUS list lasted from 2004 to 2008, and then morphed into a Fragile States list (2009–10); today presented as a 'List of Fragile and Conflict-Affected Situations' (2020). Between 2011 and 2020 the World Bank operationalized fragility to include not just the CPIA scores, but also the presence of multilateral peace operations as an indicator of the international community's perception of a fragile situation – a clear incorporation of a security criterion into its concept of fragility. It went even further in 2020, renaming its list that of 'fragile and conflict-affected situations' and explicitly including refugees and displaced persons 'as this signals a major political or security crisis' and using non-governmental data on conflict deaths (ACLED and UCDP datasets) (World Bank, 2022b). The explicit use of non-governmental conflict data by a multilateral institution can be traced back to the World Bank's 2011 report on *Conflict, Security and Development* which signalled the opening of the security–development nexus in the Bank's work.

What are the implications of these shifting conceptualizations and categorizations? Two things can be highlighted. The first is the World Bank's clear shift away from exclusively macroeconomic analysis for its lending policies towards the inclusion of internal political and even conflict and security-related factors. This required considerable stretching over time of the Bank's formal mandate, which stated that 'the Bank and its officers shall not interfere in the political affairs of any member; nor shall they be influenced in their decisions by the political character of the member or members concerned. Only economic considerations shall be relevant to their decisions' (IBRD, 2012). The dilemma was, however, that when aid allocations are made on the basis of performance or likelihood of return on investment, fragile states were unlikely to be privileged for donor assistance, hence new frameworks needed to be devised (Bhuta, 2015).

A fragility calculus is supremely political, and its implications for the financing of development have become more and more clear. Starting in the early 2010s, the World Bank established support to fragile states as one of its six strategic priorities (Marc et al, 2013), and, in particular, instead of merely 'working with' state institutions attention was increasingly paid to re-engineering them (Marc et al, 2013: 24). In 2011, the Bank's flagship *World Development Report*, subtitled 'Conflict, Security and Development' consolidated this logic and further focused on the security/insecurity

---

[4]   Early scores (prior to 2008) were not public, and whether or not governance indicators were included from the Worldwide Governance Indicators Project is not clear. 'The Bank defined LICUS as (i) low-income countries with overall CPIA and governance average of the CPIA ratings of 3.2 or less' (World Bank, 2022a; 2022b). All scores since 2006 are available online: www.worldbank.org/en/topic/fragilityconflictviolence/brief/harmonized-list-of-fragile-situations [Accessed 18 September 2023].

dimension of development assistance, noting that 'no low-income fragile or conflict-affected state has yet achieved a single Millennium Development Goal' (World Bank, 2011: 49). And by the publication of its joint 2018 report (with UNDP), *Pathways for Peace: Inclusive Approaches to Preventing Violent Conflict*, fragility language was virtually on every page – there are more than 300 references to fragility or fragile states in the report – which could lead one to think that the Bank's principal mission had moved far away from its original mandate towards wholesale engagement with state building under the umbrella of tackling fragility (United Nations and World Bank, 2018). In other areas too (such as the World Bank–UNHCR Joint Data Center on Forced Displacement (JDC)) the Bank is moving into subject areas far removed from its original mandate.

Second, the language of fragility, as in 'fragile and conflict-affected states', follows a double-edged logic. On the one hand, it acknowledges that many of the obstacles to economic development (however defined) go beyond considerations of violent interstate and internal conflict (civil war), to include forms of internal insecurity and large-scale subnational violence that threatens the wellbeing or security of the population (including state repression). This follows the logic of 'human security' by putting the wellbeing of the population at the centre of policy frameworks. At the same time, however, the way in which fragility is operationalized, around fragility in *low income* countries (see Table 7.1), means that the focus is primarily on African states, and that virtually every prominent fragile state is either in, or has recently experienced, large-scale violent conflict. Practically speaking, this means that the Bank's work still does not touch upon, for example, those states in regions such as Central America (Honduras, El Salvador and Guatemala, for example) that experience extremely high levels of violence and state capture by criminalized elites. Conceptually, it also fails to untangle the 'causal arrow': does low GDP per capita *cause* fragility and conflict, or are conflict and fragility a persistent cause of low growth and development? Economists tend to opt for the former argument.

OECD *states of fragility*

In parallel to the other major multilateral donor forum, the OECD, has also moved over time towards direct engagement with the language of fragility to shape its members' bilateral (and multilateral) development assistance policies. It adopted a 'multi-dimensional' concept of fragility, encompassing economic, environmental, political, societal and security dimensions (the inclusion of an environmental dimension is noteworthy and warrants some subsequent exploration). The initial conception, articulated in 2007, straddled the development–security divide, and was a harbinger of the emerging securitization of development assistance: 'States are fragile when state structures lack political will and/or capacity to provide the basic functions needed for poverty reduction, development and to safeguard the security and human rights of their population' (OECD, 2007: 2). Related to this were the efforts to expand the eligibility criteria for official development assistance (ODA) to include certain forms of security assistance, including for disarmament, demobilization and reintegration, as well as some aspects of security sector reform and arms control. But only one year later:

> We propose modifying the OECD/DAC definition of a fragile state, simply as *one unable to meet its population's expectations or manage changes in expectations and capacity through the political process*. Whether and to what degree these expectations entail poverty reduction, development, security or human rights will depend on historical, cultural and other factors that shape state–society relations in specific contexts. (OECD, 2008: 16, emphasis added)

This is a much more expansive understanding of fragility, as it focuses directly on the *political* dimension of state–society relations, rather different from either the World Bank's economic and governance (performance)-oriented vision, or the FSI's broad indicator-related focus. There is a fairly strong liberal (democratic) orientation towards this, with the implication that the population articulates its expectations through some sort of open process that can lead to interest aggregation (parties, civil society, interest groups) and arbitration via political institutions – all classic elements of representative systems, and antithetical to top-down or quasi-authoritarian rule. One possible explanation for this is that the OECD, being primarily an association of like-minded Western-oriented donors, does not have the same constraints as, for example the World Bank, or the same geopolitical logic as the FSI. There is also some evidence that donors such as Japan resist the liberal interventionist logic of the OECD's orientation towards fragility, as well as some of the other norms it promotes, in particular working closely with civil society (as opposed to state institutions) (Jütersonke et al, 2021).

The principal driver behind fragility within the OECD was its International Network on Conflict and Fragility (INCAF), and the 'push' it made to incorporate fragility concerns into development programming.[5]

---

[5] I was involved intermittently with the early efforts (2005–10) in the INCAF to bring armed violence prevention and reduction programming, as well as work on small arms and related issues (security sector programming), within the ambit of development assistance. See *Armed Violence Reduction: Enabling Development* (OECD-DAC, 2009). I was also on the 'Reference Group' for the OECD's 2020 *States of Fragility* report.

The impact of the adoption of a fragility lens on allocations of ODA has been clear. In the early 2000s, ODA to fragile and non-fragile states was roughly equal, but beginning in 2003–04 the share of ODA that went to fragile states increased sharply in both absolute and relative terms, so that it now outstrips 'regular' ODA by roughly 50 per cent. For many of the world's largest donors, aid to fragile states now exceeds two thirds of their total ODA (Desai, 2020: 13, 16). This may be in part a product of the creation of the category of 'fragile states' but the shift in allocations implies a broader policy reorientation, and one that necessarily moves away from previous governing logics such as 'poverty reduction' or 'sustainable development' or 'basic human needs'. Of course, many programmes in fragile states may address such issues – but not necessarily in the same way as if they were central to the framing of policies.

The G7+ International Dialogue on Peacebuilding and Statebuilding

What do the subjects of the fragility discourse make of being so categorized and classified? I have looked at the constitution of fragility through an external lens, in which the objects of fragility analysis have little or no input. In other words, the concept has not hitherto been *co-constitutive*, since states so characterized may resist, reject, amend or accept such characterizations, but have little or no input into the way in which the concept is constructed or used by multilateral organizations, major donor states, or even NGOs (although, for an exception, see Fisher, 2014). The major exception to this is the G7+ born out of the International Dialogue on Peacebuilding and Statebuilding, which brought together self-identified fragile states and donors around a set of principles for engaging in fragile situations called the *New Deal for Engagement in Fragile States.* The New Deal focuses on five goals (IDPS, 2011), which can be taken as reflecting its understanding of the sources of fragility (and the means to address it):

- Legitimate politics – Foster inclusive political settlements and conflict resolution.
- Security – Establish and strengthen people's security.
- Justice – Address injustices and increase people's access to justice.
- Economic foundations – Generate employment and improve livelihoods.
- Revenues and services – Manage revenue and build capacity for accountable and fair service delivery.

As Jan Pospisil (2017: 1418) argues, the G7+ initiative represents a form of resistance to the donor-led vision of state fragility (and the programmatic implications) and 'offers an auspicious entry point for southern governments to contest the principles of global liberal governance'. Perhaps – or perhaps not – especially since joint participation does not entirely eliminate the power dynamics between donor and recipient states.

To begin, the G7+ initiative defines fragility as: '[A] period of time during nationhood when sustainable socio-economic development requires greater emphasis on complementary peacebuilding and statebuilding activities such as building inclusive political settlements, security, justice, jobs, good management of resources, and accountable and fair service delivery' (G7+, 2013: 1). This definition both resembles and departs from other conceptualizations. At the outset it is time-bound – and hence not regarded as a chronic or endemic condition. It contains an implicit causal account (lacking from other indices) or theory of change: economic development *follows from* post-conflict peacebuilding and broader state-building efforts. More importantly, it treats fragility as almost purely an endogenous phenomenon, rooted in domestic political processes (and absences) disconnected from any external influences or structural conditions (effects of globalization, history of colonial rule or conquest/invasion, and so on). Given the strong implication of major bilateral donors and Western states as partners in the initiative, this absence is not surprising. And finally, it embodies a liberal teleology, in which politics must be inclusive and institutions should follow the rule of law (be accountable and fair).

Beyond the definition, however, the G7+ initiative noted two things, that 'in many countries, the term "fragility" is itself highly controversial, and many prefer to focus on "resilience" as the positive inverse of fragility' and that it 'is different in every context' (G7+, 2013: 1). At a minimum this implies some resistance to dominant formulations of fragility. But the flip to a focus on resilience is also not without problems, since, as noted earlier, it too suspends reflection on the exogenous conditions that oblige states to become more resilient when buffeted by forces (globalization, export dependence, unequal investment relationships, and so on) that create fragility in the first place. More importantly, the G7+ initiative places the onus on nationally or locally led assessments of the 'causes, features and drivers of fragility as well as the sources of resilience within a country' (IDPS, 2014: 1).[6] Aside from the process-oriented aspects (inclusive and participatory consultations), the emphasis is on context-specific analyses rather than transversal and macro-level comparisons or league tables that rank participating states. From a development policy perspective, this provides much more fine-grained

---

[6] A series of national fragility assessment reports have been made public: www.g7plus.org/fragility-assessment-reports/ [Accessed 18 September 2023].

guidance for shaping aid allocations, although it is impossible to determine if in fact this results in changed allocations.

Comparing and contrasting fragility frameworks

State fragility is a constructed concept – which is neither surprising nor problematic – but is it a completely *ad hoc* concept, in a sort of Alice-in-Wonderland 'words mean what I choose them to mean' way? Although there has been considerable convergence around a common terminology, with some actors (the FSI) abandoning the term 'failed states' and its cognates (ungoverned spaces, weak, failing, collapsed, vulnerable, quasi-states, and so on) and others (the World Bank) moving towards a shared concept of fragility, different actors use the same term, but not with any particular effort to do so in the same or a similar way. Very few compare and contrast their rankings or categorizations, let alone potentially harmonize these. Table 7.1 gives some idea of the uncertainty (and areas of convergence) around the concept and ordering function of 'fragile states'.

Only ten of the states appear on all four lists, with a further 14 states appearing on three of the four lists. That suggests considerable convergence despite definitional differences, and implies that it does not seem to matter a great deal what particular measurement or weighting strategy is followed. The absence of major divergences would also seem to reflect confirmation bias: we implicitly know fragility (and its absence) when we see it, and data analysis confirms our (great powers, donors) intuitions. At least five other things are noteworthy. First, only 12 of the 20 states that self-identify as fragile (in the G7+ initiative) appear on three or four lists – leaving almost half that seem to identify as fragile for 'other' reasons than recognized indicators. Togo, Timor Leste and Sierra Leone appear on no other fragility lists; Cote d'Ivoire and Guinea on only one other list (leaving aside the other three very small states). Second, those fragile states that appear on all lists except the self-identified G7+ Initiative list include such international pariahs or 'difficult cases' as Venezuela, Myanmar, Zimbabwe, Syria and Libya (among others), suggesting that one's ability to resist being drawn into the fragility donor orbit depends on relative power positions or the desirability of accessing donor resources.

Third, there are some significant plausible omissions from these lists. While I cannot justify these examples empirically at this point, one could plausibly ask why states such as Mexico, Hungary, Serbia or Moldova should not appear higher up the list, given, for example, their low rankings on Transparency International's Corruption Perception Index, low V-Dem democracy scores, and other evidence of weak or poor governance (Coppedge and Gerring, 2022; Transparency International, 2022). Arguably, fragility indices, despite their conceptual entailments of 'brittleness' do not adequately take into

Table 7.1: Comparison of state listings in various state fragility indices

Fragile States Index	World Bank	OECD	G7+
2020	2021	2020	**Alphabetical, self-identified as 'fragile'**
Yemen	Afghanistan	Yemen	Afghanistan
Somalia	Libya	South Sudan	Burundi
Syria	Somalia	Somalia	Central African Republic
South Sudan	Syria	Central African Republic	Chad
Democratic Republic of the Congo	Burkina Faso	Democratic Republic of the Congo	Comoros
Central African Republic	Cameroon	Syria	Cote d'Ivoire
Chad	Central African Republic	Chad	Democratic Republic of the Congo
Sudan	Chad	Afghanistan	Guinea
Afghanistan	Democratic Republic of the Congo	Haiti	Guinea-Bissau
Zimbabwe	Iraq	Burundi	Haiti
Ethiopia	Mali	Iraq	Liberia
Nigeria	Mozambique	Sudan	Papua New Guinea
Haiti	Myanmar	Republic of Congo	Sao Tome and Principe
Guinea	Niger	Mali	Sierra Leone
Cameroon	Nigeria	Venezuela	Solomon Islands
Burundi	South Sudan	Zimbabwe	Somalia
Eritrea	Yemen	Equatorial Guinea	South Sudan
Libya	Burundi	Libya	Timor Leste
Mali	Republic of Congo	Cameroon	Togo
Iraq	Eritrea	Uganda	Yemen
Niger	Gambia	North Korea	
Mozambique	Guinea-Bissau	Pakistan	
Myanmar	Haiti	Eritrea	

(continued)

Table 7.1: Comparison of state listings in various state fragility indices (continued)

Fragile States Index	World Bank	OECD	G7+
Uganda	Kosovo	Nigeria	
Venezuela	Laos	Mozambique	
Republic of Congo	Lebanon	Madagascar	
Guinea-Bissau	Liberia	Kenya	
Cote d'Ivoire	Papua New Guinea	Ethiopia	
Pakistan	Sudan	Guinea-Bissau	
North Korea	Venezuela	Bangladesh	
Liberia	OPT	Papua New Guinea	
Kenya	Zimbabwe	Mauritania	

Note: The World Bank distinguishes between high (the first four states) and medium-intensity conflict (all states down to Yemen), and 'high institutional and social fragility' contexts (the rest). After Mauritania, the OECD also includes 24 other states.

account the often brittle nature of political institutions and delivery of public goods in many Western or Northern states. Fourth, although the snapshot presentation does not track fragility indices over time, there is a great deal of stability in the overall rankings (with some noteworthy exceptions mainly related to the outbreak or termination of violent conflict). This suggests that fragility is more of a chronic condition, resistant to short-term 'fixes' such as aid allocations or international interventions. Finally, there appear to be two competing visions of fragility at work here: one which a strong domestic constituency is willing to acknowledge and (potentially) address, and one associated with authoritarian or fractured polities in which engagement with the international community is extremely limited or fraught. The latter, in particular, would appear to reject the reformist and interventionist agenda associated with fragility, and would otherwise (like Myanmar or Zimbabwe) potentially be considered 'strong' states not susceptible to disruptive shocks. In this case, 'strong' states are those in which the institutional presence is strong enough to suppress dissent, maintain regime control and resist external pressure – all of which would seem to be the opposite of 'fragile' and connote actual state *resilience*.

Conclusion

What do fragility comparisons and conceptualizations *do*? How do they constitute the socio-political world; what do they highlight and obscure, and how are they used by selected actors? Beginning at the beginning, *state failure* was clearly constructed as a security threat – as noted by Ratner and Helman or Robert Kaplan, ideas of state collapse, the 'coming anarchy' and ungoverned spaces all informed the reorientation of post–Cold War security policies in the global West around so-called new threats emanating from the Global South. In particular, these threats were regarded as *internally* generated, based on the inability of the state to provide public goods or meet basic needs – in particular security – with spillover effects for regional and international order and stability. This marked a rupture with traditional conceptions of insecurity oriented around the external capacity of a state to pose a military threat to its neighbours or beyond, and provided an interventionary blueprint for great power and multilateral governance.

But fragility comparisons were not only crucial to the construction and promotion of a particular governance object; the comparative practices of different institutions also had distributional consequences. One of the main ideas behind the OECD-DAC fragility report, as well as the G7+ initiative (and the policy frameworks that they supported), was to shift the way in which bilateral donor assistance was allocated, both in *how* development assistance was spent and in *where* it was allocated. Switzerland, for example, notes that 'around half of the countries and regions in which Switzerland is actively involved qualify as fragile' (SDC, 2022). The UK Department for International Development (as it was then called), under Claire Short, pushed very hard to include security sector reform as a development concern, and security (understood broadly) as a precondition for sustainable development achievements. And many donors, recognizing the specificities of working in fragile contexts, committed to working differently, rather than 'development assistance as usual'. The politics of comparisons were anything but neutral data-driven or statistical exercises.

Much of this work was developed and promoted through the OECD's International Network on Conflict and Fragility, which brought together key players from all major donors to develop guidance notes, lessons learned and best practice strategies to tackle fragility, as a means of influencing bilateral ODA practices (OECD, 2022). The list of publications gives a clear idea of what kinds of issues donors converged around: security, justice and rule of law, violent conflict and armed violence, and so on. Similarly, the World Bank's 'classification aims to inform strategic and operational decision-making within the World Bank Group [WBG]' (World Bank, 2022a: 1) in order to ensure that 'the WBG's strategic and programmatic focus in countries affected by FCS [fragile and conflict-affected situations]-related issues is adapted and tailored to the diverse challenges faced by these countries' (World Bank, 2022a: 1).[7] The main driver here has been the work of the Fragility, Conflict, and Violence (FCV) Group, part of the social development dimension of the Bank's organizational structure.

Although it is impossible in the scope of this chapter to trace shifts in donor allocations and practices, and to attribute them to fragility classifications, it appears that the politics of state fragility and donor assistance revolve more around the classification of a state as fragile (and hence warranting particular attention), and less around comparative rankings determining which states are more or less fragile, and in which dimensions, and how this may have changed over time (Carment et al, 2008). For example, although insecurity (conflict, violence, weak state institutions) is a key component of all conceptualizations of fragility, only 13 per cent of aid allocated in 2018 went to 'peace-related objectives, including peacebuilding, basic safety and security, governance and inclusive political processes' (Desai, 2020: 61). Since politics broadly defined is central to fragility, the relatively low attention paid to issues such as legitimacy, political institutions or service delivery suggests a disconnect between diagnosis and treatment. Aid allocations themselves are also determined by a host of considerations, including geopolitical or historical (colonial considerations), trends in donor countries and idiosyncratic factors.

With respect to the FSI, the most high-profile use is the league table of country rankings, although the developers of the Index stress that its main purpose is not a cross-sectional, but rather a longitudinal analysis of trends *within* states on different dimensions. The stated goals include conflict mitigation, early warning and risk analysis, all designed to inform decision making. Given the private nature of much of its work (which includes contextual risk assessments, responsible business practices, but also prevention of election violence and violence against women and girls), however, it is difficult to determine the balance between these three, and a perusal of the project's website suggests it is targeted mainly towards corporate clients or local actors/NGOs (FFP, no date). It would be interesting to see to what extent the FSI rankings shape any private actors' risk and investment decisions, but the available evidence suggests that trend analysis – whether based on the FSI, or shifts in the OECD and World Bank rankings over time – do *not* actually figure strongly in security policies, although, as states migrate 'out' of fragility, this may affect donor aid allocations. That the 'security logic' behind fragility is more sticky is perhaps not surprising (in contrast, for example, to Myatt and Müller's analysis of cybersecurity,

---

[7]   This is 'part of WBG commitments made in the context of the 18th replenishment of the International Development Association (IDA) and the Global Capital Increase for the International Bank for Reconstruction and Development (IBRD)' (World Bank, 2022a: 1). The background for this needs to be detailed.

Chapter 9, this volume), given the very general and abstract way in which fragility is often conceived.

In short, the deployment of the language of fragility has not been a neutral and objective descriptor of particular phenomena in the world. It facilitated and accelerated the fusion of security and development concerns, and the 'securitization' of development assistance thus displaced traditional ideas of poverty reduction or sustainable development. It also has reoriented development assistance to 'different' destination countries – potentially also moving away from provision for basic needs and working with the world's poorest or 'bottom billion' to more closely align to geopolitically sensitive contexts: states and regions regarded as posing a potential threat to Western or Northern interests or requiring sustained military interventions and commitments (Afghanistan, the Sahel, and so on). And it may also have changed (somewhat) the way in which development assistance is delivered, including through long-term engagements in fragile states, flexibility in programming, acceptance of risk of failure, and sensitivity to the negative distributional effects of large-scale development assistance projects, many of which exacerbate societal cleavages and inequalities, or enrich particular rent-seeking elites. Finally, it has doubtless prioritized a neoliberal form of governance, not only in the (mostly positive) sense of promoting inclusion, accountability and representative rule, but also in the liberal governmentality of the techniques of new public management (log frames, theories of change, output, outcome and impact indicators in programme monitoring and evaluation, and so on) to (re)engineer state institutions around the world.

References

Amburn, B. (2005) 'The Failed States Index 2005', *Foreign Policy*, 22 October, https://foreignpolicy.com/2009/10/22/the-failed-states-index-2005/ [Accessed 9 May 2023].

Bhuta, N. (2015) 'Measuring stateness, ranking political orders: indices of state fragility', in A. Cooley and J. Snyder (eds) *Ranking the World*, Cambridge: Cambridge University Press, pp 85–111.

Carment, D., Samy, Y. and Prest, S. (2008) 'State fragility and implications for aid allocation: an empirical analysis', *Conflict Management and Peace Science*, 25(4): 349–73.

Castellanet, C., Solanet, G. and Ficatier, Y. (2010) *Adapter les pratiques opérationnelles des bailleurs dans les États fragiles*, Paris: Agence Française de Développement.

Chandler, D. (2007) 'The security–development nexus and the rise of "anti-foreign policy"', *Journal of International Relations and Development*, 10(4): 362–86.

Coppedge, M. and Gerring, J. (2022) The V-Dem Dataset 2022, www.v-dem.net/data/the-v-dem-dataset/ [Accessed 18 September 2023].

Desai, H. (2020) *States of Fragility and Official Development Assistance*, OECD Development Co-operation Working Papers, No. 76, Paris: OECD Publishing.

Draude, A., Börzel, T.A. and Risse, T. (eds) (2018): *The Oxford Handbook of Governance and Limited Statehood*, Oxford: Oxford University Press.

Duffield, M.R. (2001) *Global Governance and the New Wars: The Merging of Development and Security*, London, New York, NY: Zed Books.

Etsy, D.C., Goldstone, J. and Gurr, T.R. (1995) *Working Papers: State Failure Task Force Report*, Arlington, VA: Central Intelligence Agency.

Ferreira, I.A. (2017) 'Measuring state fragility: a review of the theoretical groundings of existing approaches', *Third World Quarterly*, 38(6): 1291–309.

Fisher, J. (2014) 'When it pays to be a "fragile state": Uganda's use and abuse of a dubious concept', *Third World Quarterly*, 35(2): 316–32.

FFP (Fund for Peace) (no date) 'What We Do', https://fundforpeace.org/ what-we-do/ [Accessed 9 May 2023].

FSI (Fragile States Index) (no date) 'Methodology', https://fragilestatesin dex.org/methodology/ [Accessed 9 May 2023].

G7+ (2013) *Note on the Fragility Spectrum*, www.g7plus.org/wp-cont ent/uploads/2023/07/Fragility-Spectrum-in-English.pdf [Accessed 24 January 2024].

Grimm, S., Lemay-Hébert, N. and Nay, O. (2014) 'Fragile states: introducing a political concept', *Third World Quarterly*, 35(2): 197–209.

Gruffydd Jones, B. (2013) '"Good governance" and "state failure": genealogies of imperial discourse', *Cambridge Review of International Affairs*, 26(1): 49–70.

Helman, G.B. and Ratner, S.R. (1992) 'Saving failed states', *Foreign Policy*, (89): 3–20.

IBRD (International Bank for Reconstruction and Development) (2012) 'Political activity prohibited. Article 4, Section 10', in IBRD, *Articles of Agreement*, Washington DC: The World Bank Group, p 10.

IDPS (International Dialogue on Peacebuilding and Statebuilding) (2011) *A New Deal for Engagement in Fragile States*, https://gsdrc.org/docum ent-library/a-new-deal-for-engagement-in-fragile-states/ [Accessed 24 January 2024].

IDPS (International Dialogue on Peacebuilding and Statebuilding) (2014) *Guidance Note on Fragility Assessments*, www.pbsbdialogue.org/media/filer _public/96/fb/96fb5ae4-7b0d-4007-bf9e-1ed869db21da/rd_4_fragility_ assessment_guidance_note_final.pdf [Accessed 18 September 2023].

Jackson, R.H. (1991) *Quasi-States: Sovereignty, International Relations and the Third World*, Cambridge: Cambridge University Press.

Jütersonke, O. and Kartas, M. (2012) *Resilience: Conceptual Reflections*, Geneva: The Graduate Institute of International and Development Studies, Centre on Conflict, Development and Peacebuilding.

Jütersonke, O., Kobayashi, K., Krause, K. and Yuan, X. (2021) 'Norm contestation and normative transformation in global peacebuilding order(s): the cases of China, Japan, and Russia', *International Studies Quarterly*, 65(4): 944–59.

Kaplan, R. (1994) 'The coming anarchy', *The Atlantic Monthly*, 273(2): 44–76, www.theatlantic.com/past/docs/politics/foreign/anarchy.htm [Accessed 9 May 2023].

Kaufmann, D., Kraay, A. and Mastruzzi, M. (2010) *The Worldwide Governance Indicators. Methodology and Analytical Issues*, World Bank Policy Research Working Paper 5430, https://documents1.worldbank.org/curated/en/630421468336563314/pdf/WPS5430.pdf [Accessed 18 September 2023].

Law Insider (2023) 'Medically fragile definition', www.lawinsider.com/dictionary/medically-fragile [accessed 18 September 2023].

League of Nations (1920) *The Covenant of the League of Nations*, 20 February, https://libraryresources.unog.ch/ld.php?content_id=32971179 [Accessed 18 September 2023].

Lindemann, S. (2014) 'Was ist ein fragiler Staat?', https://www.kfw-entwicklungsbank.de/PDF/Download-Center/PDF-Dokumente-Development-Research/2014-08-21_FE_Was-ist-ein-fragiler-Staat.pdf [Accessed 18 September 2023].

Marc, A., Willman, A., Aslam, G., Rebosio, M. and Balasuriya, K. (2013) *Societal Dynamics and Fragility: Engaging Societies in Responding to Fragile Situations*, Washington DC: World Bank.

Milliken, J. and Krause, K. (2002) 'State failure, state collapse and state reconstruction: concepts, lessons and strategies', *Development and Change*, 33(5): 755–74.

Müller, T., Albert, M. and Langer, K. (2022) 'Practices of comparison and the making of international orders', *Journal of International Relations and Development*, 25(3): 834–59.

Neocleous, M. (2013) 'Resisting resilience', *Radical Philosophy*, 178: 2–5.

Nilsson, C. and Grelsson, G. (1995) 'The fragility of ecosystems: a review', *The Journal of Applied Ecology*, 32(4): 677–92.

OECD (Organisation for Economic Cooperation and Development) (2007) *Principles for Good International Engagement in Fragile States and Situations*, Paris: OECD Publishing.

OECD (2008) *Concepts and Dilemmas of State Building in Fragile Situations: From Fragility to Resilience*, Paris: OECD Publishing.

OECD (2020) *States of Fragility 2020*, Paris: OECD Publishing.

OECD (2022) 'The International Network on Conflict and Fragility (INCAF)', www.oecd.org/dac/conflict-fragility-resilience/incaf-network.htm [Accessed 9 May 2023].

OECD-DAC (Organisation for Economic Cooperation and Development-Development Assistance Committee) (2009) *Armed Violence Reduction: Enabling Development*, Paris: OECD Publishing.

Pospisil, J. (2017) '"Unsharing" sovereignty: G7+ and the politics of international statebuilding', *International Affairs*, 93(6): 1417–34.

Richardson, H.J. (1996) 'Failed states, self-determination, and preventive diplomacy: colonialist nostalgia and democratic expectations', *Temple International and Comparative Law Journal*, 10(1): 1–78.

Richmond, O.P. and Franks, J. (2008) 'Liberal peacebuilding in Timor Leste: the emperor's new clothes?', *International Peacekeeping*, 15(2): 185–200.

Roberts, A. (2015) *Fragile States: A Concept with a History*, London: British Academy.

SDC (Swiss Agency for Development and Cooperation) (2022) 'Action in Fragile States: Sustainable Support for Governments and Populations', www.eda.admin.ch/deza/en/home/themes-sdc/fragile-contexts-and-pre vention/sdc-work-fragile-contexts.html [Accessed 9 May 2023].

Stewart, F. and Brown, G. (2010) *Fragile States. Overview*, Number 3, Oxford: Center for Research on Inequality, Human Security and Ethnicity (CRISE), https://assets.publishing.service.gov.uk/media/57a08b17ed915 d3cfd000b1c/CRISE-Overview-3.pdf [Accessed 18 September 2023].

Transparency International (2022) *Corruption Perception Index*, www.trans parency.org/en/cpi/2022 [Accessed 9 May 2023].

United Nations and World Bank (2018) *Pathways for Peace*, Washington DC: World Bank.

Woodward, S.L. (1995) *Balkan Tragedy: Chaos and Dissolution after the Cold War*, Washington DC: Brookings Institution Press.

Woodward, S.L. (2017) *The Ideology of Failed States: Why Intervention Fails*, Cambridge: Cambridge University Press.

World Bank (2011) *World Development Report 2011: Conflict, Security, and Development – Overview*, http://documents.worldbank.org/curated/en/ 806531468161369474/World-development-report-2011-conflict-secur ity-and-development-overview [Accessed 9 May 2023].

World Bank (2022a) 'Classification of Fragile and Conflict-Affected Situations', www.worldbank.org/en/topic/fragilityconflictviolence/brief/ harmonized-list-of-fragile-situations [Accessed 9 May 2023].

World Bank (2022b) 'Historical Overview: The World Bank Group's Classification of Fragile and Conflict Affected Situations since 2006', https://thedocs.worldbank.org/en/doc/373511582764863285-0090022 020/original/FCSHistorialnote.pdf [Accessed 24 January 2024].

World Bank Independent Evaluation Group (2010) *The World Bank's Country Policy and Institutional Assessment: An Evaluation*, Washington DC: World Bank Group.

Zartman, I.W. (ed) (1995) *Collapsed States: The Disintegration and Restoration of Legitimate Authority*, Boulder, CO: Lynne Rienner Publishers.

8

Mapping the Dark and Ornamenting the Order: Comparisons in Global Crime Governance

Anja P. Jakobi and Lena Herbst

Statistics are often seen as an instrument of precision to map and even order political problems. This chapter shows that statistics on crime – particularly global statistics on crime – are usually estimates produced under difficult conditions. The lack of accurate knowledge (see also Schmidt, Chapter 11) ultimately leads to a range of incoherent statistics on the same phenomenon, all of which are, nevertheless, used in parallel to represent it (see also Krause, Chapter 7). While, in principle, contradictory statistics are ill-equipped to be a mapping or ordering tool, they actually serve as both. Comparisons and statistical data on crime have traditionally been criticized for their inherent problems, ranging from a weak database and political overinterpretation to even more difficult aggregation and comparison practices on the global level (see Andreas and Greenhill, 2010b). The present chapter shows that the role of statistical knowledge in political decision making on crime is often more ornamental than informative, in the strict sense of the term.

To examine the use and limits of comparisons in more detail, the chapter starts from a historical perspective, presenting the supply and demand of comparisons and numbers in global crime governance. It then turns to the role of comparisons in policy making on crime, and to what kind of assessments are common in global crime governance. In a third step, we examine the utility of statistical data on crime for mapping and ordering – showing that comparisons in particular can serve as ordering tools independently of the quality of their data.

Comparing crime: the demand for and supply of numbers

Crime has long been identified as a domestic social problem by national governments and researchers and its measurement has become more sophisticated over time despite consistent difficulties of definition. 'Crime' in fact refers to myriad different activities that also vary across time and between societies. Still, comparisons of crime rates – usually compared either with regard to numbers of incidents, numbers of victims, or the overall damage caused in monetary terms – map criminal activities from the local to the global level.

While social phenomena have been recorded in the form of censuses in some countries for thousands of years, this data has only been used to study social and economic trends and develop policies since the 18th century, as in the first US census in 1790 (Mosher et al, 2011). In addition to census data, periodic surveys were conducted by social scientists throughout the 19th century (Bidermann and Reiss, 1967). A first systematic measurement of crime, based on judicial data from 1825, was introduced in France in 1827, promoted by the so-called 'moral statistics' movement that emerged in several Western nations in the 1800s. Believing that quantitative measurements could be applied to social phenomena, Quetelet and Guerry put forward crime statistics as a means to understand and counter crime (Beirne, 1993; Stamatel, 2009; De Bondt, 2013; Maguire and McVie, 2017). Quetelet was thereby the first to recognize the dark figure of crime and noted that

> [A]ll we possess of statistics of crime and misdemeanours would have no utility at all if we did not tacitly assume that there is nearly invariable relationship between offenses known and adjudicated and the total sum of offenses committed. (Quoted in Sellin and Wolfgang, 1964: 3, partially in italics in original)

The idea of measuring crime more systematically was disseminated across Western countries: in 1834 France published standardized crime statistics; in 1857 England and Wales published a first series of national statistics; and in 1939 the US developed the Uniform Crime Report, a development towards national crime statistics based on judicial data. This report already had problems in presenting nationwide data due to differing definitions of crime, decentralized reporting procedures, differing law enforcement policies and data presentation influenced by political purposes (Mosher et al, 2011). During the 19th century police and judicial data were widely accepted as a reliable measurement of crime (Maguire and McVie, 2017: 165), but criticism of the use of this data for national crime statistics grew in the 20th century. A 1936 study by Robison on delinquent youth in New York

City drew attention to dark figures, while in 1947, a study by Sutherland emphasized that comparability would require crime statistics that are calculated in proportion to the population and include white-collar crimes (Mosher et al, 2011: 46–8). The development of self-report studies and victimization surveys were a reaction to the shortcomings of official police data and growing concern over validity and reliability (LaFree and Dugan, 2007; Barberet, 2014). Dependent on citizens' reports, official police data was challenged by the inaccessibility of the police, reporting biases with respect to certain types of crime, and citizens' mistrust of the police or fear of the police or offenders. Further challenges resulted from race or social class biases in reporting or recording practices (Mosher et al, 2011: 93; Barberet, 2014: 48). Victimization surveys and self-report studies of crime reflect the development of science and survey research, especially in political opinion polling, and a first attempt in the US was conducted in the 1920s (Mosher et al, 2011: 49). Still, self-report studies and victimization surveys proved problematic for comparative crime statistics, as they are determined by cultural norms, the legal system, underlying legal definitions, and ways of detecting, recording and counting crime. Collecting adequate data can prove difficult, especially in developing countries or in countries with many rural areas or affected by internal conflict (Mosher et al, 2011: 111; Barberet, 2014: 49).

Efforts to create internationally comparable statistics diversified and intensified after the Second World War (Lopez-Rey, 1985; Maguire and McVie, 2017). In recent decades, the United Nations Office on Drugs and Crime (UNODC) has established several data sources that contain comparable statistics developed against a common classification of crimes, such as standard homicide or drug trafficking reports. Other international and regional organizations have developed international comparative crime statistics, such as the *European Sourcebook on Crime and Justice Statistics*, Eurostat Data Collection, or the UN Survey on Crime Trends and the Operation of Criminal Justice Systems (Lewis, 2012). While the transnational nature of crime defies many traditional research methods, researchers, among them Stamatel (2009) and van Dijk (2007), encourage overcoming methodological challenges and call for the development of new data sources, including open ones. Besides the RAND database on terrorist incidents, van Dijk (2011) developed the Organized Crime Perception Index (Barberet, 2014). In addition, non-governmental organizations (NGOs) such as Transparency International publish their own comparative international statistics, the Corruption Perception Index (Transparency International, 2020) being one example.

In parallel to the creation of more adequate data, diplomatic and law enforcement efforts have been dedicated to countering crime across borders since the 19th century (Deflem, 2002). Later, both the League of Nations and the United Nations established conventions against crime, particularly drug trafficking (Bewley-Taylor, 1999; 2012). The US invested in bilateral and multilateral efforts to penalize and criminalize these and other crimes, for instance corruption, money laundering and human trafficking, as well as human rights violations (Andreas and Nadelmann, 2006; Jakobi, 2013). In 2000 the UN also adopted the Palermo Convention, identifying transnational organized crime as a common challenge to the international community (United Nations, 2000). Only in the late 20th century, however, was crime identified as an important security threat (Jakobi, 2020). The transition of Eastern European countries led not only to new opportunities for criminal activities like arms trafficking and nuclear smuggling, and the creation of new privatized security that was also engaged in illegal activities. As a consequence of these developments, transnational organized crime was increasingly defined as a new security threat that impacted not only domestic society, but also states and international security. However, in this context, neither the term 'transnational organized crime' – nor, for that matter, 'crime' in general – comes with a fixed meaning attached. It can encompass anything from illegal markets or smuggling to the funding of terrorist activities and trafficking in human organs – activities that have very different security implications. Global statistics and comparisons of crime are thus not only comparing different countries or trends – they also compare very different security risks. This is important to emphasize as an increasing number of criminal activities are framed as security threats – often due to the resources and attention that securitization brings. For instance, wildlife trafficking has increasingly been defined as security threat, entailing the militarization of countermeasures (Elliot, 2016).

The growing attention to crime in security governance is today accompanied by a large proliferation of data on crime, related trends and government 'performance' – a development visible also in other fields. Rankings and ratings, statistical categories and trend assessments all attest to the growing significance of quantitative information in global governance research and practice (see Hansen, 2012; Hansen and Mühlen-Schulte, 2012; Hansen and Porter, 2012; Kelley and Simmons, 2019). Still, statistics not only compare formerly distinct phenomena, they also create common analytical categories and country types and elucidate new social problems that were formerly unknown (Bowker and Star, 2000). Statistics reify the items they were meant to find and count – as ordering tools, they categorize the world.

Statistical knowledge about crime is today not only essential for research, but also for politics and the public (see Andreas and Greenhill, 2010a). In particular, the growing emphasis on so-called 'evidence-based policy making' (see Botterill, 2017; Cairney, 2019) has led to further demand for data, ranging from polling data to figures on crime or poverty. Numbers are often used competitively, as the political actors who have the 'bigger numbers' are more likely to be successful in promoting their agendas (Andreas and Greenhill, 2010a). This demand for numbers also requires quantification even in those issue areas that are hard to quantify, as data usually helps to mobilize people for a specific agenda (Stone, 1989). The use of quantitative data is visible today in many policy assessments at the national and international level (Kelley and Simmons, 2019).

The demand for data is also matched by a growing supply. The supply grows through digitalization, leading to a widespread use of 'process-produced data' that is reused for other purposes. At the same time, lower costs of data generation via online surveys and desk research contribute to more data, also because activists and interest groups increasingly use these tools. The importance of data and the requirement to produce 'evidence' for political issues also have consequences for the demand for and dissemination of data. These factors enhance the availability, but not necessarily the quality of data. While data is central to research, politics and the public, not all of this data is of adequate quality to enable acceptable comparisons. There are quality problems too with the interpretation and presentation of data. A recent case of irregularities in World Bank rankings shows that a report on business friendliness presented its findings in a way that favoured China due to political influence on and by its staff (Shalal and Lawder, 2021; World Bank, 2021).

Crime statistics: mapping, ordering and assessing

The idea of 'seeing the world as it is and not as we wish it to be' has long been a rationalist mantra and seemingly neutral, statistical knowledge generally supports such an endeavour. In a realist tradition, crime could still be considered a domestic security threat that has little effect on the foreign policy of states or the international system as a whole. However, as soon as crime relates to core security issues, industries or decision-making processes, it could influence state behaviour at the international level. Arms trafficking, terrorism or proliferation financing are therefore of relevance even to realists with little involvement in 'low politics'. Likewise, the influence of criminal organizations on a government might effectively undermine the rational and structured decision making that many realist assumptions about balancing are based on. Comparative practices and statistical figures on crime mostly concern illegal activities that are at the margins of realist theorizing. Independent of their volatile quality, statistics on crime are a mapping tool representing the 'reality of crime'. Sometimes, comparative information is presented in a ranking order – for instance when corruption rankings are published, or when the US government presents three tiers of states that are actively countering human trafficking (or not doing so). However, only in some cases, are the implications of the ranking comparable to those of mapping tools like arms statistics (see Giegerich and Hackett, Chapter 3 in this volume), which are more concerned with mapping 'capabilities' instead of deficits.

Like other mapping tools, these comparative figures also create a specific order – order in the sense of rankings, but also a normative order linked to ideas of a well-ordered society and good governance on the one hand, and malpractice on the other. For instance, prominent statistical comparisons on corruption bring a specific idea of good governance with them that is taken as a benchmark to evaluate varying societal practices across countries. At the same time, crime statistics are also an ordering tool as they shape reality and the perceptions of a global audience: more information about crime can lead to greater awareness of crime, but this does not necessarily translate into an impression of personal safety or collective security. The salience of crime in the public eye does not necessarily correspond to the actual number of crimes committed.

Comparisons of transnational organized crime are often presented as trend or performance assessments, yet distribution assessments and scenarios exist as well. Each of these assessments comes in different varieties: *trend assessments* consist of longitudinal analyses of criminal activities, comparing a specific criminal activity over several years. This is, however, often done by means of a proxy – for instance measuring seizures of narcotic drugs or counting suspicious financial transaction records. It is not always clear whether identified 'trends' pertain to available data or 'real' trends in the underlying crime. Trend assessments also compare crimes against each other, for instance how the global market for specific synthetic drugs develops against the market for other narcotic drugs, as in the *World Drug Report* (UNODC, 2021a). Regions or countries can also be compared in their trends. For instance, countries in the Andes have been the main source of coca, but trend assessments show that the main exporting countries have changed over time, and that Colombia has been the source of worldwide growth in cocaine production in recent years (UNODC, 2021b: 52).

Trend and distribution assessments can thus be interlinked to better understand the location and procedure of illicit activities. *Performance* assessments examine how countries (or subnational agencies) perform in countering crime. Performance metrics have become a standard in many organizations, and are a tool of insight for outsiders that lack in-depth, qualitative information to compare and evaluate an organization (Muller, 2018: 39–47). Some international statistics have been adapted to performance rankings by linking input to outcome statistics (Cussó and D'Amico, 2005). Being an ordering tool, performance statistics often lead to a change in the activities of organizations, which are apt to focus mainly on the activities that are assessed while neglecting others, even if those are central to the mission of the organization in question (Muller, 2018). Moreover, even without faking data, categories are frequently interpreted in a way that benefits the actors assessed, so that comparisons are weaker than they suggest: studies have shown that there are different ways to collect and interpret national statistical data, and statisticians may select the most favourable (Aragão and Linsi, 2020). Unlike in the US, illegal markets are included in some European GDP calculations (McGinty, 2019), raising the question of why an illegal market can bolster a national economy in the statistics, while at the same time crime constituting a threat to the society. Global comparisons are also used to assess performance in crime governance. For instance, the corruption indices of Transparency International provide a ranking of countries that counter corruption, and the Financial Action Task Force (FATF) listing of non-cooperative countries and territories singles out countries with a deficit in implementing anti-money laundering laws. The US government has listings of cooperative and non-cooperative countries in countering drug trafficking or human trafficking (Friman, 2010; 2015). Countries also assess themselves, for instance in anti-corruption peer reviews in which countries are compared against standards (Jongen, 2018).

While trend and performance assessments are frequent tools for comparison, global crime governance sometimes also relies on distribution and scenario assessments, particularly in the analysis of illegal markets and their governance. For instance, *distribution assessments* refer to market size or the distribution channels of illicit goods. Analysing drug trafficking frequently relies on information on 'global streams' and 'regional hubs' that may change over time. For instance, as overviews show, West Africa has developed as a hub for cocaine trafficking into Europe, while heroin is either distributed from central Asia through Balkan hubs or via the Northern Route into European markets (UNODC, 2021a).

Scenario assessments are frequently used in arguments about changing regulation, particularly the legalization of illicit markets: proponents of legalized drug markets frequently present a comparison of legal and illegal markets, underlining the possibilities of control and taxation in legalized markets. For instance, economists have underlined the benefits of a legalized, regulated market for organ supply compared to the current situation of unregulated illegal supply (see, for example, Becker and Elías, 2007). Scenarios can also be found in organizations like the FATF that develop 'typologies' based on investigations, which embody typical schemes of the newest criminal methods in money laundering (FATF, 2020a).

Taken together, comparisons are a frequent tool in crime governance (see Table 8.1). As these cases show, however, the varying assessments outlined in the introduction to this volume are interlinked: distribution assessments can be combined with trend assessments to gain insights into changes in the structure of a global illegal market. Trend assessments of crime can also be

Table 8.1: Comparative assessments in crime governance

Type of assessment	Examples of objects compared	Examples of crime governance
Trend assessment	Years, countries, crimes	Trends in drug seizures
Performance assessment	Years, countries, implementation	Anti-corruption implementation
Distribution assessment	Market exchange, regions, countries	Regional hubs for illegal markets
Scenario assessment	Present and future, regulation	Legalization of illegal markets

combined with performance assessments of crime governance to assess the effectiveness of governance instruments.

Part of the ubiquity of statistics and metrics, most of these assessments are based on quantitative data. In that sense, knowledge of 'numbers' and the development of common indicators are crucial to actually comparing objects. At the same time, the quality of these indicators has important consequences for comparisons when used as mapping tools, but less so as ordering tools, as the following section suggests.

Comparative data on crime: ordering irrespective of mapping?

The need for a 'clear picture' of the magnitude of crime is an understandable demand given not only the threats emanating from it, but also the substantial resources devoted to countering it. Qualitative studies range from a focus on ethnic crime groups to detailed studies of conflict diamonds (see Paoli, 2003; Varese, 2013; Global Witness, 2017). They show a large variance in how crime is committed, what criminal incentives are and how criminals evade law enforcement (see von Lampe, 2016). As a mapping tool, qualitative information is often criticized as 'anecdotal' or less representative, while quantitative information allows an overview, mapping the field of crime and its governance. Still, while quantitative data helps justify agendas and governance efforts, its capacity to map crime is, in fact, severely restricted (Andreas and Greenhill, 2010b; Jakobi, 2020: 26–31). Aggregate statistics, whether on population or GDP, are to some extent estimates based on samples that are then recalculated to represent the overall society and economy. As crime is hidden, the dark figure of crime remains a problem, but difficulties multiply when crime takes place across borders. One way to assess transnational crime is therefore to rely on seizures, counting the amount of drugs, weapons or other illegal goods found. Seizures give clear evidence of a crime, even when the network to which those involved belong is not necessarily exposed. However, a varying figure for seizures is also difficult to interpret as an increase could in this case be caused either by investigative successes or larger quantities of illegal shipments. Other methods to estimate market flows rely on the knowledge of market mechanisms. In local drug markets, the quality and street price of specific drugs can be a good indicator of whether or not there are larger or lower quantities on offer – since the price is adjusted accordingly. While this does not give an adequate measure, it is, for instance, seen as an unwanted outcome of the war on drugs that street prices for drugs in the US are comparatively low, indicating that prohibition and enforcement have not been successful. Other methods to assess drug use are wastewater measurements to find traces of human drug consumption, which say little about individual consumption levels or smuggling patterns, but more about consumption in the population of a specific city. All these – and other – problems exist in parallel to the difficulties that national crime statistics already exhibit. The growing availability of online information has resulted in a further growth in numbers that appear to measure crime. The increasing amount of data, however, has not necessarily brought in an increasing amount of reliable data, and more data does not necessarily result in more knowledge.

However, the political use of data on crime is widely unaffected by debates on data quality and many numbers are presented, repeated and believed without further examination: This is particularly evident in the field of money laundering. Since the late 1980s, the global anti-money laundering regime has developed into one of the most comprehensive, multi-level governance efforts in crime governance, which includes financial markets, institutions and professions worldwide. This regime developed independently of serious data sources revealing the magnitude of money laundering. In the late 1990s an expert group was convened to estimate the amount of money laundered. The group dissolved after the researchers agreed that there was no serious way to estimate this amount, and difficulties in estimating the magnitude of the problem have remained ever since (Levi et al, 2018). The global body against money laundering – the FATF – still mentions estimates from the IMF (see FATF, 2019) that have never been published as an IMF paper, but were simply alluded to by its then president:

In 1998 Michel Camdessus, Managing Director of the IMF, stated that money laundering might amount to about 2–5 percent of global GDP. He was not in fact announcing an IMF study but explicitly stating what he thought was expert opinion. The number lives on, because people do want to have some number and nothing else seemingly as authoritative has appeared since. (Reuter, 2013: 224)

This estimate – that laundered money represents 'about 2–5% of global GDP' – has gained considerable prominence, and is still widely accepted today despite its vagueness. For instance, the UNODC website (2023) still refers to the 'estimated amount of money laundered globally in one year is 2–5% of global GDP, or $800 billion – $2 trillion in current US dollars [USD]'. Another widely cited study on money laundering is the UNODC study from 2011 that estimates that money laundering represents 2.7% of global GDP, corresponding to US$1.5 trillion (UNODC, 2011). Among other sources, Europol and the FATF still use these vague numbers today (Europol, 2021b; FACTI, 2020; FATF, 2022). What exactly the numbers are, and how they relate to the reality of crime, seems less important than producing any number as a justification for governing crime.

Comparisons among crimes and their threat potential are frequent, but results vary. While the Global Organized Crime Index finds that human trafficking constitutes 'the most pervasive of all criminal markets globally' (GI-TOC, 2021: 15), a report by the United Nations Environment Programme (UNEP) and Interpol deems drug trafficking with criminal proceeds of US$344 billion annually the biggest global crime (Nellemann et al, 2016). Trusting future predictions leads us however to cybercrime with an annual cost of US$10.5 trillion by 2025 (Morgan, 2020). Non-coherent figures, misleading data and confusing trends are thus a frequent result of comparisons in global crime governance (see Table 8.2). Reports or policy statements often remain vague, referring to crime areas as 'second largest markets', 'among the most transnational organized crime fields' or 'generating billions of criminal proceeds each year'.

Comparing the practice of using statistical information shows that in some areas of crime governance, estimated numbers gain authority or outdated studies are still seen as the most reliable source, while other areas rely on a selection of specific numbers widely used, and in others, a single source becomes widely cited.

For instance, figures on human trafficking or modern slavery, considered to be the most widespread global crime by the Global Initiative Against Transnational Organized Crime's Global Organized Crime Index (GI-TOC, 2021: 15), are various and ambiguous. One key source is the *Global Report: The Cost of Coercion* from the International Labour Organization (ILO) from 2009, cited also in the 2009 World Bank report (Makisaka, 2009), which estimates the total cost of coercion to workers to be about US$21 billion. As this sum refers to the amount of money 'stolen' from the workers, it is not comparable with data from the ILO's *Global Report* of 2005, which estimates that the 'annual profits, from human trafficking alone, were at least US$32 billion' (ILO, 2005: 56; 2009: 1). This shows that even from the same source the subject of measurement can change. Quantification even results in a 'definitive' figure of €337,462 of costs related

Table 8.2: Comparing the economic impact of crime

Crime	Economic impact
Money laundering	US$800–2,000 billion (2–5%) (UNODC, 2023) US$1,500 billion (UNODC, 2011)
Drug trafficking	US$344 billion (Nellemann et al, 2016)
Human trafficking	US$32 billion (ILO, 2005)
Environmental crimes	US$91–258 billion (Nellemann et al, 2016)
Wildlife trafficking	US$7–23 billion (Nellemann et al, 2016) US$7.8–10 billion (Europol, 2021a) US$20 billion (Interpol, 2018)
Fishery crimes	US$4.2–9.5 billion (Europol, 2021a) US$25.5–49.5 billion (Interpol, 2021) US$11–24 billion (Nellemann et al, 2016)
Illegal mining	US$12–48 billion (Nellemann et al, 2016)
Forestry crimes	US$7 billion (Europol, 2021a) US$51–152 billion (Nellemann et al, 2016)
Waste crimes	US$10–12 billion (Nellemann et al, 2016) US$26 billion (Interpol, 2022)
Cybercrime	US$945 billion in 2020 (Lewis et al, 2020) US$5,200 billion in 2019–2023 (Ghosh, 2019) US$6,000 billion in 2021 (Morgan, 2020) US$10,500 billion by 2025 (Morgan, 2020)

to every victim of human trafficking, calculated in a study of the European Commission (2020). The *Study on the Economic and Human Costs of Trafficking in Human Beings within the EU* even aimed to break the economic damage down to annual figures that link the number of registered victims to the calculation of damage over their lifetime and other figures. It considers highly abstract calculations of lost economic output, lost quality of life and service costs, including coordination and prevention measures, law enforcement, specialized victim services, and health and social protection (European Commission, 2020). Another way of calculating the economic impact is presented in the recent *Global Report on Trafficking in Persons* of the UNODC (2020). This report focuses on detected victims reported to the police in 2018, resulting in 49,032 victims of human trafficking (UNODC, 2020). However, these reported numbers seem to be very small and suggest a high number of unreported human trafficking cases. In contrast, for 2020 the Polaris Project (2022) suggests 16,658 victims of human trafficking in the US alone. Including 'human trafficking' in the idea of 'modern slavery', *Global Estimates of Modern Slavery* from the ILO and the Walk Free Foundation (2017) paints an even worse picture for 2016.

According to this report, 40.3 million persons fell victim to modern slavery with 24.9 million in forced labour and 15.4 million in forced marriage (ILO and Walk Free Foundation, 2017). These numbers are quoted by NGOs and initiatives, such as Human Rights First (2017), Safe Horizon (2022), and the Global Slavery Index (2018).

Figures for environmental crime – a term that is vaguely defined and can include any harm to nature (White and Heckenberg, 2014) – also show large variations (see Figure 8.1). A report by the UNEP and Interpol from 2016 estimates environmental crime to be worth as much as US$91 to US$258 billion, making it the fourth largest category of crime in the world (Nellemann et al, 2016: 4). This widely accepted estimate of the total costs of environmental crime derives from references to very different aspects of it. For instance, the UNEP and Interpol report (Nellemann et al, 2016: 7) suggests the illegal wildlife trade to be worth US$7–23 billion, illegal fishery US$11–24 billion, illegal mining US$12–48 billion, and waste crime US$10–12 billion. Crimes connected with illegal forestry are listed as the most harmful in economic terms – with damage amounting to US$51–152 billion. Yet, other studies on environmental crime present very different figures. A Europol (2021a) report on illegal forestry, based on a 2011 study, estimates the cost of timber crime at US$7 billion, which is only a fraction of the cost assumed by Interpol and UNEP (Nellemann et al, 2016: 7; Interpol, 2019). The same 2011 study assumes damage of US$7.8–10 billion through illegal wildlife trade (Europol, 2021a), as opposed to the lower UNEP and Interpol estimates (Nellemann et al, 2016: 7). The variation is most pronounced in the sector of illegal fishery. The highest estimated costs of unregulated fishing are US$25.5–49.5 billion as reported in an Interpol (2021) study, which is twice the estimate of the earlier UNEP and Interpol report (Nellemann et al, 2016: 7). Another Europol report (2021a) assumes fishery crimes cost US$4.2–9.5 billion. Finally, UNEP and Interpol estimate waste crime to cause global damage of US$10–12 billion, which diverges significantly from an Interpol estimate of US$26 billion for waste crime committed by the Italian Mafia alone (Interpol, 2022).

These divergences are not necessarily discussed when these figures are being used, instead many of them are quoted and disseminated without further comment by other organizations. For instance, UNEP and Interpol's estimated figure for wildlife trafficking of US$7–23 billion is also used in the latest FATF report (2020b), in the World Economic Forum report (Lehmacher, 2016) and by Conservation International (2023). The overall estimated number of profits of US$91–258 billion from environmental crimes is cited in the Eurojust report (2021). Overall, why a specific actor decides for or against quoting a specific figure remains widely untransparent. Cybercrime is one emerging crime field due to the technological advances in cyberspace and the many possibilities of exploiting them for criminal use.

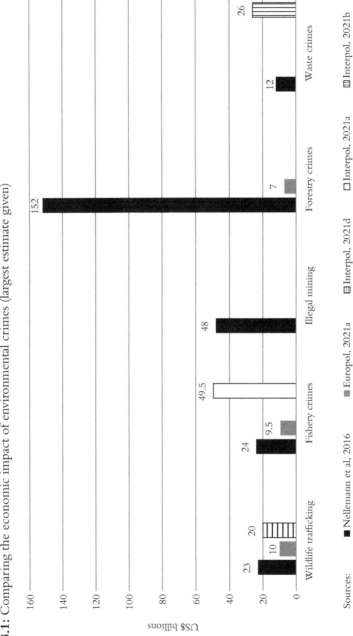

Figure 8.1: Comparing the economic impact of environmental crimes (largest estimate given)

A study by McAfee and the Center for Strategic and International Studies has become prominent and is often cited in regard to the estimation of cybercrime costs. It measures the economic impact of cybercrime to have been US$445 billion in 2014, US$600 billion in 2018, and US$945 billion in 2020 (Lewis, 2018; Lewis et al, 2020). While these figures clearly indicate an increasing trend in cybercrime costs, other sources already give higher estimates and predict criminal proceeds to rise to an unprecedented level. A 2019 study by the World Economic Forum finds that cyberattacks increased in number and costs and estimates that between 2019 and 2023 'approximately $5.2 trillion in global value will be at risk from cyberattacks' (Ghosh, 2019). A 2020 special report by Cybersecurity Ventures estimates the cost from cybercrime to have risen from US$3 trillion in 2015 to US$ 6 trillion in 2021, and predicts total costs of US$10.5 trillion annually by 2025 (Morgan, 2020).

Summarizing the observations thus far, the main function of crime statistics as an ordering tool seems to lie primarily in the mutual comparison of crimes and their significance, and in influencing agenda setting by presenting any kind of number that seems in any way plausible, and has the capacity to suggest the existence of an important problem. These comparisons also show that, despite the fact that links are increasingly being established between crimes and security, actual comparison of crime and its impact mostly relies on economic measurements – the *tertium comparationis* is the economic damage caused by different crimes, not an underlying measurement of power, security status or anything else.

Comparative data as orientation and ornament

The chapter has analysed the use of comparisons with respect to global crime and its governance. Given the significant dark figures for criminal activity, estimates of crime exhibit many difficulties, even on the local level. At the same time, global figures and comparisons between countries are increasingly common, even when data problems are acknowledged. With qualitative data being particularly – but not exclusively – used, the presentation of 'numbers' is mainly linked to trend and performance assessments, albeit distribution and scenario assessments are also common. From an academic perspective, the weaknesses of the data, however, often make it difficult to use them as a mapping tool that realistically depicts the prevalence of crime and the effectiveness of countermeasures. Different statistics on the same phenomenon can co-exist, without further inspection outside small epistemic communities (see also Krause, Chapter 7). Statistical comparisons are often used to label a policy problem as being important, specifically as being 'more important than others'. The *tertium comparationis* used in order to compare the significance of crimes varies and can be the number of incidents, the number of victims, the extent of monetary damage caused, and so forth. Crimes signal societal deviance and social problems, but they are usually hidden from the public eye. For all their weaknesses, crime rates are nonetheless regularly used to evaluate the effectiveness of a government's policies, and – for instance in the case of alleged widespread corruption – can be used to cut back on foreign aid, delegitimize public institutions or mobilize against decision makers.

Yet, as Muller (2018: 39–46) emphasizes, performance assessments are intrinsically linked to mistrust and non-knowledge – they are a means to create (an often misleading) transparency for outside observers, who are not necessarily able to evaluate complex performances. While these limitations could be an argument against using statistics to assess complex performance, our research suggests that the consequences are the opposite. Rather than developing fewer performance statistics, complex performance is measured by a growing number of them, from which one can 'pick and choose' in order to construct an argument. One can find different figures for almost any crime, and all of these can have political implications independent of their quality – a finding that has also attracted significant research (for example, Heller, 2009; Andreas and Greenhill, 2010b; Reuter, 2013; Levi et al, 2018).

There is little, however, to indicate how the gap between the quality and impact of statistics could be bridged, and whether this should even be attempted. The unavailability of accurate data opens up, instead of closing, the possibility of providing low-quality but impactful data. As the drive towards 'quantification' of social phenomena continues, statistical comparisons will be an important tool to map the field and convey 'pure facts'. Statistical information will likely continue to create social facts and influence policy priorities and the distribution of resources, thus creating order, even if their importance may be based on being merely an ornament accompanying every 'solid' argument.

Taken together, the development of more and more data for political agenda setting not only raises questions as to whether any ethical lines exist in using data outside research contexts, but also whether, in the end, the development might result in 'data fatigue' on the part of the audience, or even a rejection of quantitative claims outright. It seems that evidence-based politics is possible without clear evidence, but not without clear numbers: the enormous value that comparisons have for debating global crime as a security risk stands in marked contrast to a weak database and a reduction of crime to the economic damage it causes.

References

Andreas, P. and Greenhill, K.M. (2010a) 'Introduction: the politics of numbers', in P. Andreas and K.M. Greenhill (eds) *Sex, Drugs, and Body Counts. The Politics of Numbers in Crime and Conflict*, Ithaca, NY: Cornell University Press, pp 1–22.

Andreas, P. and Greenhill, K.M. (eds) (2010b) *Sex, Drugs and Body Counts. The Politics of Numbers in Global Crime and Conflict*, Ithaca, NY: Cornell University Press.

Andreas, P. and Nadelmann, E. (2006) *Policing the Globe. Criminalization and Crime Control in International Relations*, Oxford, New York, NY: Oxford University Press.

Aragão, R. and Linsi, L. (2020) 'Many shades of wrong: what governments do when they manipulate statistics', *Review of International Political Economy*, 29(1): 1–26.

Barberet, R. (2014) 'Measuring and researching transnational crime', in P. Reichel and J. Albanese (eds) *Handbook of Transnational Crime and Justice*, Thousand Oaks, CA, London, New Delhi: SAGE, pp 47–62.

Beirne, P. (1993) *Inventing Criminology: Essays on the Rise of 'Homo Criminalis'*, New York, NY: State University of New York Press.

Becker, G.S. and Elías, J.J. (2007) 'Introducing incentives in the market for live and cadaveric organ donations', *Journal of Economic Perspectives*, 21(3): 3–24.

Bewley-Taylor, D.R. (1999) *The United States and International Drug Control. 1909–1997*, London, New York, NY: Continuum.

Bewley-Taylor, D.R. (2012) *International Drug Control. Consensus Fractured*, Cambridge: Cambridge University Press.

Bidermann, A.D. and Reiss, A.J. (1967) 'On explaining the "dark figure" of crime', *Annals of the American Academy of Politics and Social Science*, 374: 1–15.

Botterill, L.C. (2017) 'Evidence-based policy', *Oxford Research Encyclopedia of Politics*, https://doi.org/10.1093/acrefore/9780190228637.013.177 [Accessed September 2019].

Bowker, G.C. and Star, S.L. (2000) *Sorting Things Out. Classification and its Consequences*, Cambridge, MA: MIT Press.

Conservation International (2023) 'Share the facts: raise awareness to help end wildlife trafficking', Conservation International, www.conservation.org/act/share-the-facts-about-wildlife-trafficking [Accessed on 14 December 2023].

Cairney, P. (2019) 'The UK government's imaginative use of evidence to make policy', *British Politics*, 14(1): 1–22.

Cussó, R. and D'Amico, S. (2005) 'From development comparatism to globalization comparativism: towards more normative international education statistics', *Comparative Education*, 41(2): 199–216.

De Bondt, W. (2013) 'Evidence based EU criminal policy making: in search of matching data', *European Journal of Crime Policy Research*, 20(1): 23–49.

Deflem, M. (2002) *Policing World Society: Historical Foundations of International Police Cooperation*, Oxford: Clarendon.

Elliot, L. (2016) 'The securitization of transnational environmental crime and the militarization of conservation', in L. Elliot and W.H. Schaedla (eds) *Handbook of Transnational Environmental Crime*, Aldershot: Edward Elgar, pp 68–87.

European Commission (2020) *Study on the Economic, Social and Human Costs of Trafficking in Human Beings Within the EU*, Amt für Veröffentlichungen der Europäischen Union, https://op.europa.eu/de/publication-detail/-/publ ication/373138c5-0ea4-11eb-bc07-01aa75ed71a1/language-en [Accessed 14 February 2022].

Eurojust (2021) *Report on Eurojust's Casework on Environmental Crime*, Eurojust, European Union Agency for Criminal Justice Cooperation, www.eurojust.europa.eu/sites/default/files/2021-01/report_environm ental_crime.pdf [Accessed 14 February 2022].

Europol (2021a) 'Environmental crime', Europol, www.europol.europa. eu/crime-areas-and-statistics/crime-areas/environmental-crime [Accessed 14 February 2022].

Europol (2021b) 'Money laundering', Europol, www.europol.europa.eu/ crime-areas-and-statistics/crime-areas/economic-crime/money-launder ing [Accessed 14 February 2022].

FACTI (Financial Accountability Transparency & Integrity) (2020) *FACTI Panel Interim Report*, June, FACTI, https://uploads-ssl.webflow.com/5e0bd 9edab846816e263d633/5f6b68c7bff4ad6cf6cb53a7_FACTI_Interim_R eport_final.pdf [Accessed 14 February 2022].

FATF (Financial Action Task Force) (2019) 'How much money is laundered', www.fatf-gafi.org/faq/moneylaundering/ [Accessed 9 September 2019].

FATF (2020a) 'Money laundering and terrorist financing red flag indicators associated with virtual assets', www.fatf-gafi.org/publications/fatfreco mmendations/documents/Virtual-Assets-Red-Flag-Indicators.html [Accessed on 14 February 2022].

FATF (2020b) *Money Laundering and the Illegal Wildlife Trade*, June, www. fatf-gafi.org/media/fatf/documents/Money-laundering-and-illegal-wildl ife-trade.pdf [Accessed 14 February 2022].

FATF (2022) 'What is money laundering?', www.fatf-gafi.org/faq/mone ylaundering/ [Accessed on 14 February 2022].

Friman, H.R. (2010) 'Numbers and certification: assessing foreign compliance in narcotics and human trafficking', in P. Andreas and K.M. Greenhill (eds) *Sex, Drugs, and Body Counts. The Politics of Numbers in Crime and Conflict*, Ithaka, NY: Cornell University Press, pp 75–109.

Friman, H.R. (ed) (2015) *The Politics of Leverage in International Relations. Name, Shame and Sanction*, London: Palgrave.

Ghosh, I. (2019) 'This is the crippling cost of cybercrime on corporations', *World Economic Forum*, 7 November, www.weforum.org/agenda/2019/11/ cost-cybercrime-cybersecurity/ [Accessed 14 February 2022].

GI-TOC (Global Initiative Against Transnational Organized Crime) (2021) *Global Organized Crime Index 2021*, Vienna: GI-TOC.

Global Slavery Index (GSI) (2018) 'Highlights', Walk Free Foundation, www.globalslaveryindex.org/2018/findings/highlights/ [Accessed 14 February 2022].

Global Witness (2017) 'An inside job. Zimbabwe: the state, the security forces and a decade of disappearing diamonds', 11 September, www.globalwitness.org/en/campaigns/conflict-diamonds/inside-job/ [Accessed 1 August 2019].

Hansen, H.K. (2012) 'The power of performance indices in the global politics of anti-corruption', *Journal of International Relations and Development*, 15(4): 506–31.

Hansen, H.K. and Mühlen-Schulte, A. (2012) 'The power of numbers in global governance', *Journal of International Relations and Development*, 15(4): 455–65.

Hansen, H.K. and Porter, T. (2012) 'What do numbers do in transnational governance?', *International Political Sociology*, 6(4): 409–26.

Heller, N. (2009) 'Defining and measuring corruption: from where have we come, where are we now, and what matters for the future?', in R.I. Rotberg (ed) *Corruption, Global Security and World Order*, Washington DC: Brookings Institution, pp 27–46.

Human Rights First (2017) 'Human trafficking by the numbers', https://humanrightsfirst.org/library/human-trafficking-by-the-numbers/ [Accessed 14 February 2022].

ILO (International Labour Organization) (2005) *A Global Alliance against Forced Labour. Global report under the follow-up to the ILO declaration on fundamental principles and rights at work 2005*, www.ilo.org/wcmsp5/groups/public/---ed_norm/---declaration/documents/publication/wcms_081882.pdf [Accessed 14 February 2022].

ILO (2009) *The Cost of Coercion. Global report under the follow-up to the ILO declaration on fundamental principles and rights at work*, www.ilo.org/wcmsp5/groups/public/---ed_norm/---declaration/documents/publication/wcms_106268.pdf [Accessed 14 February 2022].

ILO and Walk Free Foundation (2017) *Global Estimates of Modern Slavery. Forced Labour and Forced Marriage*, www.ilo.org/wcmsp5/groups/public/@dgreports/@dcomm/documents/publication/wcms_575479.pdf [Accessed 14 February 2022].

Interpol (2018) 'Global wildlife enforcement. Strengthening law enforcement cooperation against wildlife crime', www.interpol.int/Crimes/Environmental-crime/Wildlife-crime [Accessed 14 December 2023].

Interpol (2019) 'Global forestry enforcement. Strengthening law enforcement cooperation against forestry crime', www.interpol.int/Crimes/Environmental-crime/Forestry-crime [Accessed 14 December 2023].

Interpol (2021) 'Environmental security programme. Strengthening law enforcement cooperation against fisheries crime', www.interpol.int/Cri mes/Environmental-crime/Fisheries-crime [Accessed 14 December 2023].

Interpol (2022) 'Environmental security programme. Strengthening law enforcement cooperation against pollution crime', www.interpol.int/Cri mes/Environmental-crime/Pollution-crime [Accessed 14 December 2023].

Jakobi, A.P. (2013) *Common Goods and Evils? The Formation of Global Crime Governance*, Oxford: Oxford University Press.

Jakobi, A.P. (2020) *Crime, Security and Global Politics. An Introduction to Global Crime Governance*, London: Palgrave Macmillan/Red Globe Press.

Jongen, H. (2018) 'The authority of peer reviews among states in the global governance of corruption', *Review of International Political Economy*, 25(6): 909–35.

Kelley, J.G. and Simmons, B.A. (2019) 'Introduction: the power of global performance indicators', *International Organization*, 73(3): 491–510.

LaFree, G. and Dugan, L. (2007) 'Introducing the global terrorism database', *Terrorism and Political Violence,* 19(2): 181–204.

Lehmacher, W. (2016) 'Wildlife crime: a $23 billion trade that's destroying our planet', World Economic Forum, 28 September, www.weforum.org/ agenda/2016/09/fighting-illegal-wildlife-and-forest-trade/ [Accessed 14 February 2022].

Levi, M., Reuter, P. and Halliday, T. (2018) 'Can the AML system be evaluated without better data?', *Crime, Law and Social Change*, 69: 307–28.

Lewis, C. (2012) 'Crime and justice statistics collected by international agencies', *European Journal of Crime Policy Research*, 18(1): 5–21.

Lewis, J.A. (2018) 'Economic impact of cybercrime', McAfee; Center for Strategic and International Studies, 21 February, www.csis.org/analysis/ economic-impact-cybercrime [Accessed 14 February 2022].

Lewis, J.A., Malekos Smith, Z. and Lostri, E. (2020) 'The hidden costs of cybercrime', Center for Strategic and International Studies, 9 December, www.csis.org/analysis/hidden-costs-cybercrime [Accessed 14 February 2022].

López-Rey, M. (1985) *A Guide to United Nations Criminal Policy*, Cambridge: Gower.

Maguire, M. and McVie, S. (2017) 'Crime data and criminal statistics: a critical reflection', in A. Liebling, S. Maruna and L. McAra (eds) *The Oxford Handbook of Criminology*, Oxford: Oxford University Press, pp 163–89.

Makisaka, M. (2009) *Human Trafficking: A Brief Overview*, Social Development Notes, No. 122, World Bank, https://openknowledge.worldbank.org/han dle/10986/11103 [Accessed on 14 February 2022].

McGinty, J.C. (2019) 'GDP doesn't include proceeds of crime. Should it?', *Wall Street Journal*, 6 December, www.wsj.com/articles/gdp-doesnt-include-proceeds-of-crime-should-it-11575628201 [Accessed 14 February 2022].

Morgan, S. (2020) 'Cybercrime to cost the world $10.5 trillion annually by 2025', *Cybercrime Magazine*, 13 November, https://cybersecurityv entures.com/hackerpocalypse-cybercrime-report-2016/ [Accessed 14 February 2022].

Mosher, C.J., Miethe, T.D. and Hart, T.C. (2011) *The Mismeasure of Crime* (2nd edn), Los Angeles, London, New Delhi, Singapore, Washington DC: SAGE Publications.

Muller, J.Z. (2018) *The Tyranny of Metrics*, Princeton, NJ, Oxford: Princeton University Press.

Nellemann, C., Henriksen, R., Kreilhuber, A., Stewart, D., Kotsovou, M., Raxter, P., Mrema, E. and Barret, S. (eds) (2016) *The Rise of Environmental Crime: A Growing Threat to Natural Resources, Peace, Development and Security*, United Nations Environment Programme; RHIPTO Rapid Response– Norwegian Center for Global Analyses, www.unep.org/resources/report/ rise-environmental-crime-growing-threat-natural-resources-peace-deve lopment-and [Accessed 14 February 2022].

Polaris Project (2022) 'Myths, facts, and statistics', https://polarisproject. org/myths-facts-and-statistics/ [Accessed 14 February 2022].

Paoli, L. (2003) *Mafia Brotherhoods. Organized Crime, Italian Style*, Oxford: Oxford University Press.

Reuter, P. (2013) 'Are estimates of the volume of money laundering either feasible or useful?', in B. Unger and D. van der Linde (eds) *Research Handbook on Money Laundering*, New York, NY: Edward Elgar Publishing, pp 224–31.

Shalal, A. and Lawder, D. (2021) 'IMF chief called out over pressure to favor China while at World Bank', *Reuters*, 17 September, www.reuters. com/business/sustainable-business/world-bank-kills-business-climate-rep ort-after-ethics-probe-cites-undue-pressure-2021-09-16/ [Accessed 14 February 2022].

Safe Horizon (2022) 'Human trafficking statistics and facts', www.safehori zon.org/get-informed/human-trafficking-statistics-facts/#definition/ [Accessed 14 February 2022].

Sellin, T. and Wolfgang, M.E. (1964) *The Measurement of Crime and Delinquency*, New York, NY: John Wiley.

Stamatel, J.P. (2009) 'Contributions of cross-national research to criminology at the beginning of the 21st century', in M.D. Krohn, N. Hendrix, G. Penly Hall and A.J. Lizotte (eds) *Handbook on Crime and Deviance*, New York, NY: Springer, pp 3–22.

Stone, D.A. (1989) 'Causal stories and formation of policy agendas', *Political Science Quarterly*, 104(2): 281–300.

Transparency International (2020) Corruption Perception Index, www.trans parency.org/en/cpi/2020 [Accessed 14 February 2022].

United Nations (2000) Resolution adopted by the General Assembly (A/RES/55/25). United Nations Convention against Transnational Organized Crime, www.unodc.org/documents/treaties/UNTOC/Publications/TOC%20Convention/TOCebook-e.pdf [Accessed 10 January 2023].

UNODC (United Nations Office on Drugs and Crime) (2011) 'Illicit money: how much is out there?', www.unodc.org/unodc/en/frontpage/2011/October/illicit-money_-how-much-is-out-there.html [Accessed 14 February 2022].

UNODC (2020) *Global Report on Trafficking in Person*, www.unodc.org/unodc/en/data-and-analysis/glotip.html [Accessed 14 February 2022].

UNODC (2021a) *World Drug Report*, www.unodc.org/unodc/en/data-and-analysis/wdr2021.html [Accessed 14 February 2022].

UNODC (2021b) *World Drug Report. Booklet 2: Global Overview of Drug Demand and Drug Supply*, www.unodc.org/unodc/en/data-and-analysis/wdr-2021_booklet-2.html [Accessed 14 February 2022].

UNODC (2023) 'Money laundering', https://www.unodc.org/unodc/en/money-laundering/overview.html [Accessed 24 January 2023].

Van Dijk, J. (2007) 'The international crime victims survey and complementary measures of corruption and organized crime', *Crime Prevention Studies*, 22: 125–44.

Van Dijk, J. (2011) 'Quantitative criminology: crime and justice statistics across nations', in C.J. Smith, S.X. Zhang and R. Barberet (eds) *Handbook of Criminology: An International Perspective*, London: Routledge, pp 3–52.

Varese, F. (2013) *Mafias on the Move – How Organized Crime Conquers New Territories*, Princeton, NJ: Princeton University Press.

Von Lampe, K. (2016) *Organized Crime: Analyzing Illegal Activities, Criminal Structures, and Extra-legal Governance*, Thousand Oaks, CA: Sage.

White, R.D. and Heckenberg, D. (2014) *Green Criminology: An Introduction to the Study of Environmental Harm*, New York, NY: Routledge.

World Bank (2021) 'Statement on release of investigation into data irregularities in doing business 2018 and 2020', 16 September, www.worldbank.org/en/news/statement/2021/09/16/statement-on-release-of-investigation-into-data-irregularities-in-doing-business-2018-and-2020 [Accessed 14 February 2022].

The Cybersecurity Ecosystem and the Datafication of Threats and Capabilities

Madeleine Myatt and Thomas Müller

Introduction

The digital revolution has fundamentally reshaped the world in recent decades, making cyberspace and its key element, the internet, crucial to how economies, societies and politics operate. In this process, cyberspace has also become an object of security politics. The rise of cybersecurity – that is, activities geared towards anticipating, preventing and countering threats to users operating in and through cyberspace as well as to the underlying information technology (IT) infrastructure – has been undergirded by narratives that highlight the distinctiveness of cyberspace compared to other domains of security and emphasize the growing importance of developing political responses to cyber threats.

In this chapter, we explore the ecosystem of actors that produce and publish representations of threats and capabilities in cyberspace. How knowledge about cyber threats is produced and circulated is a question that has gained increasing attention in research on cybersecurity politics in recent years (see, for example, Dunn Cavelty, 2013; Stevens, 2020; Egloff and Dunn Cavelty, 2021; Maschmeyer et al, 2021; Slayton, 2021). This research has shed light on several facets of the use of comparative practices, such as the origins of computer risk management metrics (Slayton, 2015), the use of analogies and metaphors (Betz and Stevens, 2013; Branch, 2020) and big data analytics as an instrument used to identify actors that deviate from the usual patterns of activities (Aradau and Blanke, 2018; Shaurya and Singh, 2021). Little attention, though, has been paid to the production of knowledge about the evolving patterns of threats and capabilities in cyberspace. Yet, these comparative practices are just as crucial to cybersecurity politics, especially as they form the basis for arguments about which threats are trending and which states are improving their capabilities and enhancing their power. In particular, rankings of cyber threats and the cyber capabilities of states have become prominent tools through which actors seek to trigger policy developments and steer investments in cybersecurity resources.

Against this background, we analyse the ecology of publishers of comparative knowledge on threats and capabilities that has emerged in cyberspace. These publishers form three interrelated, yet distinct clusters: the first produces reports on the evolving patterns of cyber threats, the second evaluates the cybersecurity capacities of states and the third compares the cyber power of states. The production of comparative knowledge is much more datafied – that is, based on big data and data analytics in general – in the first cluster than in the other two. Drawing on sociological and IR approaches, we use the concept of ecosystems to tease out how the conditions of cyberspace have shaped the emergence of the ecology of publishers and help to explain differences in the comparative practices across the three clusters. The chapter thus contributes primarily to the first of the three themes highlighted in the introduction to this volume: how comparative knowledge is produced. Like other chapters (notably those of Jacobi and Herbst (Chapter 8), Bueger (Chapter 6), and Krause (Chapter 7)), it highlights the fragmented nature of the production of comparative knowledge and the ambiguity that this fragmentation entails. In addition, the chapter also provides insights into the other two themes: how comparative knowledge becomes politically relevant and how it (re)shapes politics. The three clusters produce representations of cybersecurity that reinforce and give substance to the narrative of a 'fast evolving cyber threat landscape' – to quote the 2016 Cyber Defence Pledge of the North Atlantic Treaty Organization (NATO, 2016) – that undergirds and shapes cybersecurity politics, which in turn generates further demands for comparative knowledge.

The chapter is structured as follows: after introducing our understanding of ecosystems and the ways they are represented through comparative practices, we map the ecology of publishers of comparative knowledge, distinguishing three clusters revolving around cyber threats, cybersecurity capacities and cyber power respectively. We then discuss two factors that help to explain the evolution of this ecology: the unequal distribution of relevant resources among the producers of representations and the effects of the struggle among states over the governance of the internet. While sharing a common narrative of a constantly evolving threat landscape, the three clusters differ in the logics of comparison they employ, resulting in dissimilar representations of the distribution of cyber capabilities.

Representational work in ecosystems

Is the volume of threats in cyberspace increasing, remaining stable or decreasing? Are the types of threats changing? Such questions can only be answered because there are actors that do representational work – that is, that produce abstract accounts of the patterns of threats and that successfully convince other actors that these accounts tell them something meaningful about the evolving state of cybersecurity. By doing so, the actors 'present' cyberspace in particular ways, emphasizing certain aspects while bracketing others (Bueger, 2015: 7). Like maps, the representations give actors an overview. But they also contribute to the construction of cyberspace as a governance object, that is, an issue that is deemed to have problematic aspects that require political action (see Allan, 2017). Comparative practices are fundamental to this representational work. To discern trends in the volume and types of threats over time, actors have to develop classifications of threats, collect data about threat incidents and analyse changes in the frequency of the threats – put differently, they have to assess similarities and differences between threats both at different moments in time and across these moments.

The starting point for our analysis of the role of comparative practices is the argument that cyberspace is not only the reference object of this representational work but also the social setting that shapes which actors do what forms of representational work. For this argument, we draw on a broad understanding of cyberspace as an ecosystem populated by a variety of actors that build, maintain use and/or seek to (re)shape the globalized network of computers and other digital technologies that has emerged in the last decades. Among these actors are tech companies, hackers, internet users, cybersecurity companies and various national, transnational and international governance institutions. The ecosystem metaphor is widely used among cybersecurity practitioners. The US Department of Homeland Security (2011: 2), for instance, described cyberspace in the following way: 'Like natural ecosystems, the cyber ecosystem comprises a variety of diverse participants – private firms, non-profits, governments, individuals, processes, and cyber devices (computers, software, and communications technologies) – that interact for multiple purposes'. Practitioners, though, generally only use the term in a loosely defined sense to stress the diversity of actors involved in cyberspace and, relatedly, its complexity and the dynamic interplay between the actors, their practices and the technologies they use.

One key challenge of cybersecurity politics is the diversity of concepts and meanings. Different actors or communities of interests/expertise address the issue at hand with different emphases, normative evaluations and priorities. This has a significant impact on the way cybersecurity is assessed and the ecosystem is mapped (see also Calderaro and Craig, 2020: 920). Moreover, it has implications for the definition of cyber threats, the question of which threat perceptions are prioritized, which capacity-building elements are in the limelight and which sources of cyber power are used as points of references in comparisons. Put differently: it matters which actors do the representational work.

Two discussions in IR are particularly productive for giving the metaphor more substance and adapting it for the analysis of the representational work. The first is about organizational ecologies in world politics. The metaphor of ecosystems directs analytical attention to how environments shape the populations of actors that live in them. Ecological theorizing tries to explain why some populations thrive while others do not. In organizational ecology, the populations are different types of organizations (see Hannan and Freeman, 1989). Such theorizing has recently been applied to IR to analyse why the number of non-state actors involved in global governance activities is growing while the number of international organizations stagnates. Several factors are postulated: some organizations have institutional features that give them advantages over others. Non-state actors notably do not require negotiations among states to set up governance arrangements. Moreover, there are dynamics related to organizational density: the more organizations of one type exist, the easier it is for them to legitimate their activities vis-à-vis their environment, but at the same time the more intense their competition over valued resources becomes (Abbott et al, 2016). In this competition, organizations seek to find niches – for example, new governance domains and tasks – which allow them to thrive. Furthermore, there are interactional dynamics – so-called 'regulatory processes' – in play: 'positive regulation' in which actions by one type of organization enable activities by others types in a niche, 'negative regulation' in which the activities of one type of organization make it harder for other types to establish themselves in that niche and 'double-negative regulation' in which the activities of one type of organization prevent another type from establishing itself in a niche, which in turn leaves that niche open for a third type of organization (Lake, 2021: 349). Organizational ecology is in this sense not only about which type of organization is more numerous but also – and this is the more important aspect for present purposes – about the interplay of the activities of different types of organizations and the different governance arrangements that this interplay brings about.

The second discussion relates to the ecologies of indicators. The last three decades have witnessed a proliferation of quantitative forms of representation such as indices or rankings in many policy domains in world politics. A growing literature seeks to explain this proliferation and its effects (see Broome and Quirk, 2015; Kelley and Simmons, 2019; Rumelili and Towns, 2022). One explanation developed in this literature emphasizes the 'self-reinforcing' dynamics of the 'ecology of indicators': 'as more indicators are produced, aggregations of indicators become more reliable, more indicators are used, more indicators are produced, and so on' (Davis et al, 2012: 85). This explanation actually fuses two arguments. First, it postulates an enabling dynamic similar to the 'positive regulation' process mentioned earlier. The representational work already done by some actors facilitates and enables the representational work that other actors want to do – provided that the former actors make their representations available to the latter actors, for instance by publishing them. Second, it suggests that this enabling dynamic fuels an increasing use and production of representations in a given domain. Put differently: the representational work not only becomes easier, it also becomes more prevalent.

What the indicators literature has not yet discussed is what dampens this dynamic. Building on the organization ecology literature, the assumption would be that organizations produce and publish representations because they deem this representational work conducive to their success in the competition over resources such as public attention, market shares or political influence. In this logic, the proliferation of representations would slow down once organizations came to regard the production and publication of representations as no longer giving them advantages in the competition over resources.

Thus conceptualized, an ecosystem perspective helps to analyse and explain the conditions and dynamics that shape which organizations do which representational work in cyberspace. As the first step in the analysis, the next section identifies and maps three distinct, though interrelated, clusters of producers of representations.

Three clusters of representational work

In the last three decades, cybersecurity has morphed from a solely technical issue of securing computer networks into a political issue of promoting security in cyberspace. In this process, the prevalent understanding of cyber threats has broadened to encompass not only – as initially – crimes committed in computer networks but also attacks on critical infrastructures as well as cyber conflicts in which states come under attack by other states or non-state actors (see Carr, 2021: 54–7). In this process, cybersecurity has evolved into a broad field of application, incorporating technical, legal and organizational measures, with more cooperation across the public/ private divide. Cyber threats assessments, in turn, have broadened beyond patterns of cyberattacks to include a wide range of aspects, for example the level or lack of technological and legal enforcement assets, privacy and data protections, threat intelligence exchange formats and infrastructural gaps.

As part of this process, a growing number of organizations have started to publish – some regularly, others irregularly – representations of various aspects of cybersecurity, ranging from overviews of trends in cyber threats through surveys of cybersecurity sentiments and estimations of the costs caused by cyberattacks to comparisons of cyber capabilities. The indicators and data collection methodologies vary across the different attempts to produce comparative knowledge, which has also led to a discourse on the value and shortcomings of the representations (see, for instance, Yarovenko et al, 2020).

In what follows, we do not aim to map the ecology of all of these organizations but focus more narrowly on three aspects – patterns of threats, cybersecurity capacities and cyber power – that are at the heart of cybersecurity politics. Interrelated but nonetheless distinct clusters of producers of representations have emerged for each of these three aspects: first, from the 2000s onwards, a cluster mapping and tracking of the patterns of threats based on a more comprehensive, datafied understanding of these patterns than previous computer risk management metrics (for these see Slayton, 2015), then in the 2010s a cluster evaluating the cybersecurity capacities of states and, in the last few years, a cluster developing representations of the distribution of cyber power. We discuss each of these clusters – summarized in Table 9.1 – in turn.

The *threats cluster* is both the oldest of the three clusters and the one with the highest density of organizations. Many companies active in the cybersecurity market publish some sort of statistics about the volume of and trends in cyber threats. A number of these companies, including big tech companies such as IBM and Microsoft and companies specializing in cybersecurity services such as CrowdStrike, FireEye Mandiant, Kaspersky and Symantec, regularly issue reports on the evolving patterns of threats. Cybersecurity companies publish statistics on the patterns of threats in order to secure valued resources, such as more customers and a reputation as cybersecurity experts in public debates. They dominate the cluster because they have a decisive advantage over other types of organization. By providing cybersecurity services to a large number of private, commercial and also public customers, they operate expansive networks of digital sensors and often state-of-the-art analytical tools that allow them to amass the key resource for statistical overviews of cyber threats: data on incidents – such as 'indicators of compromise' (IoCs) and 'indicators of attack' (IoAs)[1] – compiled through the monitoring, recording and aggregating of malicious activity from the open, deep and dark web.

Organizations such as research institutes, think tanks or international organizations lack such networks of sensors deployed to numerous endpoints. Hence, most of these organizations do not have access either to the same

---

[1]   IoCs are signs of an attack such as login anomalies or suspicious file changes while IoAs are clues suggesting that an attack is planned.

Table 9.1: Three clusters of representational work in cybersecurity

Cluster	Emergence	Prevalent organizations
Threats	2000s	Cluster dominated by cybersecurity companies, including
		• Microsoft (Security Intelligence Report/Digital Defense Report, published since 2005)
		• Kaspersky (Security Bulletin, published since at least 2007)
		• FireEye Mandiant (M-Trend reports, published since 2011)
		One international organization, the EU (via ENISA), aggregates such reports to produce 'Thread landscape' reports (since 2012)
Cybersecurity capacity	2010s	Cluster features a diverse cast of organizations producing comparative frameworks:
		• Cyber Readiness Index (Potomac Institute, first version 2013, second version 2015)
		• Cybersecurity Capacity Maturity Model for Nations (GCSCC, University of Oxford, UK, launched in 2014, revised in 2016 and 2021)
		• Global Cybersecurity Index (GCI, four editions published by ITU so far in 2015, 2017, 2019 and 2021)
		• National Cyber Security Index (e-Governance Academy, Estonia, produced since 2016)
Cyber power	late 2010s/ early 2020s	Cluster still in formation, with representations published so far by a research institute and a think tank:
		• National Cyber Power Index (Belfer Center, Harvard University, US, published in 2020)
		• Cyber Capabilities and National Power: A Net Assessment (IISS, UK, published in 2021)

amount of aggregated threat intelligence data or the respective analytical tools. They have dealt with this unfavourable setting in two ways. The first is to use the available quantitative and qualitative data published by cybersecurity companies as a base for producing their own representations. The European Union Agency for Cybersecurity (ENISA) has chosen this way. Since 2012 it has regularly published 'Thread Landscape' reports in which it tracks changes in cyber threats and ranks them according to their prevalence. In 2020, for instance, it listed malware, web-based attacks, phishing, web application attacks and spam as the top five cyber threats. In addition to such classifications of cyber threats, mostly based on quantifiable data, ENISA also produces detailed reports on specific cyber threats such as ransomware attacks. The second way is to compile their own incident databases. The US-based Center for Strategic and International Studies (CSIS), for instance, has maintained a list of 'Significant Cyber Incidents' on its website since 2015 (see CSIS, 2023). Another US-based think tank, the Council on Foreign Relations (CFR), compiles a list of state-sponsored cyber operations (see CFR, 2023).

The *cybersecurity capacity cluster* consists of organizations that evaluate the cybersecurity capacities of states, that is, their defensive cyber capabilities. In 2007 the Secretary-General of the International Telecommunication Union (ITU), the United Nations' specialized agency for information and communication technologies, launched the Global Cybersecurity Agenda to promote cybersecurity efforts worldwide. The ITU translated the five working areas of the Global Cybersecurity Agenda – namely legal measures, technical measures, organizational structures, capacity building and international cooperation – into a five-dimensional framework of indicators. The resulting ranking, the Global Cybersecurity Index (GCI), has so far been published in four editions: the first in 2015, the second in 2017, the third in 2019 and the fourth, which evaluates 194 countries, in 2021 (see ITU, 2015; 2017; 2019; 2021). The governance niche also attracted other organizations. Among the most prominent: the US-based Potomac Institute proposed a Cyber Readiness Index in 2013 and published a revised version in 2015, while the Global Cyber Security Capacity Centre (GCSCC) of the University of Oxford developed a Cybersecurity Capacity Maturity Model for Nations (CCM) in 2014 which it has since revised twice (see GCSCC, 2021). Both organizations designed their comparative frameworks as multi-dimensional benchmarking tools meant to guide states in their cybersecurity capacity development. What sets them apart from the CGI is that they did not aggregate the benchmarking scores into overall rankings. The e-Governance Academy (no date) developed another ranking, the National Cyber Security Index (NCSI), which covers about 160 states and is distinct from the periodically published CGI in that it has been updated constantly since its launch in 2019. The e-Governance Academy is a non-profit foundation jointly created by the Estonian government, the Open Society Institute and the United Nations Development Programme.

The most recent of the three clusters is the *cyber power cluster*. This cluster goes beyond the cybersecurity capacity cluster by considering and comparing both the defensive and offensive cyber capabilities of states. Debates about cyber power and cyber powers have been going on for some time. In 2011, notably, a Cyber Power Index for the 19 state members of the G20 was published by the Economist Intelligence Unit in cooperation with Booz Allen Hamilton, but this index covered only defensive cyber capabilities. Fully developed comparative frameworks considering both defensive and offensive capabilities have only been published in the last few years, one by a research institute and another by a think tank. In 2020 Harvard University's Belfer Center presented a National Cyber Power Index which, based on 32 intent indicators and 27 capability indicators, quantitatively ranks 30 states according to their cyber power (see Voo et al, 2020b). In 2021 the International Institute for Strategic Studies (IISS) published a qualitative net assessment in which it sorted 15 states into three tiers according to their relative cyber power (see IISS, 2021).

The factors shaping the co-evolution of the three clusters

An ecosystem perspective suggests two factors that explain why the three clusters differ in their mix of organizations and why certain types of organization, and not others, dominate the representational work on the patterns of threats, the worldwide levels of cybersecurity capacity and the distribution of cyber power respectively. The first factor is unequal resources; the second, political struggles that prevent international organizations from occupying and dominating some of the clusters. These factors account for the dominance of cybersecurity companies in the first cluster, the absence of UN and ITU activities in the first and third cluster as well as the facilitating role that the first cluster plays for the third cluster.

Unequal resources

As already briefly mentioned, private software and hardware companies like Microsoft, IBM and Intel or cybersecurity companies such as Deepwatch, Fireye Mandiant, Infosec, Kaspersky and Palo Alto Networks have a special resource that most other organizations – apart from the intelligence services of some cyber powers – lack. Their networks of digital sensors give them a privileged and in many respects exclusive access to incident-level data on cyber threats, which in turn makes them the key gatekeepers to knowledge about cyber threats. They selectively share this knowledge with a wider audience through various channels including reports, statistics, working groups or expert hearings.

Civil society actors like non-governmental organizations (NGOs) often lack the resources to extensively collect data. This creates dependencies either on the publicity of data or on other actors producing data and statistical indicators which they can then use for the development of their own representations. They can, though, partly compensate for this disadvantage by developing analytical frameworks and data process methodologies based on open-source intelligence practices. Prominent examples are the CFR's 'Cyber Operations Tracker' and the CSIS's list of 'Significant Cyber Incidents' which both monitor cyber operations based on publicly assessable data. An example of a non-state actor using open-source intelligence to map the patterns of capabilities is the British NGO Privacy International. In its report *The Global Surveillance Industry* (Privacy International, 2016), it reconstructed the surveillance industry in five states (Germany, Israel, Italy, the UK and the US), tracking how private companies sell surveillance technologies to state actors.

The struggle over internet governance

All three clusters produce comparative knowledge in an ecosystem shaped by political struggles. These struggles have existed since the early days of the internet (see Mueller, 2017). A key point of contention is the nature of the governance of the internet. The US and the EU prefer a multi-stakeholder model in which various actors – including states, private companies and international organizations – partake in the management of an open internet. As the internet was created mainly by actors from the West, its governance mostly resembles this model. However, states such China and Russia lobby for a different model, one based on the principle of cyber sovereignty and the control of states over the internet. The debate over the governance of the internet thus features two competing camps, one advocating a liberal model, the other a sovereigntist model (see Flonk et al, 2020 and Price, 2018).

The struggles involve not only questions about the nature of governance, but also disputes over the technical infrastructure of the internet, as these have implications for how the internet works and can be controlled. The technical dimension is sometimes overlooked, but it is crucial to how open the internet is and how information is exchanged. Its bases are globally standardized data communication protocols. Internet Protocol (IP) addresses are crucial to the global internet expansion, but IP addresses are not an infinite resource. This regularly triggers controversial debates on new technical standards and management frameworks (Denardis, 2009: 1–3). The proposal for a new top-down internet protocol 'New IP, Shaping Future Networks', put forward by a Huawei-led group in the ITU in 2019, is one of the latest examples in a series of efforts to change the way the internet works in the name of making cyberspace fit for the high pace of the digital transformation and the integration of emerging technologies (see Murgia and Gross, 2020).

This struggle also affects cybersecurity politics. The Budapest Convention, signed in 2001, is a key framework document for the struggle against cybercrime. The convention was negotiated under the aegis of the Council of Europe but is open to all states (see Holder, 2022). China and Russia, though, are seeking to supersede it with a new cybercrime treaty and they have succeeded in convincing a majority of emerging and developing countries to join their endeavour. UN members are currently negotiating a possible UN convention on cybercrime. Western states fear that such a convention could, if cybercrimes are defined too broadly and data privacy and human rights are not adequately protected, help authoritarian regimes expand their control over cyberspace, thus undermining rather than strengthening the security of individuals (see for instance European Data Protection Supervisor, 2022). The struggles have made it difficult for international organizations such as the UN and the ITU, despite having mandates for (cyber) security governance, to establish an epistemic infrastructure tracking patterns of cyber threats or evaluating the cyber power of states.

Moreover, the struggles are part of a broader geopolitical struggle in which the US and other Western states compete with China and Russia over power in and over the international order. This geopolitical struggle has become more intense in the past decade, making questions of relative cyber power more relevant politically. The struggles have therefore not only prevented international organizations such as the UN and the ITU from positioning themselves as key knowledge producers in the three clusters. They have also increased the demand for comparisons of cyber power. The Belfer Center and the IISS have moved to occupy the resulting niche.

Enabling effects with side effects

The three clusters differ in the representations that they produce. Some clusters, though, have enabling effects on the work of other clusters. In particular, the first cluster facilitates the production of comparative knowledge in the third. The lists of cyber incidents compiled by the CFR and the CSIS were used by the Belfer Center and the IISS as a source for their own assessments of the cyber power of states. The Belfer Center drew on the CFR's list to discern the objectives that states pursue in offensive cyber operations, which then informed the design of its indicator framework for the measurement of the distribution of cyber power (Voo et al, 2020a: 6). In addition, the CSIS's list serves as the basis for its count of 'state-based cyber attacks', which in turn forms part of its capability indicators (Voo et al, 2020b: 61). The IISS (2021: 129) in turn used the CSIS's list as one of its sources.

Put differently: some clusters depend on the work of other clusters. One corollary is that the clusters that draw on the other clusters carry over biases inherent in the latter's work. To continue with the example of the CFR's and CSIS's lists: the estimated number of state-sponsored cyber operations is most likely higher and covers more countries than these lists suggest, but accurate data is collected and shared only within the community of intelligence services or between specific allies. The CFR and CSIS, in other words, face resource constraints that might lead to certain biases in their representation of the patterns of incidents. What is more, the perception of cyber threats remains a contested political issue and takes different meanings depending on the community or actor addressing the issue. The lists of the two organizations are informed by Western perceptions. It is therefore not surprising that their lists repeat and feed into the narrative set out in Western national security reports, according to which non-Western states – especially China, Russia, Iran and North Korea – are the states that most frequently conduct offensive cyber operations (see Figure 9.1).

A common threat narrative, but dissimilar logics of comparisons

The dynamics of the ecosystem not only influence the co-evolution of the three clusters and the mix of organizations in each, they also shape the comparative approaches pursued in each of them. While all three clusters share a common narrative of a constantly evolving threat landscape, this narrative is the product of the comparative practices of the first cluster and the background for the comparative practices of the other two. Though interrelated, their representational work is nonetheless distinct, with niche logics fostering disparate logics of comparisons. We discuss these different logics, summarized in Table 9.2, in this section.

The organizations dominating the first cluster have the resources to compile and analyse huge amounts of data on cyber incidents. They often use figures for detected or blocked attacks to showcase their cybersecurity capabilities. Kaspersky's 2021 report, for instance, notes that its cybersecurity tools 'blocked 687,861,449 attacks launched from online resources across the globe' between November 2019 and October 2021 (Kaspersky, 2021) while Microsoft's 2021 report highlights that its tools blocked 9 billion 'endpoint threats', 31 billion 'identity threats' and 32 billion 'email threats' between July 2020 and June 2021 (Microsoft, 2021: 4). At the centre of the reports, however, is usually not an analysis of trends in the overall volume of cyber incidents but the disaggregation of the incident data into different types of threat and the discussion of the characteristics of and trends in those types. Put differently: the narrative that the reports want to sell is less a general 'cyber incidents are on the rise' story, rather a more differentiated story about which cyber threats are becoming more prevalent and dangerous and which less so. Underlying this story is a portrayal of cybersecurity as an ongoing contest between 'defenders' and 'attackers', in which the defenders learn to counter certain threats, the attackers in reaction seek new ways to achieve their aims, which in turn forces the defenders to step up their cybersecurity activities, and so on (see, for example, Microsoft, 2021: 5). The narrative, in short, is one of a constantly evolving threat landscape. ENISA buys into this narrative by structuring its aggregated overviews of the patterns of cyber treats in terms of top threats.

Figure 9.1: Number of state-sponsored cyber operations by country, 2005–2020

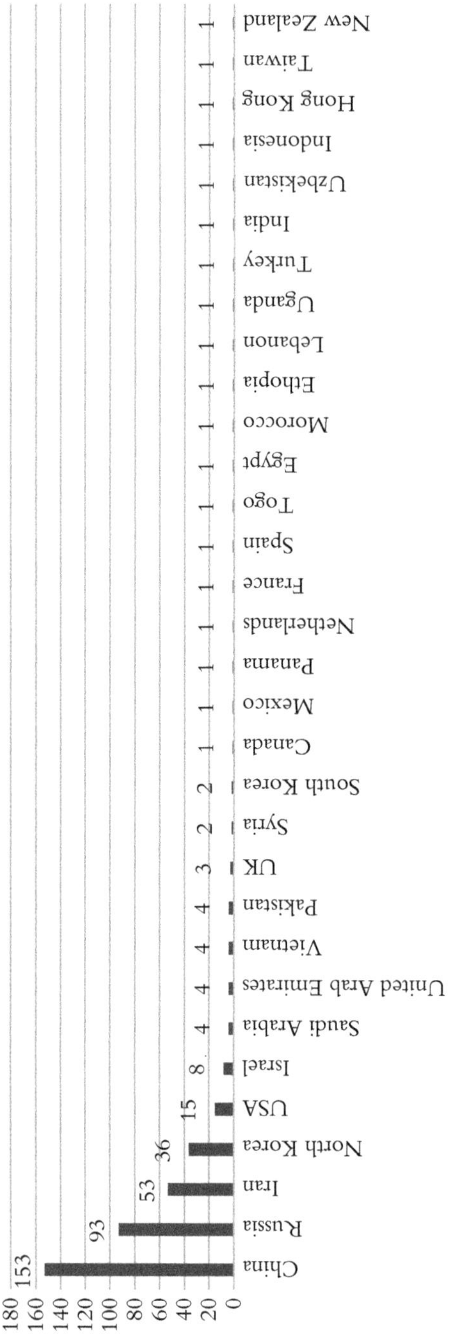

Source: See CFR (2023)

Table 9.2: Three distinct logics of comparison

	First cluster: threats	Second cluster: cybersecurity capacity	Third cluster: cyber power
Comparisons serve to analyse	Prevalence of different threats	Cybersecurity capacity levels	Cyber power differentials
Objective of representational work	Guide development of more capable cybersecurity measures	Create a comparative dynamic fostering the diffusion among states of best practices in cybersecurity	Help policy makers navigate the interstate competition in cyberspace by clarifying the nature and distribution of cyber power
Data sources	Digital sensors/ telemetry	Questionnaires, strategy documents, statistical databases	Questionnaires, strategy documents, statistical databases
Comparative approach	Big data analysis	Multi-dimensional frameworks of indicators	Multi-dimensional frameworks of indicators

The first cluster's representational work is not the only factor shaping the discourse on cybersecurity. Similarly important are episodes such as the cyberattack on Estonia in 2007, the Stuxnet attack on Iran's nuclear programme in 2010, the Snowden revelations in 2013 or the Russian interference in the US elections in 2016 that prompted public and political debates about the changing nature of cyber threats and the best ways to deal with them. Nonetheless, it is the first cluster's representational work that provides much of the publicly available knowledge on the patterns of threats in cyberspace. In so doing, it feeds and shapes the narrative of an evolving threat landscape that informs the representational work in which the other two clusters engage.

The organizations forming the second cluster seek to motivate and steer efforts by states to improve their cybersecurity capacities. They tend to leave the representation of the patterns of threats to others – and thus mainly to the first cluster – and instead seek to position themselves in the governance niche of cybersecurity capacity building. The ITU's ranking publications are a case in point. The publications briefly highlight some threat statistics at the beginning to underscore the importance of cybersecurity, but the ITU's own representational work centres on developing and updating a ranking of the cybersecurity capacities of states. The rationale is to promote best practices in cybersecurity. The Global Cybersecurity Index (GCI) is meant to provide 'the right motivation to countries to intensify their efforts in cybersecurity' (ITU, 2015: iii) and to serve as a 'useful capacity development tool' that identifies 'areas for improvement' and highlights 'best practices for strengthening national cybersecurity' (ITU, 2021: iv). The University of Oxford's GCSCC (2021: 2) similarly describes the purpose of its benchmarking framework as to help 'nations understand what works, what does not work and why, across all areas of cybersecurity'. As part of this positioning strategy, both organizations note that states have been making progress in improving their cybersecurity capacities and seek to portray themselves as facilitators and shapers of this progress while emphasizing the need for further capacity-building efforts 'in the face of changing threats' (GCSCC, 2021: 2; see also ITU, 2021: iv). The e-Governance Academy (no date) uses a different strategy for positioning itself in the governance niche. Rather than stressing best practices, it designs its ranking as a 'global live index' meant as 'a comprehensive cyber security measurement tool that provides accurate and up-to-date public information about national cyber security'. In line with this objective, instead of publishing its ranking periodically, as the ITU does, it constantly updates it on its website.

The third cluster has emerged in reaction to the absence of cyber power rankings in the debate about offensive cyber activities among states. The organizations in this sense seek to fill a niche created by political developments but not so far occupied by other organizations. They build on the general narrative of an evolving threat landscape. The IISS (2021: 171), for instance, emphasizes the 'rapidly evolving nature of cyber threats and opportunities'. However, their perspective on cyber threats is narrower than that of the other two clusters as they focus on a subset of cyber threats: attacks by states, or state-sponsored groups, on other states. The Belfer Center and the IISS not only invoke these attacks to underscore the relevance of their representational work but – as mentioned – also use them as empirical material for the development of their comparative frameworks. Differing from the second cluster, the logic of comparison is not primarily geared towards helping states improve their cybersecurity capabilities but towards teasing out power differentials in order to help policy makers navigate the interstate competition in cyberspace. While they integrate into their representations some of the indicators developed by the organizations in the second cluster, the Belfer Center and the IISS situate their representations in the practice of measuring power and classifying powers that has been part of great power politics for centuries. Consistent with this practice, they focus on the states deemed to be most important, which distinguishes them again from the representational work done in the second cluster which seeks to cover the cybersecurity capacities of all states.

Resource constraints partly explain why only the first cluster is characterized by a strong datafication of the comparative practices. The differences in the comparative practices are, however, also the result of niche strategies, with the producers of comparative knowledge in both the second and third cluster seeking to position themselves in niches that are distinct from the first cluster dominated by cybersecurity companies. The diverging niche logics – fostering worldwide cybersecurity capacity building versus understanding interstate competition in cyberspace – go a considerable way towards explaining the differences in the logic of comparison of the second and third cluster. As Table 9.3 shows, the dissimilar logics lead to differing representations of the distribution of cyber capabilities. Only 13 of the GCI's top 20 states appear in the National Cyber Power Index (NCPI) and only 9 were included by the IISS in its Net Assessment. Only 6 of the NCSI's top 20 states appear in the NCPI and only 3 in the IISS' Net Assessment. China, to highlight the most prominent example, is absent from the top 20 of the two cybersecurity capacity rankings but appears in the top 10 of the two power rankings. A closer look at Table 9.3, however, also reveals that the niche dynamics have so far not fostered a common comparative approach within the two clusters. Neither the two cybersecurity capacity rankings nor the two cyber power rankings depict the same order of states. The cybersecurity capacity rankings, though, diverge more strongly (with only 8 states appearing in both top 20 lists) than the cyber power rankings (with 9 states in both top 15s). One explanation would be that the competition over attention and influence begets differentiation – the organizations seek to produce representations that differ from those of their competitors – which in turn translates into diverse representations and contributes to the continuing ambiguity of the distribution of cyber capabilities.

Conclusion

Cybersecurity politics features many comparative practices. In this chapter, we have shown that the widespread notion of cyberspace as an ecosystem can be analytically productive to explain how comparative knowledge is produced on three key aspects of cybersecurity politics: the patterns of cyber threats, the cybersecurity capacities of states as well as the distribution of cyber power. An ecosystem approach helps to tease out how a combination of three factors – (1) differences in resources, (2) political struggles preventing stronger roles for international organizations and fostering demands for different kinds of comparative knowledge and (3) strategies to carve out distinct niches of cybersecurity expertise – has given rise to three clusters of representational work populated by different types of organizations and characterized by different logics of comparison.

In addition to shedding light on how social settings shape the production of comparative knowledge, the chapter also probes into how comparative knowledge becomes politically relevant. The three clusters share a common threat narrative that emphasizes constantly changing patterns of threats and thus both feeds and legitimizes demands for political efforts to improve cybersecurity capabilities. The ecosystem approach highlights how

Table 9.3: A comparison of the top 20 states in four prominent rankings

Rank	Global Cybersecurity Index 2021	National Cyber Security Index 2022	National Cyber Power Index 2020	IISS Net Assessment 2021
1	US	Greece	US	US the sole first-tier state
2	Great Britain	Lithuania	China	Seven second-tier states
3	Saudi Arabia	Belgium	Great Britain	(listed alphabetically):
4	Estonia	Czech Republic	Russia	Australia, Canada, China, France, Great
5	South Korea	Estonia	Netherlands	Britain, Israel and
6	Singapore	Germany	France	Russia
7	Spain	Portugal	Germany	
8	Russia	Spain	Canada	
9	UAE	Poland	Japan	Seven third-tier states
10	Malaysia	Finland	Australia	(listed alphabetically):
11	Lithuania	France	Israel	India, Indonesia, Iran, Japan, Malaysia, North
12	Japan	Sweden	Spain	Korea, Vietnam
13	Canada	Denmark	Sweden	
14	France	Saudi Arabia	Estonia	
15	India	Croatia	New Zealand	
16	Turkey	Slovakia	South Korea	
17	Australia	Netherlands	Switzerland	
18	Luxembourg	Malaysia	Singapore	
19	Germany	Italy	Malaysia	
20	Portugal	US	Vietnam	

Note: The most recent version of each ranking was used. In the GCI, some states share the same ranks, which the table indicates through merged cells.

organizations take advantage of these demands by strategically positioning themselves in two niches of cybersecurity politics through the publication of comparative frameworks: the debate about cybersecurity capacity building and the debate about interstate competition in cyberspace.

Comparative practices have political effects. The three clusters sustain a threat narrative that legitimizes demands for more cybersecurity activities. Cybersecurity politics constitute a promising case study for probing deeper into the effects of comparisons in future research. Both the cybersecurity capacity cluster and the cyber power cluster feature organizations that opt for quantitative comparative frameworks as well as organizations that opt for qualitative ones. The relative success of these organizations will thus provide insights into the impact that different comparative practices generate.

References

Abbott, K.W., Green, J.F. and Keohane, R.O. (2016) 'Organizational ecology and institutional change in global governance', *International Organization*, 70(2): 247–77.

Allan, B.B. (2017) 'Producing the climate: states, scientists, and the constitution of global governance objects', *International Organization*, 71(1): 131–62.

Aradau, C. and Blanke, T. (2018) 'Governing others: anomaly and the algorithmic subject of security', *European Journal of International Security*, 3(1): 1–21.

Betz, D.J. and Stevens, T. (2013) 'Analogical reasoning and cyber security', *Security Dialogue*, 44(2): 147–64.

Branch, J. (2020) 'What's in a name? Metaphors and cybersecurity', *International Organization*, 75(1): 39–70.

Broome, A. and Quirk, J. (2015) 'Governing the world at a distance: the practice of global benchmarking', *Review of International Studies*, 41(5): 819–41.

Bueger, C. (2015) 'Making things known: epistemic practices, the United Nations, and the translation of piracy', *International Political Sociology*, 9(1): 1–18.

Calderaro, A. and Craig, A. (2020) 'Transnational governance of cybersecurity: policy challenges and global inequalities in cyber capacity building', *Third World Quarterly*, 41(6): 917–38.

Carr, M. (2021) 'A political history of cyberspace', in P. Cornish (ed) *The Oxford Handbook of Cyber Security*, Oxford: Oxford University Press, pp 49–66.

CFR (Council on Foreign Relations) (2023) Cyber Operations Tracker, www.cfr.org/cyber-operations/ [Accessed 4 December 2023].

CSIS (Center for Strategic and International Studies) (2023) Significant Cyber Incidents, www.csis.org/programs/strategic-technologies-program/significant-cyber-incidents [Accessed 4 December 2023].

Davis, K.E., Kingsbury, B. and Merry, S.E. (2012) 'Indicators as a technology of global governance', *Law & Society Review*, 46(1): 71–104.

Denardis, L. (2009) *Protocol Politics: The Globalization of Internet Governance*, Cambridge, MA: The MIT Press.

Dunn Cavelty, M. (2013) 'From cyber-bombs to political fallout: threat representations with an impact in the cyber-security discourse', *International Studies Review*, 15(1): 105–22.

Egloff, F.J. and Dunn Cavelty, M. (2021) 'Attribution and knowledge creation assemblages in cybersecurity politics', *Journal of Cybersecurity*, 7(1): 1–12.

e-Governance Academy (no date) National Cyber Security Index, https://ncsi.ega.ee/ [Accessed 11 February 2022].

European Data Protection Supervisor (2022) *Opinion 9/2022 on the Recommendation for a Council Decision Authorising the Negotiations for a Comprehensive International Convention on Countering the Use of Information and Communications Technologies for Criminal Purposes*, 18 May, https://edps.europa.eu/system/files/2022-05/2022-05-18-opinion_on_international_convention_en.pdf [Accessed 10 May 2023].

Flonk, D., Jachtenfuchs, M. and Obendiek, A. (2020) 'Authority conflicts in internet governance: liberals vs. sovereigntists?', *Global Constitutionalism*, 9(2): 364–86.

GCSCC (Global Cyber Security Capacity Centre) (2021) *Cybersecurity Capacity Maturity Model for Nations*, https://gcscc.ox.ac.uk/files/cmm20 21editiondocpdf [Accessed 11 February 2022].

Hannan, M.T. and Freeman, J. (1989) *Organizational Ecology*, Cambridge: Cambridge University Press.

Holder, M. (2022) 'Cyberspace in a state of flux: regulating cyberspace through international law', *Groningen Journal of International Law*, 9(2): 266–80.

IISS (International Institute for Strategic Studies) (2021) *Cyber Capabilities and National Power: A Net Assessment*, 28 June, www.iiss.org/blogs/resea rch-paper/2021/06/cyber-capabilities-national-power [Accessed 11 February 2022].

International Telecommunication Union (ITU) (2015) *Global Cybersecurity Index and Cyberwellness Profiles*, Geneva: International Telecommunication Union.

ITU (2017) *Global Cybersecurity Index 2017*, Geneva: International Telecommunication Union.

ITU (2019) *Global Cybersecurity Index 2018*, Geneva: International Telecommunication Union.

ITU (2021) *Global Cybersecurity Index 2020: Measuring Commitment to Cybersecurity*, Geneva: International Telecommunication Union.

Kaspersky (2021) *Kaspersky Security Bulletin 2021. Statistics*, 15 December. https://securelist.com/kaspersky-security-bulletin-2021-statistics/105205 [Accessed 11 February 2022].

Kelley, J.G. and Simmons, B.A. (2019) 'Introduction: the power of global performance indicators', *International Organization*, 73(3): 491–510.

Lake, D.A. (2021) 'The organizational ecology of global governance', *European Journal of International Relations*, 27(2): 345–68.

Maschmeyer, L., Deibert, R. and Lindsay, J.R. (2021) 'A tale of two cybers – how threat reporting by cybersecurity firms systematically underrepresents threats to civil society', *Journal of Information Technology & Politics*, 18(1): 1–20.

Microsoft (2021) *Digital Defense Report*, October, https://query.prod.cms. rt.microsoft.com/cms/api/am/binary/RWMFIi?id=101738 [Accessed 11 February 2022].

Mueller, M. (2017) *Will the Internet Fragment? Sovereignty, Globalization and Cyberspace*, Cambridge, MA: Polity.

Murgia, M. and Gross, A. (2020) 'Inside China's controversial mission to reinvent the internet', *Financial Times*, 27 March, www.ft.com/content/ ba94c2bc-6e27-11ea-9bca-bf503995cd6f [Accessed 10 May 2023].

NATO (North Atlantic Treaty Organization) (2016) 'Cyber Defence Pledge', Press Release 124, 8 July, www.nato.int/cps/en/natohq/official_ texts_133177.htm [Accessed 11 February 2022].

Price, M. (2018) 'The global politics of internet governance. A case study in closure and technological design', in D.R. McCarthy (ed) *Technology and World Politics. An Introduction*, London: Routledge, pp 126–45.

Privacy International (2016) *The Global Surveillance Industry*, July, www.priva cyinternational.org/sites/default/files/2017-12/global_surveillance_0.pdf [Accessed 31 March 2023].

Rumelili, B. and Towns, A.E. (2022) 'Driving liberal change? Global performance indices as a system of normative stratification in liberal international order', *Cooperation and Conflict*, 57(2): 152–70.

Shaurya and Singh, M. (2021) 'Cyber threats of modern era', in V.E. Balas, A.E. Hassanien, S. Chakrabarti and L. Mandal (eds) *Proceedings of International Conference on Computational Intelligence, Data Science and Cloud Computing. IEM-ICDC 2020*, Singapore: Springer, pp 659–70.

Slayton, R. (2015) 'Measuring risk: computer security metrics, automation, and learning', *IEEE Annals of the History of Computing*, 37(2): 32–45.

Slayton, R. (2021) 'Governing uncertainty or uncertain governance? Information security and the challenge of cutting ties', *Science, Technology & Human Values*, 46(1): 81–111.

Stevens, T. (2020) 'Knowledge in the grey zone: AI and cybersecurity', *Journal of Digital War*, 1(1): 164–70.

US Department of Homeland Security (2011) *Enabling Distributed Security in Cyberspace: Building a Healthy and Resilient Cyber Ecosystem with Automated Collective Action*, 23 March, www.dhs.gov/xlibrary/assets/nppd-cyber-ecosystem-white-paper-03-23-2011.pdf [Accessed 12 May 2023].

Voo, J., Hemani, I., Jones, S., DeSombre, W., Cassidy, D. and Schwarzenbach, A. (2020a) *Reconceptualizing Cyber Power: Cyber Power Index Primer*, Cambridge, MA: Belfer Center for Science and International Affairs.

Voo, J., Hemani, I., Jones, S., DeSombre, W., Cassidy, D. and Schwarzenbach, A. (2020b) *National Cyber Power Index 2020: Methodology and Analytical Considerations*, Cambridge, MA: Belfer Center for Science and International Affairs.

Yarovenko, H., Kuzmenko, O. and Stumpo, M. (2020) 'Strategy for determining country ranking by level of cybersecurity', *Financial Markets, Institutions and Risks*, 4(3): 124–37.

PART III

How Comparisons Reshape Competitive Dynamics

10

'The Old World Fought, the Modern World Counts': Naval Armament Policies, Force Comparisons and International Status, 1889–1922

Kerrin Langer

At the end of the 19th century, naval and military force comparisons were omnipresent in policy papers, parliamentary speeches, diplomatic negotiations, newspapers, magazines, pamphlets and posters. The codification of status claims and relative strength in force ratios, the visualization of relative strength and the status hierarchy through comparisons and the conclusions derived from these visualizations with regard to status, power and security influenced political and military decision making, domestic discourse and international relations alike. For example, perceptions of the distribution of status and power, which decided on influence in diplomatic negotiations, were no longer only subject to a 'sense of place' (Pouliot, 2016: 71–85) but standing within the status hierarchy was quantified and visualized in numerical comparisons. Further, force ratios, comparisons and the conclusions derived from them served not only as a basis to determine demands in arms control negotiations and national budget planning (Albert and Langer, 2020), but served equally as a means to legitimate these demands in the struggle over the distribution of status, power and security (arms control negotiations) or national resources (proceedings on defence spending). I further argue that comparative practices, perceptions of relative naval strength and the status hierarchy influenced the dynamics of the naval arms competition among the great powers that prevailed in different stages of intensity between 1889 and 1914 (Bönker, 2012: 2) and that loomed on the horizon again from 1918 onwards (Maurer, 2021: 314), fuelled by concerns about relative standing within the status hierarchy of the great (naval) powers.

Although the interrelation between status seeking and naval power in the late 19th and early 20th century and its impact on naval arms competition has been widely recognized and studied among scholars both in International Relations (IR) and history (see Renshon, 2017; Jaschob, 2018; Murray, 2019; Bönker, 2012), there has so far been little research into naval force comparisons as an internationally shared practice to depict the status hierarchy. Jaschob (2018: 68), for example, writes that 'states permanently evaluate their status position in comparison to other countries' which can lead to status claims, and emphasizes, like Renshon (2017), the relative standing within the status hierarchy as important for German status seeking through naval build-ups. However, both scholars almost entirely neglect contemporary comparative practices in their research. In the historical research, while comparative practices like naval standards feature prominently in argumentation for the action–reaction model as the explanation for the arms competition from 1889 onwards (see Kennedy, 1980: 415–70; Marder, 1940: 105–205) or against the action–reaction model as the true reason for the naval build-ups and the competition, which often comprises some deeper analyses of comparative practices (Rose, 2011: 171–89; Mullins, 2016: 3–11, 43–81, 104–76), scholars do not refer to these comparisons as a means to depict the status hierarchy.

The aim of this chapter is precisely to contribute to the research on comparative practices as a means to depict the status hierarchy that underpinned the naval armament policies of Great Britain, France and Germany and how these comparisons influenced the naval competition between these and the other great powers in the period between 1889 and 1922. I proceed in three steps. In the first I give an overview of the interrelation between status and naval power to describe the rationale behind the naval build-ups and comparative practices. I further show how contemporaries reflected on status comparisons and relative naval strength as a means to fight the 'cold war' (Bernstein, 1914: 8888). In the second, I explore practices of status comparison and comparative orders as a means to mobilize support for naval armaments. In the last, I answer the question as to how and why status comparisons had the power to influence the naval arms competition.

Status, naval power and the 'strategy of peace'

'Prestige', Sir Walter Harcourt said in 1898, 'is the consideration in which nations or individuals are held by their fellows' (quoted in *Daily News*, 1898). Over 100 years later, Deborah Larson and her co-authors (2014: 7) defined *status*, a term I use as an analytic umbrella term for contemporary *prestige* with all its equivalents (Lebow, 2008: 487–99) as the 'collective beliefs about a given state's ranking on valued attributes'. Both definitions imply that recognition by others is crucial for the possession of status or, as historian Jost Dülffer (2003: 56) has prominently expressed it: a great power is one that has been recognized as such by the other great powers. Dülffer's conclusion points to one of the ways in which the recognition of status becomes visible in international politics: belonging to a 'defined club of actors'. The second way status becomes visible is through 'relative standing within such a club' (Larson et al, 2014: 7). This relativity points to the competitivity of status and implies that the members of the defined club serve as a group of peer competitors (Renshon, 2017: 33, 36).[1]

In the last decades of the 19th century, naval power[2] emerged as one of the most important means of acquiring status, as well as power and security in the globalized world. The necessity of naval forces was no longer determined by defensive and strategic needs alone, but status and power considerations too (Johnson, 2011: 140). Based on the experience of Great Britain, whose empire and world power status depended, in the perception of the time, on her naval power (Lambert, 2018: 4–8, 288–305; Epkenhans, 1992), the shared belief emerged among the great powers that in the 'age of empire' naval power, especially large battleship fleets, was crucial for the recognition and preservation of great or even world power status by peer competitors (Alfaro Zaforteza, 2019; Bönker, 2012: 23–100). While a powerful navy was still a means to protect maritime borders, trade routes, citizens abroad and colonial possessions, status as a great naval power and relative standing within the naval hierarchy would secure political, economic and colonial interests and a fair share in the distribution of the world in peace. This would guarantee the future existence of the nation or the empire in a world in which there would be only rise or decline (Rüger, 2007: 211; Johnson, 2011: 138–40; Hobson, 2002: 164, 296–97; Bönker, 2012: 1–3, 23–4). Naval officers, politicians, journalists and

---

[1] For a broader discussion of status in IR and the difficulties of measuring status see Musgrave and Ward (Chapter 5) and Beaumont (Chapter 2) in this volume.

[2] A comment on seapower, sea power and naval power: Seapower (one word) refers to 'maritime imperial great powers' whose 'culture and identity' is shaped by the sea and who depend 'on the control of ocean communications for cohesion, commerce and control' (Lambert, 2018: 4). Sea power (two words), a term shaped by Alfred T. Mahan, refers to a 'type of grand strategy' and a state that possesses powerful naval forces and a flourishing and strong economy. Naval power, therefore, refers to the strategic instrument (McCranie, 2021: 14–16; Lambert, 2018: 10). In the period investigated in this chapter, the latter terms – sea power and naval power – were used mostly synonymously, and the status hierarchy was measured in terms of ships. Therefore, I use the term naval power in a broad sense that includes sea power as well. For a discussion of the three terms see Lambert (2018: 4–16).

pressure groups promoted this perception of naval power, also known as navalism, with great success. Especially in Great Britain, Germany and the United States the interlinkage between naval power and status had a powerful influence on defence policy. In Great Britain every real or assumed attempt by other great powers to alter the naval hierarchy was perceived as a threat to Britain's position as the leading world power and a way downwards (Lambert, 2018: 3, 295–9). Even liberal governments, which were traditionally dedicated to politics of 'peace, retrenchment and reform', were influenced towards spending large sums on the navy in order to secure their status as the greatest naval power, which would in itself contribute to the security of Great Britain and the Empire (Johnson, 2011). In Imperial Germany, it was the pursuit of world power status in combination with status dissatisfaction (Renshon, 2017: 206–18) or the 'struggle for recognition', as Michelle Murray put it (Murray, 2019), and in the United States the belief that 'the United States were destined to rule the world' (Bönker, 2012: 45, see also pp 23–6, 42–6) that facilitated the influence of navalist ideas on defence politics and in the fierce struggle over the distribution of financial resources.

What has been already suggested in the previous section is the contemporary belief that status as a great naval power and relative standing within the naval hierarchy unfolded its potential especially in peace time. Naval power, demonstrated through the level of naval armaments up to the geographical presence of warships, were, in the perception of the time, 'modern' means to achieve political aims like economic and territorial expansion or to assert political influence (Brailsford, 1918: 163–4, 169). German Admiral Alfred von Tirpitz called it the 'political importance of sea power' (von Tirpitz, 1896; translation: Hobson, 2002: 227) and Arthur Lee the 'strategy of peace' (Lee, 1912: 928). Apart from standing within the status hierarchy, ideas of deterrence and coercion were what turned navies into political instruments and enabled the powers to make use of their status as naval powers (see, for example, Mackinder 1912: 920–21; Hollweg, 1921; Rowlands, 2019: 10–12; Rüger, 2007: 205–6).

This 'strategy of peace' was, in the contemporary perception, linked to the naval arms competition. For British MP Halford Mackinder, the impact of naval power in peace was one of the reasons for the ongoing 'competition of Fleets', which for German historian Hans Delbrück, was itself 'a surrogate for war' (Hobson, 2002: 47). Journalist Henry Brailsford (1918: 18) concluded that 'a power which has been forced by the deficiency of its own armaments to accept a diplomatic reverse, at once sets to work to beggar itself in the effort to recover its lost prestige'. However, this substitute for war was still perceived as war (Hobson, 2002: 39–57; Bönker, 2012: 73–96); 'dry warfare', 'armed peace' (Brailsford, 1918: 163), 'silent warfare' (Lee, 1912: 935) and 'cold war' were terms used to express this phenomenon, the latter by Eduard

Bernstein, a German social democratic politician. He used the term 'cold war' for the first time in 1893 (Hobson, 2002: 45) in a journal article and repeated it in the Reichstag over 20 years later when he spoke of 'this silent war, this cold war ... the war of armaments, of outdoing in armaments' (Bernstein, 1914: 8888).

The battles in this war were won through displaying and visualizing naval power. On the one hand, this was achieved through the demonstration of power in the naval theatre (Rüger, 2007). Fleet reviews, ship launches, movies, visits to foreign ports like the world tour of the American *Great White Fleet* from 1907 to 1909 (Bönker, 2012: 216–17) and other forms of representation were the means to create these 'impressions' (Rüger, 2007: 203–10). On the other hand, naval force comparisons played an important role in the visualization of naval power. For contemporaries, the 'bloodless war' was fought through the level of armaments, the 'calculation of power on one side and of power on the other' (Middlemore, 1912: 1228), the 'balance of forces' (Mahan, 1910: 8) and the status hierarchy derived from it. Similar views were expressed by Delbrück and Brailsford (Delbrück, 1899 [1902]: 524; Hobson, 2002: 46–8). Brailsford (1918: 17–19) in his analysis concluded that continual mutual observation generated knowledge about the military capabilities of potential adversaries, while at the same time, the military and naval estimates of the nations were printed and publicly available. Armament levels and military and naval estimates had become the new means of great power rivalry. And comparisons were central to this: 'Behind every acute diplomatic discussion there goes on a calculation with maps and balance sheets and statistics. ... The computing of these elements tends to replace actual warfare. The old world fought; the modern world counts' (Brailsford, 1918: 18–19). Comparisons often served a dual function: they visualized the status hierarchy and relative strength and therefore contributed to the perception of status and deterrence. For all the different ways of demonstrating naval power it was 'about image and perception, not necessarily truth' (Rowlands, 2019: 18). This becomes even more evident when we look at the specific comparative practices that mirrored status concerns and status aspirations in the context of naval armament policies, which will be explored in the next section.

Naval force comparisons, naval standards, status and naval armament debates

The most important status marker for naval power and the prime means of measuring naval power and great power status from the end of the 19th century well into the interwar period were the number and/or tonnage of battleships or 'ships of the line' (Dülffer, 2003: 52; Bell,

2000: 1–48, 126–37). After the launch of HMS *Dreadnought*, and the adoption of this type of battleship by the other countries, there was a common understanding that naval power was from then on primarily measured in *Dreadnought*-types (Bell, 2012: 13). Additionally, from around 1900 onwards and especially after the advent of so-called 'battle cruisers' in 1906, large armoured cruisers were often incorporated in these comparisons (see Nauticus, 1907: 47; Hythe, 1913: 94), due to their increasing ability to fight in the line of battle (Buchanan, 1904: 1281). Like all comparisons, they were, however, neither objective nor neutral. What was compared, who was compared, the method, the timeframe and the numbers used for the comparison depended on the position and aim of the one using and/or making the comparison (Steinmetz, 2019), a fact that was already reflected in contemporary debates (see, for example, Pretyman, 1904: 1059–61). Comparisons based on the number and tonnage of battleships or capital ships as a means to assess the status hierarchy and the potential for deterrence, secondly, did not necessarily say anything about relative fighting power, which depended on several other factors like artillery, speed or the age of the ship (for example HC Deb, 1909a; 1909b; 1909c) or actual naval strength (for example Beresford, 1910: 82), which was determined not only by battleships, but by cruisers and auxiliary craft like destroyers or submarines (Rose, 2011: 178–9) or other factors like geographical position (see, for example, Beresford, 1910: 92–5). These facts were also mirrored in discussions over the focus and emphasis on battleships for naval strategy, which was disputed, negotiated and shifting throughout the period covered in this chapter and beyond (Hobson, 2002; Bönker, 2012: 102–24). However, battleships and battleship comparisons in combination with the interpretation of these comparisons with respect to the security, power and status of the country remained central to the political debate, due to the prevailing strategy of the decisive battle (Bönker, 2012: 102–24), the battleship/capital ship as status symbols (Bell, 2012: 87–98; Tooze, 2014: 11) and the expectations evoked in the public through years of propaganda (Morgan-Owen, 2021). Battleship comparisons not only depicted the status hierarchy and gave a general picture of naval power and relative strength, but also served as a way to simplify discussion and to provide a simple, easily understandable method for measuring naval power in debates and public agitation (Rose, 2011: 177–89).

In the next two subsections I explore further ways in which comparisons were used as a means to depict the status hierarchy in the political debate. The first was by legitimizing budget demands with reference to the status hierarchy and relative naval strength; the second was by using so-called 'naval standards' to enable status aspirations to become part of naval policies.

The status hierarchy

Within the context of securing funds for the navy in Great Britain, France and Germany, referring to the status hierarchy was principally about the hierarchy of great naval powers. Comparisons were used to make the hierarchy visible. However, making explicit comparisons to support statements on the status hierarchy was not imperative in parliamentary speech. Sometimes, tables of comparisons or comparative knowledge had already been provided as further material for debates by the navy departments (see, for example, Admiralty, 1906; Nauticus, 1899; Bos, 1904). Additionally, tables and diagrams of battleship strength were published in newspapers, magazines, books, brochures and pamphlets (the examples are numerous). These comparisons were also at the disposal of parliamentarians when they debated the naval estimates. These tables and diagrams in turn often, but not always (see, for example, Rousseau, 1908; *Chicago Daily Tribune*, 1899), depicted the status hierarchy through a specific ordering from the highest- to the lowest-ranked of the countries that were being compared (see, for example, *Chicago Daily Tribune*, 1899; Rassow, 1901: 24–6; Neuhaus-Wilmersdorf, 1906: 210; Office of Naval Intelligence, 1909; Hythe, 1912: 79, 88).

There were two ways contemporaries referred to the naval hierarchy: the first was to talk in terms of first-, second- or third-class naval powers, comparable to great, middle and small powers; the second, to talk about the first, second, third … rank within the hierarchy of (great) naval powers.

The former was especially relevant to the German Navy and the legitimation of demands for further battleship construction in the early 1890s. In the plenary sessions of the Reichstag in 1889, 1890, 1891 and 1892 the question of status was discussed through debates on the rank Germany should pursue as a naval power, on whose naval power Germany's should legitimately be compared with, reflections on how to determine when a country was a first-, second- or third-class naval power, due to the absence of a 'normed scale' [*Normalskala*] (Hahn, 1892: 4465; see also von Hollmann, 1891: 1940) and therefore of a determination of the number of battleships necessary for each of these classes (Rickert, 1890a: 937–8) and on the importance of naval power for Germany's status as a great and world power. Although there was a consensus that Germany should be among the second-class naval powers, there was no consensus that it was imperative to give the navy the number of battleships it demanded in order to preserve this rank. However, neither the comparisons used in these debates nor warnings of a potential fall to the status of a third-class naval power were able to persuade a majority in the Reichstag to vote for the naval estimates as proposed by Secretary of the Navy Hollmann in 1891 (Haußmann, 1891: 1949; Sondhaus, 1997: 185–90). The reference to classes of naval powers proved to be disadvantageous to the naval leadership and parliamentarians who supported the navy, because

Hollmann's statements to the Budget Commission evoked fears that the navy actually wanted Germany to become a first-class naval power (von Bennigsen, 1891: 1935) which was unthinkable at the beginning of the 1890s for most of the Reichstag and the public (Rickert, 1890b: 913–14). Only at the end of the 19th century did German promoters of naval power become successful enough to shift the traditional focus on the army in defence spending to the navy between 1897 and 1912 (Stein, 2007: 208–96) so that Germany rose to become a first-class naval power and the second naval power around 1913 (Hythe, 1913: 85).

As deputy Oscar Hahn argued in 1892 (4456), there was indeed a 'common understanding' about who was and what it meant to be a first-, second- or third-class naval power and with regard to these attributions the 'sense of place' remained. However, as regards rank within the hierarchy of the group of naval powers, the quantified visualization provided by comparisons of battleship or capital ship strength enabled naval officials, governments and parliamentarians to explicitly determine the naval hierarchy, to visualize the need for further build-ups or criticize them and to make use of it in the debates.

Concerns over losing its place as the second naval power without heavy investment in battleship building featured prominently in French naval debates between 1889 and 1906 (see, for example, De Dompierre d'Hornoy, 1889: 1419; Chautemps, 1891: 2467; Thomson, 1906: 2674). For example, deputy Charles Bos who presented the estimates for the French navy for 1905 feared that the German and the US navies were set to overtake the French in the ranking of the naval powers within the next ten years, a conclusion he based on extensive comparisons of French and German battleship and cruiser strength as well as ship numbers of the US navy (Bos, 1904: 1588). He stated this again in his report on the navy estimates for 1906 and drew the conclusion that France would become a naval power of the fourth or fifth rank in 1919 unless it started to increase its battleship numbers. Although he only made explicit comparisons with Germany, his warning of France's decline to the fourth or fifth rank indicates that he thought in terms of a status comparison of all the great naval powers (Bos, 1905: 1292). A status comparison that ranked all the great naval powers based on the number of battleships and large armoured cruisers can, for example, be found in the report of the Naval Commission on the naval programme in 1900 (Le Moigne, 1900: 1072–5). While Germany, as the example of 1905 and 1906 shows, featured prominently as the main danger to France's status position, it was actually the US navy that became the second naval power in 1907 (Nauticus 1907: 47; Thomson 1909: 2123). Nevertheless, the focus on Germany remained, for example in 1909, when deputy Amédée Bienaimé based his warning that France 'will fall … to the fifth rank' on an explicit comparison of the number of French and German battleships and armoured cruisers, while only referring to American and Japanese shipbuilding without giving explicit numbers (Bienaimé, 1909: 1846). While the reference to the ranks within the naval hierarchy were often explicit, the comparisons they were based on were less often explicitly communicated in the debates, as they could be found in additional publications (see, for example, Chaumet, 1908: 1235–38; Painlevé, 1911: 1471, 1474–80). All the warnings of a decline, combined with demands for more money, better organization and reforms, did nothing to change the fact that France gradually lost its position as the second naval power. Consequently, from around 1907 onwards most of the deputies and the naval leadership accepted the 'humiliating' relegation to the fourth rank (Chaumet, 1907: 1402). It was France's financial situation in conjunction with the naval build-ups of the other powers, the status of the navy in national security policy as well as the structurally conditioned inconsistent and partly chaotic French naval policy that caused the decline of French naval power (Ropp, 1987; Walser, 1992: 172; Masson, 2002: 64). Although the references to French status and the status hierarchy were unable to stop French decline, they altered French naval policy nevertheless. It helped those who promoted a battleship navy after decades of struggle over the building policy to regain increasing influence from 1900 onwards, actually resulting in the cessation of all armoured cruiser construction and the building of only battleships of the *Dreadnought*-type as laid down in the naval law of 1912 (Walser, 1992).

Naval standards

The second way in which status aspirations became part of naval policies through comparisons was as so-called 'naval standards', like the famous British two-power standard. Naval standards can be defined as a specific type of comparison. Although it was argued that they were based on strategic needs, that was not necessarily the case and attaining the defined battleship standards, like battleships comparisons in general, did not indicate the actual relative naval strength of a country (Bell, 2000: 2–4; Rose, 2011: 177–89). They were mainly policy instruments to communicate status claims and/or to serve as benchmarks to assess the building policy within the political debate and were an important means of mobilizing the public, parliamentarians and the government to secure funds for the navy (Bell, 2000: 3). Because of the mobilizing effects of these standards German Secretary to the Navy von Tirpitz wanted to publicly announce in 1911 that Germany was aiming at a battleship fleet with a ratio of 2 to 3 to that of Great Britain. This ratio had been the rationale behind the German battleship programme since 1900, but had been kept secret (Hobson, 2002: 247–60). Tirpitz now hoped that he could use this standard to gain support for a further amendment to the fleet law. However, chancellor Theobald von Bethmann-Hollweg banned Tirpitz from declaring this standard as official German policy in order to avoid a further deterioration in Anglo–German relations (Epkenhans, 1991: 105–6).

Apart from their role as benchmarks, the naval standards' ratios implicitly or explicitly codified status aspirations, which were, in turn, communicated through these standards. Especially in this context they were ratios that set the minimum or maximum strength of the number and/or tonnage of battleships with regards to one or more competitors. In 1921, former German Vice-Admiral Carl Hollweg called this way of codifying status aspirations 'political fleet arithmetic' (Hollweg, 1921: 1). For example, the two-power standard,[3] which shaped British naval policy between 1889 and 1909/1912 (it was publicly abandoned in 1912, internally in 1909; Marder, 2013: 182–5) defined that the strength of the Royal Navy 'should at least be equal to the naval strength of any two other countries' (Hamilton, 1889: 1171), which effectively meant the numerical expression of the British claim to naval supremacy (Ashmead-Bartlett, 1889: 1321). The varying French standards from 1889 to 1906 (EMG, 1909) were an expression of the aim to remain the second naval power and the American claim of a 'navy second to none' which was set by the General Board in 1914 and officially communicated in 1916 likewise codified status aspirations (Bönker, 2012: 83–4).

Status comparisons and the naval arms competition

The comparative practices and orders that were used to legitimize further ship building and the contemporary references to the influence of the 'balance of forces', the prevalence of computation and comparisons indicate that, in the competition over status, it was not only important to have battleships or any other class of ships. How many battleships one had in relation to the one's peer competitors was equally important. In other words: the naval build-ups of, for example, Great Britain, France, the United States and Germany were about their relative standing in the status hierarchy. The higher one stood in this hierarchy, the more influence one could exert and altering it through naval build-ups could, in the end, even mean a peaceful transition of command of the sea (Rüger, 2007: 205–6). Although mutual observation of, and reference to, the military capabilities of peer competitors can be described as 'the normal condition of military relations' (Buzan and Herring, 1998: 79), it was the relativity of status and concerns about standing within the status hierarchy, together with concerns about technological advantages

---

[3]   The definitions varied over time. The variability of the two-power standard actually allowed governments and parliamentarians to choose the definition and interpretation that served their argument at best (Bell, 2000: 3–6).

(Hobson, 2002: 25–44), which all heightened after the launch of HMS *Dreadnought* (Keefer, 2016: 262–8) that led to the dynamics of the global arms competition between 1889 and 1914 and is reflected in the contemporary perception of the 'cold war'. The competition was driven by status anxieties and status dissatisfaction and was therefore one expression of the belief in the power of status. While there were different contemporary perceptions about the effects of naval arms competition on the stability of the international system (Hobson, 2002: 39–57), these discussions about its influence and the attempts to end it through arms control (Keefer, 2016) indicate the relevance of this 'general multilateral competition' (Keefer, 2016: 4) to international security politics between 1889 and 1914. Naval power as relevant status marker or the 'mania for a fleet', as one critic called it (Snowden, 1914: 2134) not only influenced the naval policies of, and competition among, the great powers, but involved middle and small powers in the same way (Grant, 2007: 116–34, 146–69; Keefer, 2016: 4–8, 140–58). As far as the great powers are concerned, when arms competition started in 1889 (Parkinson, 2008: 5), the stable status order began to move. The bipolar naval rivalry between Great Britain and France began to influence the whole group of great powers due to the rise in the significance of naval power. This gave rise to a particular dynamic. It does not mean that all the great powers were equally involved at all times in direct competition with each other throughout the whole period (Bönker, 2012: 2; Osterhammel, 2009: 676), nevertheless, as the competition was about relative standing within the naval hierarchy and technological advantages, even bipolar competition or races influenced the competition within the whole group.

As the competition was about status and relative standing, the question is, what effect did the comparative practices outlined earlier have on naval arms competition? Recent research has denied the influence of comparative practices on the Anglo–German dreadnought race due to their role as instruments in the political mobilization process rather than as the main basis for Great Britain's decision to build a certain number of *Dreadnought*-type battleships and battle cruisers (Rose, 2011). However, I argue that the perception of relative naval strength was not the only driving force behind the naval arms competition, but that the status hierarchy assessed through naval force comparisons and the practice of self-comparison itself, due to its mobilizing effect, were drivers too. This does not mean that comparisons automatically intensified competition. They equally had the potential to end the direct competition between two or more competitors. I want to further substantiate my argument about the influence of status comparisons on the naval competition from two perspectives: an analytical perspective based on recent research on rankings and the British contemporary reflection on naval standards.

The research on rankings during recent decades has shown that rankings are a driver behind competitive dynamics (Brankovic et al, 2018: 270). Rankings are regularly published, visualized and quantified zero-sum comparisons that '[produce] status competition between the ranked entities' (Brankovic et al, 2018: 276). An 'imagined public', relativity, the scarcity of status, shared understandings about valued goods and the unit of comparison as well as 'actors' perception and motivations' all contribute to competitive dynamics triggered by rankings (Brankovic et al, 2018: 284). Although the status comparisons and naval standards studied in this chapter are at best proto-rankings, the research on rankings helps us to think about the effects of comparisons on the naval competition. First, there was the shared understanding that battleships were the means to measure naval power and assess the status hierarchy, which contributed to the effect that emerged from the comparisons. Second, for most of the period, the status comparisons and naval standards were zero-sum, meaning that there could be only one supreme naval power (Great Britain) and the ranks within the hierarchy were not shared. This only changed after the First World War when, due to financial struggles and the fear of a new arms race, Great Britain was willing not only to share the position of the supreme naval power with the United States, which publicly claimed its goal of having a navy 'second to none' in 1916, but to codify this status equality in a legally binding agreement at the Washington conference in 1922 which settled the 'peaceful transition' (Schake, 2017) of naval supremacy (Bell, 2000: 618; Maurer, 2021; Tooze, 2014: 394–407). Third, the quantification of the status hierarchy in terms of the number and/or tonnage of battleships and cruisers that had previously been subject to the 'sense of place', in combination with the visualization of the hierarchy in tables, diagrams (for example, Nauticus, 1899: 357–8; Office of Naval Intelligence, 1909; Hythe, 1913: 79, 88) and graphic portrayals (for example Neuhaus–Wilmersdorf, 1906: 210) encouraged the powers to pursue naval build-ups in order to alter or maintain their relative positions and to enhance or maintain the status and security they derived from naval power. Comparisons were not only a means to assess relative standing but served as a powerful tool to illustrate that a country's status position was in danger or had not been reached yet. Fourth, it was the publication of these comparisons (some of them, like *Brassey's Naval Annual* or the German *Nauticus*, annually[4]) in combination with the expectation evoked in the public and among policy makers that status as a naval power was imperative

---

[4]   *Brassey's Naval Annual* was published between 1886 and 1992, the title changed over the years (Ranft, 1986: v–vi). The *Jahrbuch für Deutschlands Seeinteressen*, which was commonly known under the title *Nauticus* after its editor, was published anonymously by the German Imperial Naval Office between 1899 and 1914 (Bönker, 2012: 209).

for the future of the nation and empire in general, and a specific rank was achieved or preserved in particular, that fuelled competitive dynamics.

However, comparisons did not automatically intensify the competitive dynamics or escalate competition into an arms race. On the one hand, it was the rationale behind the comparisons that determined whether status comparisons and naval standards had an impact on armaments policies and the intensification or escalation of competition. It was the shared idea that naval power and the naval hierarchy were important for great power status and political and diplomatic influence in peacetime that led to references to the status hierarchy, depicted in comparisons and codified status claims as benchmarks, influencing governments, parliamentarians and the 'imagined' public in favour of voting for ship building funds. Without this rationale the warning that, without further ship building the country's rank in the status hierarchy would either be in danger or would not have been reached yet, as demonstrated through comparisons, would have made no sense. On the other hand, there were several other, often interlocking factors (Buzan and Herring, 1998) such as technological change, reactions to the change in alliances or external threats, the expectations of public opinion, the decision to employ the 'strategy of armaments' (Hobson, 2002: 39–44) that brought about intensified competition or the arms race, and increased the influence of the military-industrial complex or domestic struggles over financial resources (Rose, 2011).

Last but not least, the naval standards as codified status aspirations or even a codified status hierarchy not only had the potential to get a spiral of reciprocal armament going, as was at least implied in the standards and the status comparisons, there was also the possibility that they might contribute to the stabilization of the system. In combination with expectations evoked in the public and parliament that they had to be met (Morgan-Owen, 2021: 413), the standards were a strong motivation for further build-ups, for example during the Anglo–German naval race between 1906 and 1912. No matter what the reason for the initial decision to enter into competition had been, the moment it was ongoing, comparisons contributed to the specific dynamic that kept the competition running (Hobson, 2002: 44). The Anglo–German naval race is, however, also an example of standards being able to end an arms race and stabilize relations at least for some time either informally or formally. In the Anglo–German case, the informal reciprocal acceptance of the 10:16 (in British terms) or 2:3 (in German terms) ratio for new construction ended the arms race, but not the competition, although no formal agreement was ever made (Epkenhans, 2007). A second example would be the formal Anglo–American codification of the status hierarchy after the First World War mentioned earlier.

The possibility of naval standards intensifying or easing competition was also reflected in the contemporary British perceptions of the impact of naval standards. Both positions were of course highly embedded in the debate on naval expenditure, and the political struggle for influence and political positions. On the one hand, there were those who believed that naval standards prevented competition and arms races because they deterred others from competing with Great Britain. The standards made it clear to every other nation that competition with Great Britain was useless because British naval policy was bound to a definite standard which showed that Great Britain was absolutely determined to keep its supremacy (see Chamberlain, 1893: 1876–7). The two-power standard, for example, not only expressed the British claim to naval supremacy, it was also a quantitative expression of the belief that the British building programme of 1889 would end the arms race that loomed on the horizon before it actually began (for example, Hamilton, 1889: 1190–1; Goschen, 1889: 1195).

On the other hand, based on the perception that armaments only led to armaments, the naval standards were perceived as a driver behind the naval competition due to an action–reaction model. In 1889, Henry Labouchere (Liberal) for example understood the two-power standard as 'a gauntlet thrown down to Europe, threatening, in effect, that "whatever you spend we will spend double"' (Labouchere, 1889: 1299). In the perception of Labouchere and others, the consequence, however, was not an end to the naval competition, but an intensification of it (Cremer, 1893: 1886; Labouchere, 1895: 1295; Robertson, 1899: 1012). With regard to the status hierarchy, many of those who believed that armaments only led to more armaments, not only in Great Britain, but, for example, also in Germany and the United States, further argued that all the build-ups and the money spent were useless, because 'in the end the relation between us and the other powers would be the same as it was before this competition began' (Labouchere, 1896: 488; see also Carnegie, 1909: 3; Richter, 1899: 3368).

Conclusion

Historical evidence clearly shows that referring to status comparisons and naval standards was a highly relevant legitimization practice in the political debates to secure funds for the navy. They were further perceived as an important means to make use of naval power in peace and to fight the 'cold war' that contemporaries were convinced they were experiencing. In both contexts the underlying rationale was that status as a naval power and standing within the status hierarchy mattered if a great power were to exert influence and to assert its interests in diplomatic negotiations and the distribution of the world. These comparisons, however, which shaped naval security politics between 1889 and 1922, did so not necessarily through an objective assessment of relative naval strength, which was quite difficult, but because of their influence on the perception of the current and future distribution of status as well as perceptions of power and security that were not primarily dealt with in this chapter.

These comparisons and standards further influenced naval arms competition because this competition was fuelled first of all by status concerns and relative standing within the status hierarchy of the naval powers. Second, status comparisons were used as a prime means to mobilize for new ship construction, which, in turn, kept the arms competition going. Whether or not these comparisons and standards were able to intensify competition or enabled an arms race, however, depended on the influence the rationale of naval power as a status marker had within a country and on several other factors, of which financial capabilities and the deliberate decision to embark on competitive build-ups were the most important. Although there was a tendency for comparisons to intensify the competition and rivalry among the great powers, there are examples where comparisons and standards were able to constrain bilateral competition. The latter was, for example, the case in France after the turn of the century, when Great Britain, due to its supremacy, no longer served as a 'useful element of comparison' for French battleship strength (Bos, 1905). A second example is to be found in the few years after the First World War when the will to end the looming arms race before it started was so strong a motivation in Great Britain that it agreed to the codification of equality with the United States at the Washington conference.

References

Admiralty (ed) (1906) *Fleets. Great Britain and Foreign Countries*, London: Eyre and Spottiswoode.

Albert, M. and Langer, K. (2020) 'Die Geschichte des Streitkräftevergleichs in der internationalen Politik: Machtvergleiche und die Macht des Vergleichens', *Zeitschrift für Internationale Beziehungen*, 27(2): 34–64.

Alfaro-Zaforteza, C. (2019) 'The age of empire, 1870–1914', in A. James, C. Alfaro-Zaforteza and M.H. Murfett (eds) *European Navies and the Conduct of War*, Abingdon, New York, NY: Routledge, pp 130–56.

Ashmead-Bartlett, E. (1889) Speech, 6 May, *Hansard* [Parliamentary Debates. House of Commons] III/335.

Bell, C.M. (2000) *The Royal Navy, Seapower and Strategy between the Wars*, Basingstoke: Palgrave Macmillan.

Bell, C.M. (2012) *Churchill and Sea Power*, Oxford: Oxford University Press.

Beresford, C. (1910) Speech, 14 March, *Hansard* [Parliamentary Debates. House of Commons] V/15.

Bernstein, E. (1914) Speech, 15 May, *Stenographische Berichte des Reichstags* 295.

Bienaimé, A. (1909) Speech, 6 July, *Journal officiel de la République française* [Débats Parlementaires/Chambre] 1909.

Bönker, D. (2012) *Militarism in a Global Age. Naval Ambitions in Germany and the United States before World War I*, Ithaca, NY: Cornell University Press.

Bos, C. (1904) 'Rapport fait au nom de la commission du budget chargée d'examiner le projet de loi portant fixation du budget général de l'exercice 1905 (Ministère de la marine)', *Journal officiel de la République française* [Documents Parlementaires/Chambre] 1904, Annexe No. 1951.

Bos, C. (1905) 'Rapport fait au nom de la commission du budget chargée d'examiner le projet de loi portant fixation du budget général de l'exercice 1906 (Ministère de la marine)', *Journal officiel de la République française* [Documents Parlementaires/Chambre] 1905, Annexe No. 2666.

Brailsford, H.N. (1918) *The War of Steel and Gold. A Study of the Armed Peace* (10th edn), London: G. Bell & Sons, Ltd.

Brankovic, J., Ringel, L. and Werron, T. (2018) 'How rankings produce competition: the case of global university rankings', *Zeitschrift für Soziologie*, 47(4): 270–88.

Buchanan, T. (1904) Speech, 29 February, *Hansard* [Parliamentary Debates. House of Commons] IV/130.

Buzan, B. and Herring, E. (1998) *The Arms Dynamic in World Politics*, London: Lynne Rienner.

Carnegie, A. (1909) *The Path to Peace. Reprinted from the London "Times" of June 19, 1909* (slightly revised), New York, NY: The Peace Society of the City of New York.

Chamberlain, J. (1893) Speech, 19 December, *Hansard* [Parliamentary Debates. House of Commons] IV/19.

Chaumet, C. (1907) 'Rapport fait au nom de la commission du budget chargée d'examiner le projet de loi portant fixation du budget général de l'exercice 1908 (Ministère de la marine)', *Journal officiel de la République française* [Documents Parlementaires/Chambre] 1907, Annexe No. 1235.

Chaumet, C. (1908) 'Rapport fait au nom de la commission du budget chargée d'examiner le projet de loi portant fixation du budget général de l'exercice 1909 (Ministère de la marine)', *Journal officiel de la République française* [Documents Parlementaires/Chambre] 1908, Annexe No. 2020.

Chautemps, E. (1891) Speech, 7 December, *Journal officiel de la République française* [Débats Parlementaires/Chambre], 1891.

Chicago Daily Tribune (1899) 'Comparative Naval Strength of Nations', *Chicago Daily Tribune*, 29 January, p 37.

Cremer, W. (1893) Speech, 19 December, *Hansard* [Parliamentary Debates. House of Commons] IV/19.

Daily News (1898) 'Judged by results. Lord Salisbury's foreign policy. Speech by Sir W. Harcourt', *Daily News*, 9 May, p 8.

De Dompierre d'Hornoy, C. (1889) Speech, 17 June, *Journal officiel de la République française* [Débats Parlementaires/Chambre] 1889.

Delbrück, H. (1899 [1902]) 'Zukunftskrieg und Zukunftsfriede', in H. Delbrück (ed) *Erinnerungen. Aufsätze und Reden*, Berlin: Georg Stilke, pp 498–525.

Dülffer, J. (2003) 'Vom europäischen Mächtesystem zum Weltstaatensystem um die Jahrhundertwende', in J. Dülffer *Im Zeichen der Gewalt. Frieden und Krieg im 19. und 20. Jahrhundert* (edited by M. Kröger, U. Soénius and S. Wunsch), Köln: Böhlau, pp 49–65.

Epkenhans, M. (1991) *Die wilhelminische Flottenrüstung 1908–1914. Weltmachtstreben, industrieller Fortschritt, soziale Integration*, München: Oldenbourg.

Epkenhans, M. (1992) 'Seemacht = Weltmacht. Alfred T. Mahan und sein Einfluß auf die Seestrategie des 19. und 20. Jahrhunderts', in J. Elvert, J. Jensen and M. Salewski (eds) *Kiel, die Deutschen und die See*, Stuttgart: Steiner, pp 35–47.

Epkenhans, M. (2007) 'Was a peaceful outcome thinkable? The naval race before 1914', in H. Afflerbach and D. Stevenson (eds) *An Improbable War. The Outbreak of World War I and European Political Culture before 1914*, New York, NY: Berghahn, pp 113–29.

EMG (État-Major Général) (1909) 'Quelle doit être la composition de la flotte en cuirassés, croiseurs-cuirassés, croiseurs protégés, contre-torpilleurs, torpilleurs, sous-marins et autres bâtiments?', in *SHD, MV* [Marine Vincennes], BB8 2424/13.

Goschen, G. (1889) Speech, 07 March, *Hansard* [Parliamentary Debates. House of Commons] III/333.

Grant, J.A. (2007) *Rulers, Guns, and Money. The Global Arms Trade in the Age of Imperialism*, Cambridge, MA: Harvard University Press.

Hahn, O. (1892) Speech, 29 February, *Stenographische Berichte des Reichstags* 120.

Hamilton, G. (1889) Speech, 07 March, *Hansard* [Parliamentary Debates. House of Commons] III/333.

Haußmann, C. (1891) Speech, 09 March, *Stenographische Berichte des Reichstags* 116.

HC Deb (1909a) 16 March, *Hansard* [Parliamentary Debates. House of Commons] V/2.

HC Deb (1909b) 17 March, *Hansard* [Parliamentary Debates. House of Commons] V/2.

HC Deb (1909c) 18 March, *Hansard* [Parliamentary Debates. House of Commons] V/2.

Hobson, R. (2002) *Imperialism at Sea. Naval Strategic Thought, the Ideology of Sea Power, and the Tirpitz Plan, 1875–1914*, Boston, MA: Brill.

Hollweg, C. (1921) 'Seemacht', *Deutsche Allgemeine Zeitung*, 23 November, p 1.

Hythe, V. (1912) 'Comparative strength/Comparative tables', *The Naval Annual*, (1912): 69–90.

Hythe, V. (1913) 'Comparative strength/Comparative tables', *The Naval Annual*, (1913): 76–96.

Jaschob, L. (2018) *Status im internationalen System. Das Deutsche Reich und sein Statusstreben in Europa 1890–1914*, Baden-Baden: Tectum Verlag.

Johnson, M. (2011) 'The liberal party and the navy league in Britain before the great war', *Twentieth Century British History*, 22(2): 137–63.

Keefer, S.A. (2016) *The Law of Nations and Britain's Quest for Naval Security. International Law and Arms Control, 1898–1914*, Cham: Springer International Publishing.

Kennedy, P.M. (1980) *The Rise of the Anglo-German Antagonism, 1860–1914*, London: Allen & Unwin.

Labouchere, H. (1889) Speech, 06 May, *Hansard* [Parliamentary Debates. House of Commons] III/335.

Labouchere, H. (1895) Speech, 18 March, *Hansard* [Parliamentary Debates. House of Commons] IV/31.

Labouchere, H. (1896) Speech, 09 March, *Hansard* [Parliamentary Debates. House of Commons] IV/38.

Lambert, A.D. (2018) *Seapower States. Maritime Culture, Continental Empires and the Conflict That Made the Modern World*, New Haven, CT: Yale University Press.

Larson, D., Paul, T.V. and Wohlforth, W.C. (2014) 'Status and world order', in T.V. Paul, D. Larson and W.C. Wohlforth (eds) *Status in World Politics*, Cambridge: Cambridge University Press, pp 3–29.

Le Moigne, A. (1900) 'Rapport fait au nom de la commission de la marine chargée d'examiner: 1° le projet de loi relatif à l'augmentation de la flotte; 2° la proposition de loi de M. Fleury-Ravaria sur le même objet', *Journal officiel de la République française* [Documents Parlementaires/Chambre] 1900, Annexe No. 1599.

Lebow, R.N. (2008) *A Cultural Theory of International Relations*, Cambridge: Cambridge University Press.

Lee, A. (1912) Speech, 22 July, *Hansard* [Parliamentary Debates. House of Commons] V/41.

Mackinder, H. (1912) Speech, 22 July, *Hansard* [Parliamentary Debates. House of Commons] V/41.

Mahan, A. (1910) 'Britain and the world's peace', *Daily Mail*, 31 October, p 8.

Marder, A. (1940) *The Anatomy of British Sea Power. A History of British Naval Policy in the Pre-Dreadnought Era, 1880–1905*, New York, NY: Alfred A. Knopf.

Marder, A. (2013) *From the Dreadnought to Scapa Flow. The Royal Navy in the Fisher Era 1904–1919* (1st vol), Barnsley: Seaforth Publishing Pen & Sword Books Ltd.

Masson, P. (2002) *La Puissance Maritime et Navale au XXe Siècle*, Paris: Le Grand livre du mois.

Maurer, J.H. (2021) 'David Lloyd George and the American naval challenge: Great Britain and the Washington Conference', *Diplomacy & Statecraft*, 32(2): 310–29.

McCranie, K.D. (2021) *Mahan, Corbett, and the Foundations of Naval Strategic Thought*, La Vergne, TN: Naval Institute Press.

Middlemore, J. (1912) Speech, 24 July, *Hansard* [Parliamentary Debates. House of Commons] V/41.

Morgan-Owen, D. (2021) 'Strategy, rationality, and the idea of public opinion in Britain, 1870–1914', *Historical Research*, 94(264): 397–418.

Mullins, R.E. (2016) *The Transformation of British and American Naval Policy in the Pre-Dreadnought Era. Ideas, Culture and Strategy*, edited by J. Beeler, Cham: Springer International Publishing.

Murray, M. (2019) *The Struggle for Recognition in International Relations*, Oxford: Oxford University Press.

Nauticus (ed) (1899) *Jahrbuch für Deutschlands Seeinteressen*, Berlin: Mittler und Sohn.

Nauticus (ed) (1907) *Jahrbuch für Deutschlands Seeinteressen*, Berlin: Mittler und Sohn.

Neuhaus-Wilmersdorf, E. (1906) 'Die Seeinteressen des Deutschen Reiches', *Illustrierte Zeitung*, 08 February, pp 208–11.

Office of Naval Intelligence (ed) (1909) *Information Concerning Some of the Principal Navies of the World: A Series of Tables Compiled to Answer Popular Inquiry*, Washington DC: Government Printing Office.

Osterhammel, J. (2009) *Die Verwandlung der Welt. Eine Geschichte des 19. Jahrhunderts*, München: Beck.

Painlevé, P. (1911) 'Rapport fait au nom de la commission du budget chargée d'examiner le projet de loi pourtant fixation du budget générale de l'exercice 1912 (ministère de la marine)', *Journal officiel de la République française* [Documents Parlementaires/Chambre] 1911, Annexe No. 1244.

Parkinson, R. (2008) *Late Victorian Navy. The Pre-Dreadnought Era and the Origins of the First World War*, Suffolk: Boydell Press.

Pouliot, V. (2016) *International Pecking Orders. The Politics and Practice of Multilateral Diplomacy*, Cambridge: Cambridge University Press.

Pretyman, E. (1904) Speech, 04 August, *Hansard* [Parliamentary Debates. House of Commons] IV/139.

Ranft, B. (ed) (1986) *Ironclad to Trident. 100 Years of Defence Commentary, Brassey's 1886–1986. Centenary Vol. of Brassey's Naval Annual*, London: Brassey's Defence Publishers

Rassow, H. (1901) *Deutschlands Seemacht* (10th edn), Elberfeld: Baedeker'sche Buch- und Kunsthandlung u. Buchdruckerei, in Bundesarchiv RM 3/9816.

Renshon, J. (2017) *Fighting for Status. Hierarchy and Conflict in World Politics*, Princeton, NJ: Princeton University Press.

Richter, E. (1899) Speech, 14 December, *Stenographische Berichte des Reichstags* 168.

Rickert, H. (1890a) Speech, 10 January, *Stenographische Berichte des Reichstags* 112.

Rickert, H. (1890b) Speech, 9 January, *Stenographische Berichte des Reichstags* 112.

Robertson, E. (1899) Speech, 16 March, *Hansard* [Parliamentary Debates. House of Commons] IV/68.

Ropp, T. (1987) *The Development of a Modern Navy. French Naval Policy, 1871–1904*, edited by S. Roberts, Annapolis, MD: United States Naval Institute.

Rose, A. (2011) *Zwischen Empire und Kontinent. Britische Außenpolitik vor dem Ersten Weltkrieg*, München: Oldenbourg Wissenschaftsverlag.

Rousseau, A. (1908) 'Enquête Maritime. La situation navale', *Le Temps*, 13 May, p. 1.

Rowlands, K. (2019*) Naval Diplomacy for the 21st Century. A Model for the Post-Cold War Global Order*, London: Routledge.

Rüger, J. (2007) *The Great Naval Game. Britain and Germany in the Age of Empire*, Cambridge: Cambridge University Press.

Schake, K. (2017) *Safe Passage. The Transition from British to American Hegemony*, Cambridge, MA: Harvard University Press.

Snowden, P. (1914) Speech, 18 March, *Hansard* [Parliamentary Debates. House of Commons] V/59.

Sondhaus, L. (1997) *Preparing for Weltpolitik. German Sea Power before the Tirpitz Era*, Annapolis, MD: Naval Institute Press.

Stein, O. (2007) *Die deutsche Heeresrüstungspolitik 1890–1914. Das Militär und der Primat der Politik*, Paderborn: Schöningh.

Steinmetz, W. (2019) 'Introduction. Concepts and practices of comparison in modern history', in W. Steinmetz (ed) *The Force of Comparison. A New Perspective on Modern European History and the Contemporary World*, New York: Berghahn, pp 1–32.

Thomson, G. (1906) Speech, 22 November, *Journal officiel de la République française* [Débats Parlementaires/Chambre] 1906.

Thomson, G. (1909) Speech, 16 July, *Journal officiel de la République française* [Débats Parlementaires/Chambre] 1909.

Tooze, J.A. (2014) *The Deluge. The Great War, America and the Remaking of the Global Order, 1916–1931*, London: Lane.

von Bennigsen, R. (1891) Speech, 07 March, *Stenographische Berichte des Reichstags* 116.

von Hollmann, F. (1891) Speech, 07 March, *Stenographische Berichte des Reichstags* 116.

von Tirpitz, A. (1896) Letter to Albrecht von Stosch, 13 February, in V. Berghahn and W. Deist (eds) (1988) *Rüstung im Zeichen der wilhelminischen Weltpolitik. Grundlegende Dokumente 1890–1914*, Düsseldorf: Droste, pp 114–17.

Walser, R. (1992) *France's Search for a Battle Fleet. Naval Policy and Naval Power 1898–1914*, New York, NY: Garland.

11

Force Comparison and Conventional Arms Control at the End of the East–West Conflict

Hans-Joachim Schmidt

Introduction

This chapter looks at how comparative practices interact with security governance, using as an example the negotiations for the Treaty on Conventional Armed Forces in Europe (CFE Treaty). The aim of these negotiations was to regulate the conventional military balance in Europe and the agreed means to do so were quantitative limits for key weapon systems. Comparisons of relative military capabilities were accordingly central to the negotiations on the arms control framework.

By examining the political disputes shaping the negotiations on the CFE Treaty, this chapter provides insights into both how comparative knowledge is produced and how it shapes security politics. To illustrate the production of comparative knowledge, the chapter shows how the members of the North Atlantic Treaty Organization (NATO) and the Warsaw Treaty Organization (WTO) step by step negotiated a common comparative framework comprising, in particular, definitions of key weapon systems, counting rules, statistics of actual holdings of these weapon systems as well as limits for future holdings. With regard to the effects of comparative practices, the chapter highlights a complex interplay between these practices, the governance frameworks with which they were intertwined and the political changes that these frameworks were meant to manage. The initial assessment was that the military situation was characterized by an imbalance favouring the WTO and that equal limits for NATO and the WTO would remedy the problem. Soon, however, the political changes brought about by the end of the Cold War – in particular the peaceful unification of Germany, the dissolution of the WTO and the end of the Soviet Union – raised new problems for the negotiators, prompting changes both in the arms control framework and the comparative practices underpinning it, notably a redefinition of the notion of parity and a shift from alliance limits to national limits.

The initial assessment: a conventional imbalance

Military force comparisons between NATO and the WTO gained in importance after the Soviet invasion of Afghanistan in the winter of 1979/80. In the US, the Pentagon used this military aggression to exaggerate the Soviet Union's regional (particularly in Europe) and global military strength in its publications on 'Soviet Military Power' in 1981 and between 1983 and 1991. The Soviet Union answered with its own one-sided military force comparisons in 1982, 1984 and 1987 that were meant to demonstrate the global military superiority of the US and NATO (see Soviet Union Ministry of Defence, 1987). In addition, NATO published two military force comparisons in 1982 and 1984 under the title 'NATO and the Warsaw Pact: Force Comparisons' with a more balanced but still one-sided view, as Gaby Schlag shows in Chapter 4 of this volume. Both the Pentagon and NATO particularly emphasized the quantitative conventional military superiority of Soviet and WTO forces as a central concern for military stability and security in Europe.

Several years before, two formats of arms control talks had been launched in the context of the détente process of the Conference on Security and Co-operation in Europe (CSCE) talks between 1973 and 1975. The first were the negotiations on Mutual and Balanced Force Reductions (MBFR) in Central Europe[1]; the second the negotiations on military Confidence Building Measures (CBMs) for the whole of Europe including all neutral and non-aligned countries and the deployed forces of US and Canada. In the 1980s, the CBM talks were thematically broadened and renamed the Confidence and Security Building Measures (CSBMs) talks.

After his election as General Secretary of the Communist Party of the Soviet Union, Mikhail Gorbachev started reforms under the new labels of glasnost and perestroika. To get the necessary financial flexibility for these reforms, he strove to reduce the immense costs of the arms race between East and West. In 1986 his government and all other WTO members accepted

---

[1] The MBFR negotiations related to forces stationed in four NATO countries (Belgium, Luxemburg, Netherlands and West Germany) and in four WTO countries (Czechoslovakia, East Germany, Hungary and Poland). Guided by the principle of parity, the West demanded asymmetric reductions of soldiers towards common ceilings and the East demanded symmetric reductions of soldiers to preserve its military doctrine of conventional superiority.

the Stockholm Agreement on CSBMs with politically binding measures and, as an entirely new feature, on-site inspections. In 1988, the legally binding Intermediate-Range Nuclear Force Treaty (INF Treaty) entered into force, stipulating the complete worldwide disarmament of all Soviet and US land-based nuclear-capable missiles with an intermediate range (defined as 500 to 5,500 km). This enhanced nuclear stability and security in Europe. With the treaty, the Soviet Union for the first time agreed to asymmetric reductions. The treaty was complemented by the voluntary withdrawal or dismantlement of nearly all land-based tactical nuclear missiles (Lance, Hades, FROG, SS-12, Pershing 1) belonging to the two alliances in Europe.

But the strong conventional imbalance with its negative consequences for stability and security still existed. In 1987 the members of NATO and the WTO initiated negotiations on a mandate for new conventional arms control efforts for the whole of Europe defined as the area from the Atlantic to the Urals. These negotiations led to a convergence of the comparative practices of the two military alliances (Hartmann et al, 1994: 25–6). The two sides selected five major weapon systems – namely tanks, artillery systems, armoured combat vehicles, combat aircraft and combat helicopters – as central elements for the comparison of conventional military land and air power and published statistical data relating to them. This rapprochement facilitated conventional arms control and disarmament. At the end of 1988, Gorbachev announced the unilateral withdrawal of five Soviet divisions from the German Democratic Republic (GDR; 25 per cent of all Soviet divisions in the GDR), thus signalling that he was ready to reduce the conventional imbalance. Moreover, he accepted the principle of parity between both alliances in the Mandate for Negotiations on Conventional Armed Forces in Europe concluded on 10 January 1989 (Hartmann et al, 1994: 5, 19–20).

In parallel, the MBFR talks were concluded. Although they ended without an agreement, these talks had contributed to the Soviet policy change just mentioned. They established for the first time a permanent communication channel to discuss military security and stability and were repeatedly used for other purposes if no other communication channel was suitable or available (Boysen, 1986: 500–501). The talks provided a forum where both sides could explain their ideas and views about military security and stability and answer questions from the other side. This helped to expand mutual understanding and to establish some kind of trust. The West had introduced the principle of military parity in these talks.

However, the CFE negotiations from March 1989 to the full ratification of the CFE Treaty in November 1992 not only faced the political challenge of overcoming the quantitative conventional imbalance between NATO and WTO. They soon also had to deal with the implications of the peaceful unification of the two German states, each of them in a different alliance, and the dissolution of the WTO. This had a deep impact on the principles, norms, rules and procedures of the CFE Treaty.

Such strong political challenges could have hampered or even ruptured arms control. This was not the case with the CFE talks. The political and military interest in the treaty on both sides was too high, though for different reasons: NATO countries wanted to end the destabilizing Soviet conventional military superiority in Europe whereas the Soviet Union was no longer able to preserve this military advantage for political, economic and financial reasons and therefore sought to establish a new modus vivendi with NATO countries based on the principle of parity and the norm of a stable and secure balance of forces at a lower level (50 per cent below the sum of all conventional land forces) between both alliances. This way, the CFE talks defined a new performance standard for the future European security order.

Force comparison and arms control

As the editors point out in the introduction to this volume, comparisons can be used for different kinds of assessments. Arms control negotiations such as the CFE talks intertwine two types: performance assessments and distribution assessments. The participating states evaluate the military balance in terms of their potential military performances should they enter a war against each other. But to regulate the military balance, they generally operationalize abstract performance standards (for example, a principle of parity) through distributional rules for a select number of weapon systems deemed crucial for military performances in case of a war (for example, equal limits for certain weapon systems).

Force comparisons – that is, comparisons of military power in the sense of probable military performances – are a complex task. They involve not only counting weapon systems and soldiers, but also have to factor in aspects such as military doctrines, political intentions as regards the use of force as well as qualitative factors such as the quality of weapon systems, the quality of command-and-control systems and the morale of the soldiers.

Arms control sets special conditions for force comparisons. For arms control, only those military items can be identified and counted that have sufficient visible differences to other categories and weapons, otherwise their identification and verification is impossible. This was no problem for CFE because the size and the differences of the selected weapon categories and systems were huge enough.

Arms control, therefore, always covers only a selective part of military power. Doctrines and many qualitative military factors are usually omitted because they are either less visible, even invisible, or difficult to define and evaluate in an objective and intersubjective way for arms control purposes. But it would be wrong to say that arms control cannot cover qualitative factors in a force comparison. The selection of weapon categories and systems and the negotiation of detailed definitions for them always captures the qualitative aspects of military items as well. In connection with the envisioned goals of arms control the acts of selection and definition amount to a statement about what is militarily and politically valued. In the case of CFE, the military and political value of the five selected weapon categories (main battle tanks, armoured combat vehicles (ACVs), artillery pieces of 100 mm calibre and above, attack helicopters and combat aircraft) was high because both alliances regarded these weapon categories as the major elements in the conventional military strength of their land and air forces. After the signature of CFE and the publication of statistics on the five weapon categories (and some additional subcategories[2]), the agreed categories became the new definitions underpinning regular military force comparisons such as the International Institute for Strategic Studies' *The Military Balance* in the following years.

This points to another important difference between military force comparisons and arms control. Military force comparisons often involve an element of uncertainty that can be used to strengthen deterrence. Arms control tries to reduce uncertainty and wants to strengthen security by increasing transparency, accountability and stability. Peace is then based on trust rather than unstable deterrence. If successful, arms control talks lead to informal, political or legal agreements. The higher their political and military value, the higher the political status of the military balance codified in such agreements even if the real military balance looks different. When military threat perceptions wane, military force comparisons can lose their value and perhaps even cease to be undertaken. This raises the question: Can common weapons definitions agreed during arms control negotiations alter previous practices of military force comparison and even be used to reshape the military security agenda of European states?

Which weapon systems are covered, limited, reduced or disarmed in which area of application depends on the goals that states are pursuing through arms control negotiations. In contrast to the previous MBFR talks, the area of application covered the entire land territory from the Atlantic to the Ural Mountains including all European islands of the CFE states parties (see article 2 (B), in OSCE, 1990: 3). This definition underscores that maritime forces were excluded from the talks and thereby the major

---

[2] The category 'armoured combat vehicle' was divided into three subcategories (armoured personnel carrier, armoured infantry fighting vehicle and heavy armament combat vehicle). The category of combat helicopter was divided into two subcategories (attack helicopter and combat support helicopter). The subcategory attack helicopter was further divided into specialized attack helicopter and multi-purpose attack helicopter (see OSCE, 1990: 2–6).

military advantage of NATO as a maritime alliance. This was justified by the argument that maritime forces cannot be used to conquer and hold foreign land territory. The jointly selected and defined five weapon categories covered the most important weapon systems of land and air forces. Because the WTO was, in contrast to NATO, first and foremost a land power, its most important military weapon systems in Europe were covered by the treaty. This asymmetric military outcome favoured NATO and underlined that Soviet political power was weaker.

The main goal of CFE was to prevent the 'launch of surprise attacks' and the start of 'large-scale offensive actions' between alliance forces (see OSCE, 1990: 1). For this purpose, the negotiators divided the territory of both alliances into three different regions starting from the centre of Europe with the lowest limitations for the three weapon categories (tanks, ACVs, artillery pieces) of land forces. The limitations were higher in the other two regions towards the Ural Mountains (for WTO) and towards the Atlantic (for NATO) thereby enhancing military stability. Additionally, a certain number of the weapons in these three categories were to be stored in 'designated permanent storage sites' in the three regions, in order to provide an early warning if they were ever activated and moved out of the storage sites. The fourth zone, the so-called 'flank' regions in the North and South of the area of application were separately limited to prevent the destabilizing transfer of weapons from the other three regions into the flanks. The two air force categories (attack helicopters, combat aircraft) were not placed under regional constraints because of their high mobility as flight systems.

As mentioned earlier, the initial goal was a stable and secure balance of forces at a lower level, defined as 50 per cent below the sum of all conventional forces, between both alliances. This included a 10 to 15 per cent reduction of NATO forces. By stipulating this goal, the CFE's mandate created a new shared performance standard. The question, though, was whether this standard would prevail in light of the political changes – in particular German unification, the dissolution of the Warsaw Pact, the end of the Soviet Union – that were beginning to unfold. How the CFE talks coped with the changes will be discussed in what follows.

From parity between military alliances to rough parity between NATO and the Soviet Union

German unification and the limitation of German armed forces

German unification raised four major questions for the CFE negotiations:

1. What would be the future military status of a unified Germany? The options discussed were neutrality outside any alliance, membership of

both alliances, membership in one alliance (NATO) or withdrawal from the military structure of NATO like Spain and France at that time.

2. Should the German armed forces be limited under either the CFE or the 2+4 Treaty?
3. What should be the overall personnel limit for the German armed forces?
4. How should stationed forces be limited, including those of the US, France, Great Britain and the Soviet Union in Berlin?

A neutral status similar to Austria's was not possible for Germany because of its history and its political, economic and military strength in the centre of Europe. The Soviet idea of a combined membership in both alliances was related to its interest in saving the Eastern alliance, but was a non-starter. Only the last two options were compatible with CFE. After some discussions, the Soviet Union accepted NATO membership for the unified Germany with one important constraint: NATO should not move its military structure into the former GDR in peace time. This is the origin of Russia's later criticism of NATO's Eastern enlargements.

The Soviet Union wanted to limit German armed forces in the 2+4 Treaty. But this would have singularized Germany too much and was therefore strongly opposed by the West German government and, in particular, by the US. West Germany argued for limitations in the context of CFE in order to reduce its singularization. In the end, a compromise was found. German forces were constrained in the CFE Treaty through two separate declarations by East and West Germany and these limitations were also mentioned in the 2+4 Treaty.

The overall size of the unified German armed forces was a matter of dispute. The Soviet Union demanded a limit of 200,000 to 250,000 soldiers. This was not acceptable to Germany because Chancellor Kohl wanted to preserve the conscription system and therefore needed a minimum strength of 300,000 men. The German Defence department wanted 400,000 to 420,000 soldiers. At the Kohl–Gorbachev Meeting in the Caucasus on 15–16 July 1990, Gorbachev accepted a German compromise proposal of 370,000 soldiers for all forces and 345,000 for land and air forces (see Kohl, 1990). However, personnel limits were not part of the CFE negotiations although Germany had tried hard to include them for a certain time in order to reduce its singularization. Consequently, it pressured the other CFE participants to accept legally binding national personnel limits for land and air forces in the CFE-1A negotiations which were completed in 1992. Because the US wanted only a politically binding CFE-1A agreement, Germany was the only CFE member that had to accept legally binding personnel limits for its forces, including a limit of 25,000 men for naval forces which were excluded from CFE. In the end, Germany thus had to accept some kind of singularization in return for support for its unification.

To pave the way for the complete withdrawal of all Soviet forces from East Germany, West Germany pushed for the withdrawal of the forces of all four powers (US, France, UK and Soviet Union) stationed in Berlin. Chancellor Kohl paid more than 12 billion Deutschmark for the accelerated Soviet withdrawal which was finished at the end of August 1994. Since then, the Eastern part of Germany has been free of stationed forces.

The successful negotiation of a peaceful unification between West Germany and East Germany, a former member of the Eastern alliance, had a tremendous impact on the desire of the other East European WTO member states to peacefully leave their alliance. It accelerated this process and raised the fear that the parity approach between the two alliances could collapse. The signing of the 2+4 Treaty on 12 September 1990 led to a growing interest on the part of the East European states in higher national limits because they wanted to leave the WTO.[3] And the Soviet Union redefined the original principle of parity between the two alliances as a balance between itself and NATO.

This outcome can be interpreted as a special regulation of the distribution of military forces geared towards alleviating fears about a stronger unified Germany in the centre of Europe. At the same time, the peaceful German unification undermined the alliance approach to the regulation of the distribution of military forces because it created an example for other WTO members wanting to leave their alliance. It thereby risked the new performance standard and its assessment. However, German willingness to exclude its new eastern part from NATO in peace time supported to a certain degree the new performance standard.

From alliance limits to limits for groups of states

The negotiations formally took place not between the two alliances, but between their various individual members. In the wake of the political changes mentioned earlier, the smaller members of the Eastern alliance increasingly wanted to leave the WTO and demanded the withdrawal of Soviet forces from their territory. This raised the question of whether the alliance approach to limitations still worked. On the one hand, Eastern states, particularly Czechoslovakia, Hungary and Romania opposed the alliance approach from February 1990 onwards. On the other hand, most other countries feared a breakdown of the talks if the alliance approach were to be changed. The compromise, proposed by the Eastern European participants, was to replace the term 'alliances' with 'groups of states'. This saved the

---

[3]   The WTO was formally dissolved in Prague on 1 July 1991. But it had de facto already broken up in mid-1990.

alliance approach, albeit in a more neutral way, and at the same time offered smaller WTO members the chance to distance themselves from their own alliance. Later, the national limitation approach was strengthened by the rule that changes in the national sub-limits within the groups of states were only possible with the consent of the respective states. The new term 'group of states' demonstrated that the performance standard had lost some value but could be still preserved. The growing importance of national limits at the same time heralded a shift in the distribution assessments.

Withdrawal of NATO proposals

US President Bush proposed on 29 May 1989 as an additional measure the reduction of American and Soviet forces stationed in Europe to a ceiling of 275,000 soldiers in order to accelerate the Soviet troop withdrawal from Eastern Europe (see Institute for Defense and Disarmament Studies, 1989: 407.B.175–9). This proposal was never repeated when it became clear that the WTO would dissolve and that the Soviet Union would soon be forced to withdraw all its forces from the other states parties of the Eastern group. However, the US government informally advised the Soviet and later Russian government regularly in advance about further reductions of its forces stationed in Europe. This must be seen as a further step towards weakening the Eastern military alliance and thus further undermining the new performance standard.

Increase of group limits in four weapon categories

Only the group limit of 20,000 tanks, which had been proposed by the West, was not changed during the negotiations. With regard to all other weapon categories, the first figures proposed by the West were raised to come closer to Eastern and/or Soviet demands. In the case of ACVs, NATO countries lifted their proposed limit from 28,000, which had been accepted by the WTO on 11 May 1989 (Institute for Defense and Disarmament Studies, 1989: 407.B.165–8), to 30,000 in December 1989 because they faced contradictory internal demands on the issue of light tanks. Italy wanted to include its light tanks in the category of tanks whereas France and Great Britain preferred to assign them to the category of ACVs. As the amount of these tanks was initially unclear, NATO raised its proposed limit, which the Soviet Union accepted in April 1990 (see Institute for Defense and Disarmament Studies, 1990a: 407.B.356). Later, it emerged that this increase was not really necessary and that the agreed limit was 1,800 vehicles above the actual Western holdings. However, the growing tensions within the Eastern group with regard to their national limits and reductions made it impossible to return to the original limit.

In the category of artillery, Western countries proposed a group limit of 16,500 items and the Eastern countries a group limit of 24,000. Additionally, the Soviet Union demanded the exclusion of its old T-10 and T-12 anti-tank guns which could also be used as artillery guns and the inclusion of the US recoilless 105 mm calibre anti-tank gun. In the end, all these weapon types were excluded and NATO countries accepted the WTO proposal of a limit of 20,000 items, which was 1,500 items above NATO's holdings. However, with German unification in October 1990, the unified country got 2,160 additional artillery pieces belonging to the former GDR forces, thus becoming the only NATO member that had to reduce the number of its artillery pieces.

NATO countries proposed 1,900 attack helicopters as the group limit in July 1989. The WTO members accepted this limit without clarifying the definitions and the counting rules in September 1989. Later the Eastern group proposed a 5 per cent increase to 2,000 in order to reduce the Soviet quota for the sufficiency rule from 40 to 37.5 per cent of all attack helicopters covered by the limit. The actual holdings were much lower: the Soviet Union possessed 1,481, the other members of the Eastern group 181 and the Western group 1,594 systems. The higher figure of the Western group may be one reason why the Soviet military finally demanded the exclusion of 100 Mi-24 R and K from the treaty limitations because they were unarmed and only used for the purpose of reconnaissance and targeting. NATO countries accepted this exceptional demand, thereby allowing the Eastern group a 5 per cent transgression of the helicopter limit. In this category, both sides tacitly agreed to dismantle no weapon systems.

The limitation of combat aircraft was complex and difficult because of the technical, structural and geostrategic asymmetries between Eastern and Western forces. For example, US forces had no trainer aircraft for basic training in Europe and all the fighters which protected its strategic forces were stationed in the United States. But all Soviet trainer aircraft for basic training were stationed in Europe and most of the fighters which protected its strategic forces too. This created a strong disadvantage for the Soviet Union if such forces were to be limited. Western air forces also had more dual-role fighter aircraft (fighter and attack role) whereas Soviet combat aircraft were equipped for one combat role. Additionally, Soviet land-based naval bombers were operating mainly against Western naval forces which were excluded by the CFE mandate. This explains why the Soviet Union initially wanted to limit only attack aircraft and to omit defensive fighters and all medium bombers. NATO countries, however, insisted on a limit on all attack aircraft, fighters, combat trainer aircraft and medium bombers including land-based naval bombers, arguing that their exclusion would facilitate attempts to circumvent the constraints. NATO countries proposed a group limit of 5,700 combat aircraft,

11 per cent below their own holdings of 6,400. The Soviet Union proposed a ceiling of 7,800 (excluding land-based naval bombers) and reduced it later to 6,950 systems omitting a large part of its trainer aircraft and demanding the reclassification and modification of combat trainer aircraft to unarmed trainer aircraft in order to minimize their reductions (Institute for Defense and Disarmament Studies, 1990b: 407.B.380). In the end, the West prevailed with some important exceptions. First, unarmed trainer aircraft for basic training were excluded from the treaty as demanded by the Eastern side. Second, the reclassification of Soviet combat trainer aircraft to unarmed trainer aircraft was allowed for up to 550 systems including up to 130 modern MiG 25 U within 40 months after the treaty entered into force. Third, land-based naval bombers were limited at 430 systems by a separate politically binding declaration outside the treaty, which fixed the Eastern holdings at that time. Soviet combat aircraft were finally confined to 5,150 systems with the common tacit understanding in October 1990 that the limit should be below the NATO holdings but come close to it. If adding the 550 combat trainer aircraft and 400 Soviet land-based naval bombers, the total becomes 6,100 aircraft, which was close to NATO's holdings of 6,400/5,923 systems.[4] But the Eastern side insisted on 6,800 systems for each group, a much higher figure surpassing Western holdings, in order to lower the Soviet percentage for the sufficiency rule to under 40 per cent of the total combat aircraft limit. However, with the dissolution of the WTO and the limitation of Soviet air forces this high group ceiling lost its value.

Increase of group limits for the sufficiency rule (Soviet limitations)

That the group limits lost their initial importance, mattered more for some states than for others. For NATO countries and the smaller members of the Eastern group, the constraints on Soviet forces became more important than Eastern group ceilings and they wanted these limits to be as low as possible. But for the Soviet Union, the value of Western group ceilings grew. The Soviet side was faced with a dilemma regarding its reduction liabilities. Because of its quantitative superiority, low Western (and Eastern) group limits would also mean higher costs for dismantling its own weapons. Therefore, it had an interest in ceilings beyond Western holdings as long as Soviet limits came close to NATO's actual holdings.

---

[4] In the first data exchange after the signature of the treaty the NATO countries together declared only 5,923 combat aircraft. This was due to the fact that the final counting rules for the treaty were not completely comparable with the figure of 6,400 from the last NATO force comparison. For example, roughly 130 land-based naval tactical combat aircraft were excluded by the definitions of the CFE Treaty (Dunay, 1991: 137).

Table 11.1: Sufficiency rule and its percentage of all limited forces

Weapon category	Soviet ceiling	% of all forces
Tanks	13,300	33.25
ACVs	20,000	33.33
Artillery	13,700	34.25
Combat aircraft	5,150	37.86
Attack helicopters	1,500	37.50

Source: Hartmann et al (1994: 354)

Note: These figures do not include the final lowering of Soviet ceilings by 150 tanks and 525 artillery pieces at the last meeting of the Eastern Disarmament Commission in Prague from 26–27 October 1990.

The means of constraining the size of the Soviet forces was the sufficiency rule. Its rationale was to impose limits on the Soviet Union, which possessed the numerically largest armed forces in the area of application. Most states agreed that no CFE participant should possess more than one third of all forces. NATO countries initially proposed figures of around 30 per cent to test the Soviet reformers under Gorbachev. The Eastern group proposed percentage figures between 32 and 40 per cent (see Dunay, 1991: 67). Following German unification and Soviet acceptance of Germany's NATO (and Western CFE group) membership, and in light of the impending dissolution of the WTO, Soviet delegates demanded an upgrade from one third to 40 per cent in August and September 1990 and linked it to the Eastern group of states (Institute for Defense and Disarmament Studies, 1990c: 407.B.387–8). Soviet military hardliners, who determined the Soviet positions in the final phase of negotiations, were no longer prepared to agree further compromises with the West especially with regard to attack helicopters and combat aircraft. The lifting of the group ceilings in these two categories was used to lower the percentage to under 40 per cent as Table 11.1 indicates.

This meant that the Soviet Union would possess a little more than 34 per cent of all forces on average.

Soviet weapon transfers beyond the Urals

Western intelligence services had observed the increasing transfer of Soviet conventional weapon systems from the European region to beyond the Ural Mountains from the beginning of 1990. Roughly 57,300 weapon systems were removed from Europe. This did not violate treaty regulations but undermined the cooperative and trustful spirit of the talks. Soviet diplomats first heard of these movements from their Western counterparts in September 1990. The question was what military purpose the movements had and whether the respective military units would be transferred too. If yes, then Soviet conventional superiority would be preserved and Western countries would only gain more time for an early warning. But the Soviet delegates explained that these weapon systems were moved primarily to modernize military units in the Asian parts of the Soviet Union, to maintain and repair damaged weapons and to minimize the costs of the coming reductions. In the context of the solution of the article III issue regarding the counting rules of the treaty (see Hartmann et al, 1994: 109–16), Moscow explained that it had moved 16,400 tanks, 15,900 ACVs and 25,000 artillery pieces to its Asian regions between January 1989 and November 1990. Of these 8,000 tanks, 11,200 ACVs and 1,600 artillery systems were to be used for the modernization of units stationed in these regions. A further 8,400 tanks, 14,700 ACVs and 7,000 artillery pieces would be stored either for maintenance or to replace decommissioned weapons. The expensive build-up of a new strategic reserve was not planned. Finally, the Soviet Union was willing to eliminate or convert 6,000 tanks, 1,500 ACVs and 7,000 artillery pieces between 1991 and 1995. More than 25 per cent of the transferred systems would be destroyed. With the resolution of the article III issue, the weapon systems of the naval infantry and coastal defence forces were excluded from the CFE limits. Following the disintegration of the Soviet Union the reduction liabilities of article III were transferred to its successor Russia and the reduction period was prolonged until the year 2000 (Crawford, 2001: 32). Many in the West regarded the Soviet/Russian relocation of their weaponry as a cascading system. NATO countries had established a similar system to side-step the destruction of modern military equipment. They gave these weapon systems and the reduction liabilities to other alliance members who had older types of weapons. These members got modern military systems free of charge but were forced to pay for the destruction of their older equipment. Through this procedure, NATO countries saved between 3,500 and 5,000 modern weapon systems – the exact figure was never published (Bonn International Center for Conversion, 1995: 229–35).

Exclusion of the Soviet military district Kiev from the southern flank region

In October 1990, the Soviet foreign minister Eduard Shevardnadze accepted the inclusion of the military district Kiev into the flank region and the US accepted the exclusion of the ACVs of Soviet paramilitary forces from the limits. The Soviet military, though, rejected this inclusion on the grounds that it would create too many restrictions for the southern flank. Turkey in turn criticized the absence of any limitations on the ACVs of Soviet paramilitary forces. This created a difficult situation for Washington because of the parallel crisis in the Middle East. It needed Turkish air bases for its military preparations to liberate Kuwait and Soviet support in the UN Security Council for an article VII mission. Therefore, the US arranged a triangular transaction with both parties: the military district Kiev was removed from the definition of the flank region but the Soviet Union had to accept special limits for this region – 2,250 tanks, 2,500 ACVs and 1,500 artillery pieces – which fixed the strength at that time. Turkey got its constraints on the Soviet ACVs with a limit of 1,000 for all paramilitary forces and 600 in the Flank region. Again, the Soviet Union did not have to reduce its forces. However, this special regulation gave the Soviet Union only an additional 1,000 ACVs on top of its national ceiling and the limit for the Eastern group. Furthermore, the Russian military demanded permanent storage sites in the flank region as a consequence of its complete troop withdrawals from states parties of the Eastern group. As a result, the Soviet Union stored up to 600 tanks, 800 ACVs and 400 artillery pieces in the southern part of the military district of Leningrad and 400 tanks and 500 artillery pieces in the military district of Odessa.

Growing nationalism

German unification and the incorporation of its Eastern part into NATO and the Western CFE group facilitated reductions and enabled higher national ceilings for the Eastern group. Nonetheless, conflicts about national limitations arose within it. Without the protection of the WTO or the Soviet Union every country had to organize its military security alone. This prompted demands for higher and legally binding national ceilings. Only Czechoslovakia was less concerned about these political and military changes and more oriented towards a compromise (Madejka, 1997: 61–2). What fuelled the dispute over the sufficiency rule were conflicting preferences. The Soviet Union argued for higher limits following the dissolution of the Warsaw Pact whereas the Pact's smaller former members wanted to lower them to increase their own security from Moscow. To resolve the issue, the US negotiated a bilateral solution with the Soviet Union for the Soviet ceilings in October 1990 (see Institute for Defense and Disarmament Studies, 1990d: 407.B.394). Afterwards, the major Western powers put pressure on the smaller Eastern European countries to accept a compromise without a further increase in the group limits (Hartmann et al, 1994: 131). The final agreement was only possible through an additional lowering of Soviet limits by 150 tanks and 525 artillery pieces at the last meeting of the Eastern Disarmament Commission in Prague on 26 and 27 October 1990.

In sum, German unification and the dissolution of the WTO threatened the alliance approach and with it the newly defined performance standard (alliance parity at a lower stable level). A combination of measures was developed to save the performance standard and redefine it informally as a rough balance between NATO and the Soviet Union: the switch to the 'groups of states' approach, NATO's acceptance of constraints for East Germany, increased group limits for four weapon categories, and a shift from the initially envisioned reductions to limits corresponding to existing holdings.

The changing performance assessment – the shifting military balance of power – thus made national limitations more important, and with them distribution assessments focusing on holdings of weapons systems. The finalization of distribution limits helped to stabilize European security for some time. The combination of an informal revision of the performance standard – from a parity between NATO and the Warsaw Pact to a parity between NATO and the Soviet Union – with a renegotiation of national limits, including new limits for the unified Germany, contributed to the successful management of a period of profound change in Europe.

Obsolete parity

After the failed coup against General Secretary Gorbachev in August 1991, Boris Yeltsin became the new Russian leader. Fourteen Soviet republics used the political weakness in Moscow after the coup to gain independence from the Soviet Union. In September 1991, the Soviet Union recognized the independence of Estonia, Latvia and Lithuania. At the end of the same year, Yeltsin and the leaders of Belarus and Ukraine declared the end of the Soviet Union and founded the Commonwealth of Independent States (CIS). The dissolution of the Soviet Union further changed the military balance in Europe to the advantage of NATO, the former WTO members and other Western states. The informal performance standard of a rough CFE balance between NATO and the Soviet Union became obsolete.

This further reduced the value of the signed CFE Treaty in relation to military stability and security in Europe. Nevertheless, the treaty, which had still not yet come into force, was used as the main instrument for managing the division of the Soviet armed forces peacefully. What made this difficult were contradictory demands. The three Baltic states Estonia, Latvia and Lithuania vehemently opposed their status as legal successors of the Soviet Union because they had never accepted their forceful integration into it. They had therefore refused to become parties to the CFE Treaty in order to preclude the stationing of Soviet/Russian troops on their territory. The problem was that Ukraine shared the same legal position, but the other CFE participants were unwilling to exclude it from the treaty given its status as the second strongest military power after Russia. If other former Soviet republics had taken this view, it could have risked the future of the CFE Treaty. Initially the Western states favoured CFE membership for all

11 Soviet republics in the area of application. This would also reduce the military strength of the larger former Soviet republics somewhat. At the same time, several Western states such as the US, France, the UK and Canada had never accepted the forcible integration of the Baltic states into the Soviet Union. This contributed to an ambivalent US position. It did not consider Russia as the legal successor to the Soviet Union with regard to conventional forces in order to strengthen the independence of the other former Soviet republics and the division of Soviet forces. But it supported Russia as the legal successor to Soviet nuclear forces in order to reduce the number of new nuclear states from four (Russia, Belarus, Ukraine, Kazakhstan) to one.

Fortunately, the CFE Treaty was fully in the interests of the other former Soviet republics (Belarus, Armenia, Azerbaijan, Moldova, Georgia, Kazakhstan). They regarded the CFE regime as an important instrument for strengthening their independence, getting a fair share of Soviet forces and building up their own national forces despite the Soviet/Russian wish to create a unified command for the forces of all its successor states. Ukraine likewise shared this view. This made it possible to develop a differentiated solution for the membership question.

The Baltic states and the CFE regime

On 18 October 1991 the CFE participants concluded a legal declaration that the Baltic states would not become members of the CFE regime (see Hartmann et al, 1994: 500–502). This was in the interests of Russia and all other successor states, as they were thus not forced to share Soviet weapons with the Baltic states. Nonetheless, the Soviet/Russian forces stationed in the Baltic states were covered by CFE and its verification regime. However, the Baltic states never accepted any agreement with other CFE participants to verify these forces because they wanted their complete withdrawal. The declaration explicitly emphasized that it did not prejudice the question of Ukrainian CFE membership. This solution was only possible because the Baltic states were small and militarily very weak.

The other Soviet successor states and the CFE regime

After the August coup, the Soviet Union declared its readiness to ratify CFE as soon as possible pending the conclusion of the new Union Treaty. Ukraine, however, declared its independence on 24 August 1991 before the new Union agreement was finished. This foreclosed the option of a fast ratification of the CFE Treaty by the Soviet Union, which would have bound all its successor states.

Fortunately, all concerned former Soviet republics independently declared in autumn 1991 that they recognized the signed CFE Treaty and accepted the Soviet limits as the basis for their further division. In reaction, the Western states created the North Atlantic Cooperation Council (NACC) to manage Eastern security demands and also established a High-Level Working Group (HLWG) to support the division of Soviet forces, the ratification of CFE and its implementation by the successor states. At the first meeting of the HLWG on 10 January 1992, the Western states agreed with seven successor states (Kazakhstan was absent) on a framework for this process (Institute for Defense and Disarmament Studies, 1991: 407.B.463–464).

Initially Russia demanded two thirds of all Soviet land forces and 75 per cent of all air forces to demonstrate and secure its dominance within the CIS. Yeltsin also tried to establish unified CIS forces under Russian leadership up until March 1992 which delayed the talks. These demands were strongly opposed by most other republics and, in particular, by Ukraine, which additionally demanded a conventional compensation from Russia for giving up its nuclear forces. In order to accelerate the internal talks in the CIS, the HLWG formulated a 'Road Map for bringing the CFE Treaty into force' on 20 March 1991 (Institute for Defense and Disarmament Studies, 1992: 407.B.466–467). In the same month, the Joint Consultative Group established by the CFE Treaty started talks on the Final Document for the extraordinary treaty conference at the next CSCE meeting in July 1992 to increase political pressure. The negotiations between the CIS states and the HLWG were intensified to conclude the division of Soviet forces at the next CIS summit in Tashkent on 15 May 1992.

The southern flank republics were dissatisfied with the Russian and Ukrainian proposals for the division of Soviet forces because the proposed ceilings were very low. Moldova demanded parity between all flank states and higher ceilings, which Russia rejected. And because of the conflict between Armenia and Azerbaijan about Nagorno-Karabakh, neither state would accept any limit which would be higher for the other side. However, because all the smaller southern flank republics had either internal or bilateral conflicts, neither Russia nor Ukraine were willing to give them too many weapons.

At the summit in Tashkent, the CIS states reached agreement on their shares of the Soviet forces (see OSCE, 1992a). Armenia, Azerbaijan and Georgia got the same, but significantly higher shares than in previous proposals in order to enhance stability and security in the region while Moldova was allocated somewhat lower ceilings. The compromise between the three big republics was that Russia got more for its air forces whereas Belarus and Ukraine got more for their land forces. Russia was allocated slightly below 50 per cent of Soviet land forces but got nearly two thirds (65.2 per cent) of the air forces. This reduced Russian dominance as compared to its initial demands, but the dominance still persisted.

With these shares, Russia was no longer able to preserve a rough parity with NATO forces. The new performance standard consequently lost its meaning. The CFE Treaty too lost large parts of its originally envisioned stabilizing function. The whole structure of limitations was geared towards managing the military situation between two alliances, not between the growing number of individual CFE participants. The central question was then how military stability and security could be organized between NATO and 16 newly independent East European states while there was still a Russian military dominance in Eastern Europe. The national limitations approach was further strengthened by omitting all references to the alliance approach in the Final Document of the extraordinary conference of the CFE states parties in Oslo on 5 June 1992 (see OSCE, 1992b). However, additional military measures to enhance stability between member states were absent. The adaptation of the CFE Treaty seemed necessary and urgent because of the tremendous change in the military balance and security situation in Europe. But, with the end of the East–West conflict, there was no longer a major military threat, and the US feared that continued arms control negotiations would threaten the future of NATO. The Western states, therefore, decided to first wait until 1995 to see how the new CIS states would implement their CFE obligations for military reductions before starting negotiations on how to further adapt the CFE regime.

Conclusion

The successful CFE negotiations created a new common performance standard between the two alliances with the principle of parity at a lower level. German unification and the break-up of the Eastern Alliance put this goal at risk, but it was able to survive for a short time through its informal transformation into a rough parity between NATO and the Soviet Union, which made the signature of the CFE Treaty in November 1990 possible. This provided the basis for a new distribution of military forces regulated through arms control, in particular through conventional weapon limitations and reductions. The CFE Treaty thus created a new practice of distribution assessments revolving around existing holdings and CFE ceilings. In combination with the special force limitations for a unified Germany, conventional arms control helped to stabilize the immense political change that unfolded during those years. The new performance standards and the distributional rules through which they were operationalized demonstrated that comparative practices can support the limitation and reduction of armed forces, thereby reducing military tensions and enhancing political cooperation. As a result, the traditional practice of force comparisons lost its value.

But the dissolution of the Soviet Union in 1991 made it impossible to go ahead on the basis of these performance standards. It did not, however, mark the end of the new form of distribution assessment. On the contrary, the new CFE limitations for the Soviet Union provided the basis for managing the distribution of conventional forces between eight of the fifteen successor states in the Tashkent Agreement of May 1992. When the CFE Treaty entered into force on 9 November 1992, its alliance-centred approach was outdated. The end of the Eastern military alliance and the break-up of the Soviet Union had raised the number of individual states in Eastern Europe to 17 and then to 18 with the peaceful division of Czechoslovakia into Slovakia and the Czech Republic in 1993. Distribution assessments focusing on national limits became more important for the final documents of the CFE Treaty (OSCE, 1992b). The treaty determined for more than 15 years the military security of many states in Europe. Because of the low military threat many countries even unilaterally reduced their forces below their respective CFE ceilings.

All in all, the CFE Treaty provides several insights into comparative practices and their effects on security politics. The CFE negotiations underscore how crucial comparative practices are to arms control and the management of competition. Military balances cannot be managed without a comparative framework for evaluating and regulating the distribution of military capabilities. Given the distributional implications, the development of a shared comparative framework of this kind involves complex wrangling over definitions, counting rules and limits, as the CFE negotiations illustrate. At the same time, they demonstrate that comparisons are neither per se nor always generative of competition. Rather, they can also be instrumental in ending competition and managing the transition towards more stable relations.

At the same time, the subsequent history of CFE has also demonstrated the limits of arms control. The alliance approach to limitations provided only inadequate measures for stabilizing military security between individual states. It was further challenged by the demand of East European countries to become NATO members in order to reduce their growing insecurity after the end of the WTO and the uncertain democratization of Russia. From 1996 to 1999 Russia and the NATO countries defined in principle a new performance standard through a new system of national and territorial limits[5] and took account of the controversial enlargement of NATO by precluding any new deployment of substantial military combat forces in

---

[5]   National limits constrain the forces of a single country over the whole area of application while territorial limits constrain all forces (including forces deployed with the host nation's consent) in a single country/territorial unit.

new alliance states with similar restraints on Russia in the adaptation talks of the CFE Treaty. The adapted CFE Treaty was signed in Istanbul in 1999 but never entered into force. NATO countries were not willing to link the enlargement of the alliance to the new adapted CFE Treaty and Russia was not willing to fulfil its Istanbul commitments by withdrawing all Russian troops from Georgia and Moldova thereby solving the unregulated territorial conflicts in these countries. Because both sides were unable to find a political compromise Russia suspended its participation in the CFE regime in 2007 and abandoned it in the wake of its illegal war against Ukraine on 7 November 2023 (see Russia, 2023). On the same day NATO countries suspended the operation of the CFE Treaty but kept the door open for talks about a new performance standard (see NATO, 2023).

References

Bonn International Center for Conversion (ed) (1995) *Conversion Survey 1996. Global Disarmament, Demilitarization and Demobilization*, Oxford: Oxford University Press.

Boysen, S. (1986) 'Der Beitrag der Rüstungskontrolle zur Stabilität in Europa', in E. Forndran and H. Schmidt (eds) *Konventionelle Rüstung im Ost-West-Vergleich: Zur Beurteilung militärischer Potentiale und Fähigkeiten*, Baden-Baden: Nomos Verlagsgesellschaft, pp 473–501.

Crawford, D. (2001) *Conventional Armed Forces in Europe (CFE). A Review and Update of Key Treaty Elements*, Washington DC: US Department of State.

Dunay, P. (1991) *The CFE Treaty: History, Achievements and Shortcomings*, PRIF-Report 24, Frankfurt am Main: PRIF.

Hartmann, R., Heydrich, W. and Meyer-Landrut, N. (1994) *Der Vertrag über die konventionellen Streitkräfte in Europa. Vertragswerk, Verhandlungsgeschichte, Kommentar, Dokumentation*, Baden-Baden: Nomos Verlagsgesellschaft.

Institute for Defense and Disarmament Studies (1989) *The Arms Control Reporter. A Chronicle of Treaties, Negotiations, Proposals, Weapons and Policy*, 6/1989, Brookline, MA.

Institute for Defense and Disarmament Studies (1990a) *The Arms Control Reporter. A Chronicle of Treaties, Negotiations, Proposals, Weapons and Policy*, 5/1990, Brookline, MA.

Institute for Defense and Disarmament Studies (1990b) *The Arms Control Reporter. A Chronicle of Treaties, Negotiations, Proposals, Weapons and Policy*, 7/1990, Brookline, MA.

Institute for Defense and Disarmament Studies (1990c) *The Arms Control Reporter. A Chronicle of Treaties, Negotiations, Proposals, Weapons and Policy*, 9/1990, Brookline, MA.

Institute for Defense and Disarmament Studies (1990d) *The Arms Control Reporter. A Chronicle of Treaties, Negotiations, Proposals, Weapons and Policy*, 11/1990, Brookline, MA.

Institute for Defense and Disarmament Studies (1991) *The Arms Control Reporter. A Chronicle of Treaties, Negotiations, Proposals, Weapons and Policy*, 1/1991, Brookline, MA.

Institute for Defense and Disarmament Studies (1992) *The Arms Control Reporter. A Chronicle of Treaties, Negotiations, Proposals, Weapons and Policy*, 2/1992, Brookline, MA.

Kohl, H. (1990) 'Kohl on his Caucasus meeting with Gorbachev, 17 July 1990', in K.H. Jarausch and V. Gransow (eds) *Uniting Germany: Documents and Debates, 1944–1993*, translated by A. Brown and B. Cooper, Oxford: Berghahn Books, pp 175–8.

Madejka, Z. (1997) 'How the Warsaw Pact was dissolved', *Perspectives*, 8: 55–65.

NATO (2023) 'North Atlantic Council statement on the Allied response to Russia's withdrawal from the Treaty on Conventional Armed Forces in Europe, Brussels', 7 November, Available from www.nato.int/cps/en/nat ohq/official_texts_219811.htm [Accessed 28 November 2023].

OSCE (Organization for Security and Co-operation in Europe) (1990) *Treaty on Conventional Arms in Europe*, 19 November, www.osce.org/files/ f/documents/4/9/14087.pdf [Accessed 28 November 2023].

OSCE (1992a) *Agreement on the Principles and Procedures for the Implementation of the Treaty on Conventional Armed Forces in Europe*, 15 May, https://nuke. fas.org/control/cfe/text/tashka.htm [Accessed 28 November 2023].

OSCE (1992b) *Final Document of the Extraordinary Conference of the States Parties to the Treaty on Conventional Armed Forces in Europe*, 5 June, https:// nuke.fas.org/control/cfe/text/osloa.htm [Accessed 28 November 2023].

Russia (2023) 'Foreign Ministry statement on the completion of the procedure for the Russian Federation's withdrawal from the Treaty on Conventional Armed Forces in Europe (CFE Treaty)', Moscow, 7 November, https://mid.ru/en/foreign_policy/news/1913546/ [Accessed 28 November 2023].

Soviet Union Ministry of Defence (1987) *Whence the Threat to Peace* (4th edn), Moscow: Military Publishing House.

12

'Winning the Technology Competition': Narratives, Power Comparisons and the US–China AI Race

Nike Retzmann

Introduction

Power comparisons lie at the heart of both international politics as a practice and International Relations (IR) as a scholarly discipline. In debating the measurement of power, weighing the relative importance of various power dimensions, and evaluating the distribution of power in the world – in other words, in comparing power – researchers and practitioners negotiate the meaning of the concept itself (see Guzzini, 2009). They single out certain events and processes as relevant to the distribution of power while dismissing others. Technologies are just one example of that. Throughout history, technological artefacts have time and again been perceived as critical power resources because of the way they shape warfare, trade, media landscapes and politics (Miskimmon and O'Loughlin, 2017; Horowitz, 2018; Stevens, 2018; Baum and Potter, 2019; Drezner, 2019). The meaning attached to these artefacts varies, however, among different groups of agents as well as over time. For instance, according to Jon R. Lindsay (2020: 20), '[e]very new generation of information technology inspires a new generation of military strategists to envision a new revolution in warfare'. But not all of these visions would, in retrospect, be considered to have come true.

With increasingly rapid advances in information and communication technologies, artificial intelligence (AI) has lately been at the centre of attention in this respect. As a general-purpose and enabling technology, AI will, it has been argued, transform nearly all aspects of our life and become a determining factor for world leadership. We are, according to some, on the edge of an 'AI revolution' (Horowitz, 2018: 37). However, what the discursive processes are through which AI gains such relevance is seldom questioned. Presuming that the meaning ascribed to it is not just a 'natural' consequence of AI's technical features, this chapter enquires into the links between technologies, states' perception of their standing in the world, and the foreign policy choices that they make. It demonstrates that, while AI is perceived as something new, as an epochal change, the way it is being narrated follows familiar patterns. Through an intertwined set of narratives and comparisons, AI is gaining relevance as a source of power and as the centre of a race between the US and China. This drives competitive dynamics and shapes policies, as 'winning the technology competition' (NSCAI, 2021: 156) becomes a political priority. The chapter thereby aims to contribute to this volume by providing insights into the role comparative knowledge plays in rendering an issue – in this case AI – politically relevant. It highlights how practices of comparing can shape national security discourses and reinforce competitive dynamics. In doing so, it additionally sheds light on the interplay of narratives and comparisons in the production of knowledge.

These theoretical considerations will be empirically illustrated with the case of the US National Security Commission on Artificial Intelligence (NSCAI), which was established by the US Congress in 2018. The Commission commenced its work in 2019 and was active until 2021. It was tasked with reviewing developments in AI, assessing their potential impact on US competitiveness, and providing recommendations on how to maintain technological advantages and strengthen national security (US Congress, 2018: § 1051). I argue that the NSCAI constructs a narrative of an ongoing US–China AI race and places it in the tradition of other historical technological competitions, intertwining temporal and spatial comparisons while doing so. Narrating the present as a shrinking window of opportunity, the NSCAI's account feeds into current policy decisions made by the US government.

The next section will elaborate on the relation between narratives, power comparisons and technological change from a theoretical standpoint. After that, the chapter will trace the narrative construction of the US–China AI race in the NSCAI's official reports. The last section takes a look at the legislative steps that followed the Commission's work.

Power comparisons, narratives and AI

Within both international politics and the discipline of IR, the question of how AI will impact the power of states is receiving growing attention. Often AI's relevance to the shape of the international order is simply taken for granted. Rarely is the focus shifted to the discursive processes through which technologies gain their political relevance in the first place. This chapter argues that the concept of narrative is crucial for shedding a light on how AI becomes socially constructed as a source of power. It contends that events – such as the arrival of new technologies – do not possess meaning per se, but acquire it through a process of narrative construction. This is not to argue against the materiality of events but to stress that human beings depend on storytelling to make sense of them and deduce a course of action (Hagström and Gustafsson, 2019: 388; Gadinger et al, 2014a: 23). Narrating is thus an epistemological constant that helps humans to reduce complexity, navigate their environment and maintain their ability to act.

Narratives are here defined as a subtype of discourse that is characterized by a certain set of structural elements (see Spencer, 2016: 5, 16). They can be divided into a setting, a plot and a lesson. The plot is the narrative's centrepiece. Narration is at its heart a process of emplotment in which events are brought into a temporal order that is simultaneously perceived as a causal relationship (Gadinger et al, 2014b: 73; Krebs, 2015: 11; Oppermann and Spencer, 2018: 270–71; Hagström and Gustafsson, 2019: 390). The plot is embedded in a setting that describes the where and when and holds information about the story's characters. Finally, narratives often contain a lesson at the end, a recommendation of preferrable courses of action (Hagström and Gustafsson, 2019: 390). As a cognitive process which reduces complexity, the building of a narrative is always selective. Certain events and characters take centre stage while others are sidelined or remain altogether invisible.

As Ronald Krebs (2015:12) states, we live 'in a world that is always narrated'. Narratives therefore do not stand in isolation. Rather, they are connected through ties of internarrativity – they are nested within each other, tap into or stand in conflict with one another (Viehöver, 2012: 87; Hagström and Gustafsson, 2019: 399). Not all narratives are, however, equally successful. Some narratives gain such dominance that they become almost invisible as such. Agents perceive them as 'truth' or 'common sense' and do not necessarily recognize them as constructs. Other narratives never reach this level of dominance and remain disputed (Viehöver, 2012: 77; Miskimmon and O'Loughlin, 2017; Oppermann and Spencer, 2018; Hagström and Gustafsson, 2019).

Through the way they order events and provide humans with a sense of chronology, narratives are central to the construction of temporality (see Viehöver, 2012: 75–106; Yildiz at al, 2015: 424–5;). That makes a focus on narratives a particularly promising approach to better understanding the way agents make sense of processes of change such as technological developments. The emergence of new technologies requires agents to make sense of them against the background of their knowledge. This might lead them to rethink their ideas and beliefs, but they might also find a way to harmonize what they have learned with what they already know. In other words, new technologies like AI may end up being integrated into existing narratives or may inspire new ones. The meaning of technological innovations is therefore not pre-given. Their impact on the social is not simply the consequence of their technical characteristics. In fact, as Andreas Kaminski (2010: 11) shows, many technologies exist in a discursive form – in scenarios, popular imaginations, visions and public debates – long before they have been physically realized. To some degree, this is also true for AI. In fact, as Stephen Cave and his co-authors (2020) have shown, AI narratives have a long history, reaching back to antiquity. While, particularly in recent years, there have been rapid advances in its development, some of its potential features and applications remain to be implemented. This creates uncertainties – leading agents to attempt to reduce this insecurity by engaging in anticipatory practices or, in other words, by narrating the future (see Berenskötter, 2011).

The chapter then moves away from determinist understandings of technologies that often still dominate political debates. There are two different forms of technological determinism – instrumentalism and substantivism. For instrumentalists, technologies are the mere tools of their human users and creators. Their impact on the social is therefore determined by their user's or creator's intentions, beliefs and ideologies (Feenberg, 1991: 5; McCarthy, 2015: 20). Substantivism, on the other hand, assumes that technologies possess essential characteristics which shape the social and political world (Feenberg, 1991: 7; McCarthy, 2015: 20). While these understandings still hold a considerable amount of influence in political debates and everyday discussions of technologies, scholars in IR have increasingly moved away from technological determinism. Drawing on strands of Science and Technology Studies, this chapter perceives the technological and the social as mutually constitutive (Pinch and Bijker, 1989; Sismondo, 2010: 57–71; Manjikian, 2018; McCarthy, 2018: 2, 13–14). It further contends that a narrative approach is particularly helpful to understanding how technologies gain their importance in international power politics. AI becomes a factor of relevance to the international order through a process of narrative construction. Furthermore, as Daniel R. McCarthy (2015: 33) puts it, technological development itself is 'the outcome of political decisions and struggles over the form of the object and, subsequently, the shape of the social world'. Narratives are thus key for the way AI is developed and deployed as well as regulated (Hudson et al, 2023).

Comparisons play an important role in this respect. The most evident connection is that the international distribution of power rests on comparisons. To deliberate this matter without comparing the supposed power of various agents – either implicitly or explicitly – appears difficult, if not impossible. As the chapter will demonstrate, these comparisons, however, are often embedded in narratives which provide the causal links that help agents explain why the international order looks a certain way, how it came into being and what consequences this entails. As they usually put past, present and future in relation to each other, narratives are closely connected to temporal comparisons.

Method

To further examine these links, the following section will look at the way AI has been narrated in the work of the NSCAI. The NSCAI presents an interesting case study. The very establishment of a National Security Commission tasked with reviewing the potential impact of AI on the position of the US in the world points towards the need of political agents to make sense of new technological developments. The NSCAI, furthermore, brought together agents from various sectors. Designed as an independent commission, it involved representatives of the private technology sector and researchers as well as people who had previously served in the Department of Defense and other federal entities. The Commission also held public events to engage with a broader audience. The narratives and discourse shaping, as well as emerging out of, the Commission's work are therefore potentially not limited to the political circle in a narrow sense.

The analysis focuses on the narratives laid out by the NSCAI in its official reports (NSCAI, 2019; 2020a; 2020b; 2020c; 2021). The analysis was guided by predefined categories but aimed to remain open to relevant narratives and themes emerging from the empirical material, thereby combining a deductive and inductive research design. The categories were designed to help identify the various structural elements of narratives (setting, plot, lesson) and thus reconstruct the narration. To be able to reconstruct the setting, two aspects were taken into consideration: the objects of the comparisons – that is, the agents whose power was being compared – and the timescales referred to in the material. The analysis of the plot focused on the underlying conceptions of power, statements about the distribution of power between the objects of comparison, the indicators used to put the agents' power into relation, changes in the distribution of power and, lastly, the explanations given for these changes. Finally, for the purpose of analysing the lesson to be drawn from the narrative, the chapter examines the recommendations for actions to be carried out in reaction to the described changes.

Where it appeared necessary and relevant, additional material was consulted in the *Foreign Relations of the United States* series and other national security publications by the US government in order to gain a better understanding of the internarrative links present in the NSCAI's works.

The narrative construction of the US–China AI race

The newness of AI

As Kaminski points out, new technologies are often said to have world-changing effects – history is full of claims about technological artefacts that are going to usher in a new age. Kaminski traces that back to the way new technologies disaffirm familiar world views. This leads to an apparent paradox in the way technologies are made sense of and communicated about (Kaminski, 2010: 11, 37, 68–74). Technologies are perceived as new things that break with the familiar. At the same time, the new cannot be described outside of existing systems of meaning. There is simply no way for us, as humans, to apprehend it otherwise. While new technological artefacts thus challenge existing narratives, calling the plot elements and the inherent causal links into question, in order to make sense of the change, agents have to fall back on familiar patterns of narration. This explains the contradictory argumentation of the Commission. On the one hand, the Commission claims historical incomparability: 'No comfortable historical reference captures the impact of artificial intelligence (AI) on national security. … The race for AI supremacy is not like the space race to the moon. AI is not even comparable to a general-purpose technology like electricity' (NSCAI, 2021: 7). On the other hand, these are exactly the technologies and historical occurrences the NSCAI keeps referring to: 'The Commission's attempts to predict AI's impact on national security is like Americans in the late 19th century pondering the impact of electricity on war and society' (NSCAI, 2019: 14). So, the NSCAI depicts AI as something historically unique, but simultaneously uses temporal analogies and comparisons to assess its potential impact on society. The internarrativity here is needed for agents to make sense of a new situation by linking it to what they already regard as common knowledge in spite of its postulated incomparability.

Just as Kaminski describes, the NSCAI proclaims the beginning of a new era heralded by new technologies. There are multiple references to the 'AI era' (for example NSCAI, 2019: 36; 2021: 1), the 'digital age' (see NSCAI, 2020b; 2020c; 2021) or the 'information age' (see NSCAI, 2020b). A particularly large transformative potential is ascribed to AI on the basis of it being a general-purpose technology (NSCAI, 2019: 9). Thus, the Commission predicts that AI will change every aspect of human life – from our social relations, to the economy and the nature of warfare. However, aside from that, the Commission also observes a 'new era of competition' (NSCAI, 2021: 14, 28), a 'new era of conflict' (NSCAI, 2021: 9), and an 'era of great power competition' (NSCAI, 2020b: 21). In other words, the Commission establishes a correlation between the arrival of new epoch-shaping technologies, such as AI, and a new constellation of the international order. This already presents a part of the emplotment process.

Importantly, the NSCAI always states that we are currently at the beginning of this new age. This emphasizes the epochal relevance of current events and thereby reinforces the urgency of political decisions, contributing to the impression of a 'gathering storm' (NSCAI, 2021: 46). At the same time, it implies that there is still time left to act: 'We still have a window to make the changes to build a safer and better future' (NSCAI, 2021: 21). That is an important aspect considering that the NSCAI is trying to mobilize the US government to implement its recommendations. To paint a picture of an entirely hopeless situation would not be likely to incentivize such behaviour. Instead, the NSCAI is putting forward a concept of history in which America can still 'win ... the AI era' (NSCAI, 2021: 16). The present is thereby constructed as a decisive time, a shrinking but still open window of opportunity.

Instead of reflecting on the potential positive impacts of AI, the Commission discusses almost exclusively effects that could be damaging to the US. It therefore imagines the future mainly in terms of threats. This presents, for instance, a difference to the *Global Trends* reports published by the US National Intelligence Council (NIC). Here, the picture is more nuanced. Risks connected to AI are not absent from the NIC's account, but the threat scenario does not loom as large as it does in the NSCAI's tale. Instead, the NIC highlights many positive effects AI might have (see NIC, 2008; 2012; 2017; 2021). In its evaluation on how technology will shape the global order, the NIC foresees great potential for the US, as a democracy, to sustain a leadership role (NIC, 2021: 110–11). The NSCAI, instead, presents it as certain that the US needs to take action immediately because it will otherwise be overtaken by China. While the NSCAI's narrative locates the actual change in the future, it describes its effects as already becoming tangible. This reinforces the need for action.

The competition for AI leadership

The NSCAI tells the story of a great power competition. Power comparisons play a central role here. Introducing AI as a new but crucial factor that impacts the relative distribution of power, the competition for technological innovativeness becomes a contest for global leadership. The protagonists – and main objects of comparisons – in this narration are state actors, above all the US. This might appear unsurprising given the identity of the narrator but, nevertheless, it shows that this narrative involves a process of self-assessment, of identifying and evaluating one's own position in the world. In this context, it is notable that the states the US is being compared to are often simply referred to as 'US competitors' (for example NSCAI,

2020b: 12; 2021: 586). The repeated use of the terms 'competitors' and 'adversaries' not only defines these states mainly by their positioning relative to the US, but also contributes to the construction of a threat scenario. The Commission thereby follows a typical narrative pattern by identifying a hero – the US – and a villain. As Alexandra Homolar (2022) shows, the hero–villain narrative binary is particularly common in US national security documents. She highlights how, through its special emotional appeal, this narrative structurization is particularly promising for political mobilization. The villains' role is in the present case cast with familiar agents. As the most powerful of its competitors, China becomes the main antagonist and as such dominates the NSCAI's account. Although considered to be lagging behind the US and China in several important technology fields, Russia is identified as America's second main rival. Focusing on these states, the narrative involves a rather limited set of actors. North Korea and Iran, for example, two other traditional US rivals, are hardly ever mentioned throughout the reports.

Interestingly, India is, like China, mentioned as a rising power. Unlike China, however, India is not considered a threat. The Commission's statements rather evoke the impression that India's 'fate' is still undecided in the sense that its increasingly important geopolitical position could still be used to US advantage (see NSCAI, 2020b: 215). That might be connected to the notion that the competition over AI leadership is not just one between China and the US but between democracies and authoritarian regimes: 'Artificial Intelligence (AI) is intensifying the broader geopolitical struggle between the United States and its competitors, and deepening the challenge democracies face from autocracies' (NSCAI, 2020c: 78). The contest between the two countries thus gains a normative dimension with wider consequences for world society as a whole. While in the *Global Trends* reports mentioned earlier the focus is less on interstate competition than on economic and societal challenges, the democracies-vs-autocracies narrative is present there as well. It touches upon values deeply embedded in US foreign policy discourse, namely the strength of the US' ideational power and its role in promoting democracy and liberty worldwide. The NSCAI's narratives thus draw on important aspects of US national identity as a 'beacon of liberty and opportunity around the world' (White House, 2017: 41). On the one hand, this strengthens the hero–villain binary. On the other, it can add to the story's persuasiveness as well as increase the importance of AI in the eyes of the audience. The successful deployment of the technology becomes narratively bound to American identity. This emotionalizes and reinforces the Commission's call for political action.

Through its main focus on these agents, the Commission reproduces a concept of power which perceives it as a characteristic mainly possessed by nation states. Non-state actors are only ascribed a subordinate role in this tale. To some degree this seems surprising as the NSCAI also argues that, because of the public availability of AI, it will lead to a diffusion of power among different kind of agents. At the same time, by concentrating on the competition with two main antagonists, the Commission reduces the noise, so to speak. It constructs a relatively coherent and straightforward picture and thereby pushes a clear threat scenario.

The construction of the hero–villain binary already provides us with an important element of the AI competition narrative, as does the painting of AI as a revolutionary technology. This alone, however, does not sufficiently explain AI's status in national security discourse. The way it is being tied into power comparisons plays a role as well. The development and deployment of AI gains significance as a factor on the basis of which the power of states is assessed. The NSCAI's account argues that the successful deployment of AI will decide which country gains technological leadership and scientific power. These are, in turn, considered first and foremost means to ensure economic strength and military superiority. AI's relevance to the international distribution is in this way being tied to existing narratives on economic and military power. In addition, the NSCAI ascribes great importance to what could be called ideational power. The Commission argues that AI and associated technologies might be used by nations to create and expand spheres of influence. Particularly worrisome from the NSCAI's perspective is the success of authoritarian regimes in this field, leading us back to the roles of protagonists and antagonists. It is through this military, economic and ideational potential that AI is believed to be accelerating the rise of China. For the NSCAI, a gain in power by China appears to translate directly into a weakening of the US. Through the juxtaposition of the two countries and their position in the world, the narrative follows the logic of a zero-sum game, tapping into several master narratives. The conceptualization of power politics as a zero-sum game links to realist theories. Beyond that, however, the way the Commission emphasizes the standing of China and the US in the world in the depiction of current and past events paints a picture of history as being driven by the continuous rise and fall of empires. As Linus Hagström and Karl Gustafsson (see 2019: 388) have pointed out before, this way of thinking about the course of history presents probably one of the most prominent narratives in international politics.

Consequently, the relationship between the US and China is being constructed as great power competition which is being accelerated through AI. More specifically, the current situation is being labelled a 'reemergence of great power competition' (NSCAI, 2019: 6), connecting the US–China race to the Cold War period. This narrative relation should not be dismissed as irrelevant, considering the place this time period holds in US collective memory. Success in the deployment and development of AI thereby becomes part of a much larger competition with the potential of reordering the world in its entirety.

To summarize at this point: how does AI gain its role as an object in the national security discourse? For one thing, it is its classification as a general-purpose technology and the large transformative potential that is being ascribed to it, for the military and the economy as well as society at large. But this is true for other general-purpose technologies. AI, with its many (yet) unrealized potentials, remains a source of uncertainty and leaves room for speculation. Since it seems to break with the familiar, it is claimed to usher in a new era. This era, however, correlates with what is considered the reemergence of great power competition. On this basis, the development and deployment of AI is being embedded into a threat scenario. The US fears the loss of its leadership position, while it perceives China to be on the rise. For the US, China represents a different vision of what the global order should look like. The challenge it poses to the US touches upon key elements of American identity narratives. The perception of threat is increased by historical links that are being drawn between current developments and the era of the Cold War.

Race dynamics

Whereas this establishes AI as an object of interstate competition, the contest gains special dynamics through the particular modes of comparisons that are being used. In this narrative, power comparisons are intertwined with temporal-spatial comparisons. Thus, the NSCAI states that 'strategic competitors have *caught up with* the United States technologically, and threaten U.S. military-technical superiority' (NSCAI, 2019: 29, emphasis added), that 'China *lags behind* the United States in the fundamental research and development of quantum computers' (NSCAI, 2020b: 161, emphasis added), and that 'leading indexes that measure progress in AI development generally place the United States *ahead* of China' (NSCAI, 2021: 161, emphasis added), even though 'China stands a reasonable chance of *overtaking* the United States … in the coming decade' (NSCAI, 2021: 161, emphasis added). The interweaving of these modes of comparing contributes to the construction of a US–China AI race. The notion that the development and deployment of AI is the object of a race – inherently a competition of speed – only reinforces the impression of urgency. It evokes the idea that there will be a finish line and a clear winner in the end.

The mental image of a race is of course not new in US foreign policy discourse. During the Cold War period, the 'space race' and the 'arms race' shaped US policy. Taking a closer look at government documents from the 1960s to mid-1980s dealing with these two examples, what appears remarkable is that in both cases there is a certain notion that the race is to some degree 'out of control' as if it were a higher power, a dynamic none of the agents can withdraw from, in spite of them being aware of the resources the race is consuming (see for example Wilson, 1955; Department of State, 1966; Mabon and Patterson, 1995 Gerakas, Mabon et al, 1997; Gerakas, Patterson, et al, 1997; Wilson, 2001). This is similar to the NSCAI's account – the race is simply 'there'. Its recommendations are less about how to stop a competitive dynamic, but how to best succeed in it. The Commission's account is thereby tapping into already existing narratives and thus resonates with knowledge familiar to the audience. As a result, the AI race is discursively being linked to political-technological competitions of the past (see NSCAI, 2020b: 64, 123). This is not only a vital part of making sense of the current situation. The Commission thereby also embeds the narrative of the ongoing US–China AI competition into a much larger narrative, narrating it as a continuation of previous challenges and conflicts in US history.

Interestingly, the Commission moreover expresses concerns that China is putting forward a narrative itself according to which it has already won the AI race. Even though it projects a similar outcome if the US does not take immediate action, the NSCAI conceives the narrative as damaging for the US's reputation and therefore argues in favour of actively countering it. What can be observed here, is that it is recognized by the agents themselves that the race is, at least to some degree, narratively constructed. Statements that point towards the importance of storytelling can also be found in government documents concerning the arms and space races. In a memorandum from November 1963, the then Assistant Secretary of State for International Organization Affairs, for instance, indicates how different narratives on the lunar landing play out differently in terms of competitive dynamics and outcomes:

> Chairman Khrushchev has maneuvered himself into this public position: he is not racing the Americans to the moon because life on earth is so good that he is not in that much of a hurry and, because he doesn't want to risk human life. ... If the Americans succeed in landing and recovering the first man from the surface of the moon by 1970, the resulting national prestige will be modified by the fact that we did not win 'victory' in a 'race' against the Russians; we simply – if dramatically – met a self-imposed deadline. (Cleveland, 1963)

Even so, as the NSCAI's call for a counter-narrative shows, the agents still feel the need to subject themselves to the race dynamic, with the result that narrating simply becomes another dimension of the competition.

Unsurprisingly, the idea of an ongoing race is reflected in the NSCAI's policy recommendations. The overall conclusion of the Commission's narrative is that the US cannot let its competitors win the contest as too much would be at stake. The US instead has to fully commit to the race to defend its technological leadership in the world. The NSCAI puts forward a wide array of suggestions as to how to best achieve this objective, many of them containing direct references to Chinese activities and the explicit aim to counter them. China, says the Commission, has been actively pursuing a campaign to gain AI leadership and challenge the overall US position in the world. Where the US has not yet adapted bureaucratic structures, China has formulated national strategies and policies, invested massively in technological infrastructure and its national champions, and fostered science, technology, engineering and mathematics education (NSCAI, 2021: 27). The Commission therefore recommends that the US government formulate strategies that explicitly deal with AI and its associated technologies on a federal level as well as within departments and agencies. The development and implementation of these strategies are mainly meant to help systemize and better coordinate the state's efforts, both in the domestic and the international realm. Furthermore, the Commission urges the government to build up information infrastructures in several areas related to AI and associated technologies. It argues that it is essential that government departments and academia exchange knowledge with one another as a way of fostering innovation. The NSCAI further advises the government to invest in the improvement of its technological infrastructure. This serves mainly to increase security and ensure that the US is prepared for AI-enabled warfare (NSCAI, 2021: 2, 51) but also to keep government positions attractive for a highly skilled workforce that currently is 'regularly denied access to software engineering tools' (NSCAI, 2021: 129). Aside from the government's own technological tools, the NSCAI thinks the US as a whole needs to do more to generate innovation and remain a forerunner in AI and associated technologies. The Commission formulates the express goal of staying two generations of microchips ahead of China. Furthermore, the NSCAI advocates the adoption of stricter export controls and protection policies for technology transfers to competitor states such as China or Russia. Export controls should be focused on advanced hardware since, because of its nature as a dual-use technology and the many open-source applications, it appears a futile endeavour to try controlling AI algorithms and software. US export controls should therefore concentrate on semiconductor manufacturing equipment (SME) as the basis of a variety of technological applications (NSCAI, 2020c: 63). The aim behind this is also to gain more leverage over China's AI capabilities. China is currently building up its domestic semiconductor manufacturing capabilities depending on the import of SME for that purpose (NSCAI, 2021: 498–9).

The Commission constructs the US–China AI race as a competition that requires a national effort to win it. It therefore provides a number of recommendations to improve the cooperation between the commercial sector, academia – where, according to the NSCAI, expertise in AI is predominantly located – and the government. One of the biggest weaknesses of the US, the Commission identifies, is the 'tech talent deficit' (NSCAI, 2020b: 6). In summary, the Commission believes that 'AI can no longer be relegated to a specialized field, understood by a few' (NSCAI, 2020b: 112). The government needs to actively build a skilled workforce instead of focusing solely on recruitment measures. The NSCAI argues that the talent pool could be increased if more people were to gain access to technological infrastructures in the first place. It therefore emphasizes the need 'to democratize access to compute [sic] and data to fuel AI R&D in the open research environment' (NSCAI, 2020b: 42).

However, as has been pointed out before, the AI race has been constructed as a competition with wider consequences for the international order and tied to US identity narratives. In the eyes of the Commission, the US must actively attempt to lead in setting international AI standards to ensure the protection of its values and norms. Against this background, it recommends the extension of international cooperation in AI. Emphasizing the need of democracies to counter the rising influence of autocracies, the Commission recommends establishing a Digital Coalition with democratic countries and agents from the private sector. The NSCAI additionally highlights how important it is to integrate the issue of AI into existing military and intelligence alliances to ensure interoperability between itself and its partners in the future and thereby minimize vulnerabilities.

The narrative of the US–China AI race and its political effects

The NSCAI did not invent the narratives presented here. Rather, the NSCAI and its work are embedded in a complex web of already existing and constantly evolving narratives, and its own establishment needs to be seen against this background. For a *National Security* Commission on Artificial Intelligence to be created, as Congress did through the John S. McCain National Defense Authorization Act, AI had to be constructed as a national security object in the first place. Instead, the NSCAI is one important actor among several that has interlaced various narratives and combined narrative elements to build a comprehensive account of AI's meaning for international politics and to draft scenarios for the future. Through this interlinking of existing stories, drawing on fundamental master narratives of US foreign policy, the Commission has sharpened the narrative. Its role is thus more that of an accelerator than that of an inventor. That this way of narrating AI has political consequences becomes apparent, however, in how much it is mirrored by legislative steps taken by the US government following the

Commission's work. One of the most important pieces of legislative action in this respect is the CHIPS and Science Act that was signed into law by President Biden in August 2022. The act (US Congress, 2022) contains a modified version of the United States Innovation and Competition Act of 2021 (USICA) (US Congress, 2021b). When the USICA was passed by the US Senate, President Biden remarked that '[w]e are in a competition to win the 21st century, and the starting gun has gone off. As other countries continue to invest in their own research and development, we cannot risk falling behind' (White House, 2021b). Once again, the notion of 'winning' a specific era becomes visible as well as an interlacing of temporal and spatial comparisons. The CHIPS and Science Act, which was passed with bipartisan support, has been presented as a policy priority of the Biden administration as shown by the fact that the President referred to it in his 2022 State of the Union address (White House, 2022b). The act allocates federal funds to R&D, particularly in the area of semiconductor manufacturing, and is supposed to help establish regional technology hubs and create more STEM education opportunities at all educational levels. When signing the act, Biden stated that

China is trying to move way ahead of us in manufacturing these sophisticated chips as well. It's no wonder the Chinese Communist Party actively lobbied U.S. business against this bill. The United States must lead the world in the production of these advanced chips. This law will do exactly that. (White House, 2022a)

In his 2023 State of the Union address, the president reinforced this sentiment (White House, 2023). As National Security Advisor Jake Sullivan described in front of the NSCAI, the CHIPS act is supposed to secure US supply chains in semiconductors as a key enabling technology (White House, 2021a).

The NSCAI further envisioned in its official reports a democratization of AI in order to foster innovation and make better use of the US talent pool. To that end, it recommended the establishment of a National AI Research Resource. In 2020 Congress passed the National Artificial Intelligence Initiative Act (US Congress, 2021c), which directs the White House to launch a task force that will start building this infrastructure. President Biden did so in June 2021. The official press release quotes the director of the National Science Foundation, Sethuraman Panchanathan, who, in his assessment of AI's relevance to economic power and his vision of a multi-stakeholder approach, reproduces the NSCAI position: 'By bringing together the nation's foremost experts from academia, industry, and government, we will be able to chart an exciting and compelling path forward, ensuring long-term U.S. competitiveness in all fields of science and engineering and all sectors of our economy' (White House, 2021c). The task force released its final report in January 2023 in which it set out a four-phase plan for the implementation of the National AI Research Resource (NAIRR Task Force, 2023).

These are just two examples. There are several other related initiatives currently under way, some explicitly inspired by the NSCAI's recommendations. The National Digital Reserve Corps Act (US Congress, 2021a), for instance, was introduced to Congress in 2021 and referred to the House Committee on Oversight and Reform.

Conclusion

This chapter has traced narratives that have contributed to the construction of AI as a trend of relevance to the international distribution of power and US national security. The NSCAI did not invent these narratives – in fact, it often proves difficult, if not impossible, to detect the origin of a narrative as the web of meaning it is nested in is too complex – but it has lent its voice to them and tied in certain elements, while leaving others out. By embracing this specific set of narratives, it has dismissed alternative stories and sharpened the debate. The example shows that the interplay of narratives and comparative practices plays a crucial role in the way agents make sense of and engage in competition.

The NSCAI's central narrative reaches back into the past, inserting the current developments around AI into a series of technological competitions which have already taken place, in particular during the Cold War. It narrates the current situation as the reemergence of a great power competition which correlates with the proclaimed beginning of the age of AI. It constructs AI as a revolutionary technology with a historically unmatched transformative potential while at the same time drawing on temporal analogies and comparisons to make sense of the present. Following a typical narrative pattern, the NSCAI creates a hero–villain binary which sees the US and China facing off against each other. The AI race becomes one integral part of that competition through the way it is linked to various forms of power – in particular, economic, military and ideational power. National performance in the field of AI thus emerges as a relevant factor in respect to which states are assessed. The NSCAI thus builds a threat scenario which centres around AI and carries potentially world-altering consequences. It envisions a future which is already starting to materialize – a future in which the US loses its leadership position and China continues its rise as the world's dominant superpower, resulting in the victory of autocracy over democracy. Comparative practices, in particular the choice of temporal and spatial modes of comparisons, contribute in this context to the unfolding race dynamics. They paint the competition as a contest of speed and heighten the urgency for political action. The present is thus constructed as a time of decision.

According to the NSCAI's account, the US has to act immediately to secure its position in the world and shape the international order. As recent decisions and policy initiatives of the government show, the narrative of an US–China AI race has become popular within the US foreign policy community. Feeding into US foreign policy, it is starting to have political effects. The CHIPS and Science Act of 2022 is one of the most prominent examples.

References

Baum, M.A. and Potter, P.K. (2019) 'Media, public opinion, and foreign policy in the age of social media', *The Journal of Politics*, 81(2): 747–56.

Berenskötter, F. (2011) 'Reclaiming the vision thing: constructivists as students of the future', *International Studies Quarterly*, 55(3): 647–68.

Cave, S., Dihal, K. and Dillon, S. (2020) 'Introduction: Imagining AI', in S. Cave, K. Dihal and S. Dillon (eds) *AI Narratives: A History of Imaginative Thinking about Intelligent Machines*, Oxford: Oxford University Press, pp 1–22.

Cleveland, H.M. (1963) 'Memorandum from the assistant secretary of state for international organization affairs (Cleveland) to acting secretary of state ball, Washington, 20 November 1963', in P. Claussen, E.M. Duncan and J.A. Soukup (eds) (2001) *Foreign Relations of the United States, 1961–1963, Volume XXV, Organization of Foreign Policy; Information Policy; United Nations; Scientific Matters*, Document 411, Washington DC: United States Government Printing Office.

Department of State (1966) 'Department of state policy paper, Washington, October 1966', in S.K. Holly (ed) (1999) *Foreign Relations of The United States, 1964–1968, Volume XXXIV, Energy Diplomacy and Global Issues*, Document 55, Washington DC: United States Government Printing Office.

Drezner, D. (2019) 'Technological change and international relations', *International Relations*, 33(2): 286–303.

Feenberg, A. (1991) *Critical Theory of Technology*, New York, NY: Oxford University Press.

Gadinger, F., Jarzebski, S. and Yildiz, T. (2014a) 'Politische Narrative. Konturen einer politikwissenschaftlichen Erzähltheorie', in F. Gadinger, S. Jarzebski and T. Yildiz (eds) *Politische Narrative*, Wiesbaden: Springer Fachmedien Wiesbaden, pp 3–39.

Gadinger, F., Jarzebski, S. and Yildiz, T. (2014b) 'Vom Diskurs zur Erzählung. Möglichkeiten einer politikwissenschaftlichen Narrativanalyse', *Politische Vierteljahresschrift*, 55(1): 67–93.

Gerakas, E., Mabon, D.W., Patterson, D.S., Sanford, W.F. Jr., and Yee C.B. (eds) (1997) 'National Intelligence Estimate, NIE 11–9–63', Washington, 15 July 1963, Document 295, *Foreign Relations of the United States, 1961–1963, Volumes VII, VIII, IX, Arms Control; National Security Policy; Foreign Economic Policy, Microfiche Supplement*, Washington DC: United States Government Printing Office.

Gerakas, E., Patterson, D.S. and Yee, C.B. (eds) (1997) 'Record of Meeting of the Executive Committee of the Committee of Principals', Washington, 8 July 1968, Document 252, *Foreign Relations of the United States, 1964–1968, Volume XI, Arms Control and Disarmament*, Washington DC: United States Government Printing Office, https://history.state.gov/historicaldo cuments/frus1964-68v11/d252

Guzzini, S. (2009) *On the Measure of Power and the Power of Measure in International Relations*, DIIS Working Paper, 28. Copenhagen: Danish Institute for International Studies.

Hagström, L. and Gustafsson, K. (2019) 'Narrative power: how storytelling shapes East Asian international politics', *Cambridge Review of International Affairs*, 32(4): 387–406.

Homolar, A. (2022) 'A call to arms: hero–villain narratives in US security discourse', *Security Dialogue*, 53(4): 324–41.

Horowitz, M.C. (2018) 'Artificial intelligence, international competition, and the balance of power', *Texas National Security Review*, 1(3): 36–57.

Hudson, D., Finn, E. and Wylie, R. (2023) 'What can science fiction tell us about the future of artificial intelligence policy?', *AI & Society*, 38: 197–211.

Kaminski, A. (2010) *Technik als Erwartung. Grundzüge einer allgemeinen Technikphilosophie*, Bielefeld: Transcript.

Krebs, R.R. (2015) *Narrative and the Making of US National Security*, Cambridge: Cambridge University Press.

Lindsay, J.R. (2020) *Information Technology and Military Power*, Ithaca, NY: Cornell University Press.

Mabon, D.W. and Patterson, D.S. (eds) (1995) 'Memorandum of Conversation, Washington, 10 January 1963', Document 256, *Foreign Relations of the United States, 1961–1963, Volume VII, Arms Control and Disarmament*, Washington DC: United States Government Printing Office, https://history.state.gov/historicaldocuments/frus1961-63v07/d256

Manjikian, M. (2018) 'Social construction of technology. How objects acquire meaning in society', in D.R. McCarthy (ed) *Technology and World Politics. An Introduction*, Abingdon: Taylor and Francis, pp 25–41.

McCarthy, D.R. (2015) *Power, Information Technology, and International Relations Theory. The Power and Politics of US Foreign Policy and the Internet*, Basingstoke: Palgrave Macmillan.

McCarthy, D.R. (2018) 'Introduction: technology in world politics', in D.R. McCarthy (ed) *Technology and World Politics. An Introduction*, Abingdon: Taylor and Francis, pp 1–21.

Miskimmon, A. and O'Loughlin, B. (2017) 'Understanding international order and power transition. A strategic narrative approach', in A. Miskimmon, B. O'Loughlin and L. Roselle (eds) *Forging the World. Strategic Narratives and International Relations*, Ann Arbor, MI: University of Michigan Press, pp 276–310.

NAIRR Task Force (2023) *Strengthening and Democratizing the U.S. Artificial Intelligence Innovation Ecosystem. An Implementation Plan for a National Artificial Intelligence Research Resource*, 13 January, www.ai.gov/wp-content/uploads/2023/01/NAIRR-TF-Final-Report-2023.pdf [Accessed 2 March 2023].

NIC (National Intelligence Council) (2008) *Global Trends 2025. A Transformed World*, November, www.dni.gov/index.php/gt2040-home/gt2040-media-and-downloads [Accessed 10 October 2022].

NIC (2012) *Global Trends 2030. Alternative Worlds*, December, www.dni.gov/index.php/gt2040-home/gt2040-media-and-downloads [Accessed 10 October 2022].

NIC (2017) *Global Trends. Paradox of Progress*, January, www.dni.gov/index.php/gt2040-home/gt2040-media-and-downloads [Accessed 10 October 2022].

NIC (2021) *Global Trends 2040. A More Contested World*, March, www.dni.gov/index.php/gt2040-home/gt2040-media-and-downloads [Accessed 10 October 2022].

NSCAI (National Security Commission on Artificial Intelligence) (2019) *Interim Report*, November, www.nscai.gov/wp-content/uploads/2021/01/NSCAI-Interim-Report-for-Congress_201911.pdf [Accessed 27 June 2022].

NSCAI (2020a) *First Quarter Recommendations*, March, www.nscai.gov/wp-content/uploads/2021/01/NSCAI-First-Quarter-Recommendations.pdf [Accessed 27 June 2022].

NSCAI (2020b) *Interim Report and Third Quarter Recommendations*, October, www.nscai.gov/wp-content/uploads/2021/01/NSCAI-Interim-Report-and-Third-Quarter-Recommendations.pdf [Accessed 27 June 2022].

NSCAI (2020c) *Second Quarter Recommendations*, 23 January, www.nscai.gov/wp-content/uploads/2021/01/NSCAI-Q2-Memo_20200722.pdf [Accessed 27 June 2022].

NSCAI (2021) *Final Report*, March, https://reports.nscai.gov/final-report/table-of-contents/ [Accessed 27 June 2022].

Oppermann, K. and Spencer, A. (2018) 'Narrating success and failure. Congressional debates on the "Iran Nuclear Deal"', *European Journal of International Relations*, 24(2): 268–92.

Pinch, T. and Bijker, W.E. (1989) 'The social construction of facts and artefacts. How the sociology of science and the sociology of technology might benefit each other', in W.E. Bijker, T.P. Hughes and T. Pinch (eds) *The Social Construction of Technological Systems. New Directions in the Sociology and History of Technology*, Cambridge, MA: MIT Press, pp 17–50.

Sismondo, S. (2010) *An Introduction to Science and Technology Studies* (2nd edn), Chichester: Wiley-Blackwell.

Spencer, A. (2016) *Romantic Narratives in International Politics. Pirates, Rebels, and Mercenaries*, Manchester: Manchester University Press.

Stevens, T. (2018) 'Cyberweapons: power and the governance of the invisible', *International Politics*, 55(3–4): 482–505.

US Congress (2018) John McCain National Defense Authorization Act for Fiscal Year 2019, Pub. L. 115–232, 13 August, www.congress.gov/bill/115th-congress/house-bill/5515 [Accessed 5 April 2023].

US Congress (2021a) National Digital Reserve Corps Act, H. R. 4818, 117th Cong., 29 July, www.congress.gov/bill/117th-congress/house-bill/4818?s=1&r=99 [Accessed 5 April 2023].

US Congress (2021b) United States Innovation and Competition Act of 2021, S. 1260, 117th Cong., 8 June, www.congress.gov/bill/117th-congress/senate-bill/1260 [Accessed 5 April 2023].

US Congress (2021c) William M. Thornberry National Defense Authorization Act for Fiscal Year 2021, Pub. L. 116–283, Division E, 1 January, www.congress.gov/bill/116th-congress/house-bill/6395 [Accessed 6 April 2023].

US Congress (2022) CHIPS and Science Act of 2022, Pub. L. 117–167, 9 August, www.congress.gov/bill/117th-congress/house-bill/4346/text [Accessed 15 August 2022].

Viehöver, W. (2012) '"Menschen lesbarer Machen": Narration, Diskurs, Referenz', in M. Arnold, G. Dressel and W. Viehöver (eds) *Erzählungen im Öffentlichen*, Wiesbaden: VS Verlag für Sozialwissenschaften, pp 65–132.

White House (2017) *National Security Strategy of the United States of America*, December, https://trumpwhitehouse.archives.gov/wp-content/uploads/2017/12/NSS-Final-12-18-2017-0905.pdf [Accessed 2 March 2023].

White House (2021a) 'Remarks by National Security Advisor Jake Sullivan at the National Security Commission on Artificial Intelligence Global Emerging Technology Summit', 13 July, www.whitehouse.gov/nsc/briefing-room/2021/07/13/remarks-by-national-security-advisor-jake-sullivan-at-the-national-security-commission-on-artificial-intelligence-global-emerging-technology-summit/ [Accessed 17 August 2022].

White House (2021b) 'Statement of President Joe Biden on Senate Passage of the U.S. Innovation and Competition Act', 8 June, www.whitehouse.gov/briefing-room/statements-releases/2021/06/08/statement-of-president-joe-biden-on-senate-passage-of-the-u-s-innovation-and-competition-act/ [Accessed 17 August 2022].

White House (2021c) 'The Biden Administration Launches the National Artificial Intelligence Research Resource Task Force', 10 June, www.whitehouse.gov/ostp/news-updates/2021/06/10/the-biden-administration-launches-the-national-artificial-intelligence-research-resource-task-force/ [Accessed 17 August 2022].

White House (2022a) 'Remarks by President Biden at Signing of H.R. 4346, "The CHIPS and Science Act of 2022"', 9 August, www.whiteho use.gov/briefing-room/speeches-remarks/2022/08/09/remarks-by-presid ent-biden-at-signing-of-h-r-4346-the-chips-and-science-act-of-2022/ [Accessed 17 August 2022].

White House (2022b) 'State of the Union Address 2022', 1 March, www. whitehouse.gov/state-of-the-union-2022/ [Accessed 17 August 2022].

White House (2023) 'State of the Union Address 2023', 7 February, www. whitehouse.gov/state-of-the-union-2023/ [Accessed 2 March 2023].

Wilson, C.E. (1955) 'Memorandum from the Secretary of Defense (Wilson) to the President, Washington, 28 June 1955', in D.S. Patterson (ed) (1990) *Foreign Relations of the United States, 1955–1957, Regulation of Armaments; Atomic Energy*, Volume XX, Document 42, Washington DC: United States Government Printing Office.

Wilson, J.G. (ed.) (2001) '"Memorandum of Conversation", Moscow, 12 August 1986', Document 144, *Foreign Relations of the United States, 1981– 1988, Volume XI, Start I*, Washington DC: United States Government Printing Office, https://history.state.gov/historicaldocuments/frus1981-88v11/d144 [Accessed 30 January 2024].

Yildiz, T., Gadinger, F. and Jarzebski, S. (2015) 'Das narrative Element des Politischen: Überlegungen zu einer Poetologie des Wissens in der Politikwissenschaft', *Zeitschrift für Politikwissenschaft*, 25(3): 421–32.

13

Conclusion: Comparative Ordering in Security Politics and Beyond

Thomas Müller

International Relations tends to underestimate how pervasive comparative practices are and how much they contribute to the ordering of world politics. One key reason is that there is not one stream of research on comparative practices but several parallel ones, each focusing on specific phenomena such as arms dynamics, status competition and the production of knowledge, quantitative or otherwise, about governance objects. The present volume seeks to overcome this fragmentation and prepare the ground for a more substantial dialogue between the different streams of research.

For that purpose, the various chapters have explored the uses and effects of comparative practices across both traditional security issues, such as arms competition and arms control, and security issues that have gained more prominence in recent decades, such as global crime, maritime security, state fragility, cybersecurity and artificial intelligence. Taken together, the chapters underscore the idea that the various streams of research would benefit from a common agenda. It would allow research on indicators and rankings to contextualize the rise of these different comparative practices within the ecology of those that underpin and shape world politics. Research on balance of power politics, arms dynamics and status hierarchies would gain a better understanding of how actors modulate the dynamics of the competitions over power, military capabilities and status respectively. Research on knowledge practices, in turn, would get a better grasp of a common feature of many, if not all, such practices: the identification of differences and similarities – in short, comparing – is fundamental and integral to the representation and ordering of the world.

This concluding chapter brings together the findings of these chapters and reflects on the insights that they provide into the three guiding questions identified in the introduction: how comparative knowledge is produced, how it becomes politically relevant and how it shapes global security politics. Comparative practices, though, are not a peculiarity of global security politics. They permeate all policy fields in world politics. The chapter therefore ends with some suggestions on how to broaden the debate beyond global security politics and to study the comparative ordering of world politics.

How is comparative knowledge produced?

The chapters show that the various issue areas of security politics – whether traditional or new – all feature epistemic infrastructures that produce comparative knowledge, usually in the form of statistics. Some of these epistemic infrastructures are maintained by international organizations, others by non-governmental organizations, and yet others by for-profit companies. These epistemic infrastructures are not only important as publishers of comparative knowledge, they also serve as enablers of the comparative practices of other actors. By compiling statistics on piracy incidents, cybersecurity incidents or the military arsenals of states, the epistemic infrastructures make it easier for other actors to analyse any trends behind these incidents or compare the military capabilities of selected states. Yet, as Bastian Giegerich and James Hackett (Chapter 3) and Christian Bueger (Chapter 6) underscore, the compilation of the statistics involves a range of decisions on definitions, classifications and methods of calculation that affect the outcome of the comparisons. In this sense, epistemic infrastructures not only simply serve as enablers of actors' comparative practices, they also shape these practices. They preconfigure them by publishing datasets that reflect particular methodologies for operationalizing and quantifying security issues and, relatedly, privilege some forms of comparison over others.

The chapters demonstrate that the available comparative knowledge on security issues is often ambiguous. To give but a few examples. There are differing statistics on the same crimes (see Jakobi and Herbst, Chapter 8), disputes about the number of piracy incidents (see Bueger, Chapter 6) and different rankings and lists of fragile states (see Krause, Chapter 7). These ambiguities, though, are not peculiar to more recent subfields of security politics. They have also persisted in longstanding subfields, as Giegerich and Hackett (Chapter 3) illustrate with their discussion of the different methods for calculating military expenditure. Put differently, the epistemic infrastructures on arms dynamics – that is, on the issue that for a long time has been most central to global security politics – are no more consolidated than those on newer security issues such as maritime security, global crimes, state fragility or cybersecurity.

What accounts for these ambiguities and their persistence? The authors point to three factors in particular. One is the difficulty of collecting reliable data. This can restrict the number of data producers when special resources are required that only a few actors possess, for example large networks of digital sensors in the case of cybersecurity (see Myatt and Müller, Chapter 9). It can also lead to a situation that renders data permanently ambiguous, when it forces the actors producing the comparative knowledge to rely on estimates and best guesses rather than robust figures. For instance, the different levels of transparency that states allow with respect to their military capabilities and expenditures complicates the statistical work of the IISS (see Giegerich and Hackett, Chapter 3). Similarly, the opacity of most crimes makes it hard to compile accurate statistics on them (see Jakobi and Herbst, Chapter 8). Another factor is a lack of consolidation of, and standardization among, the relevant epistemic infrastructures. Many of the subfields – from arms dynamics through maritime security and global crimes to state fragility – feature a plurality of epistemic infrastructures, with a number of different actors producing and publishing comparative knowledge, each employing their own methodology.

The third factor is the political struggle over the governance of the issues. Research on rankings discusses political contention as a factor that spurs the production of comparative knowledge. Interested actors, the argument goes, seek to influence the governance of issues by publishing comparative knowledge that supports their policy proposals, resulting in a situation characterized by a plurality of representations (see Kelley and Simmons, 2019: 496). The present volume highlights another effect of political contention. It hampers the consolidation of epistemic infrastructures, that is, the development of shared methodologies and shared institutional frameworks for the production of comparative knowledge. In the case of maritime security, for instance, disputes over the best governance architecture have prevented the consolidation of the fragmented assemblage of epistemic infrastructures (see Bueger, Chapter 6). The Cold War arms control negotiations were for a long time characterized by methodological disputes between Western and Eastern states over how to count and compare military capabilities. These disputes were only resolved in the second half of the 1980s (see Müller and Albert, 2021). In his chapter on the Treaty on Conventional Forces in Europe (Chapter 11), Hans-Joachim Schmidt unpacks how Western and Eastern states developed a shared comparative framework for the conventional balance in Europe, revealing how closely intertwined the methodological debates were with political considerations of what constituted an acceptable distribution of military capabilities.

The study of comparative practices thus underscores how fuzzy structures and governance objects are in world politics. There is no natural way of producing comparative knowledge about the distribution of power or any other governance object. Rather, which comparative practices are the most appropriate and pertinent ones to make sense of structures such as the distribution of power and status hierarchies or to produce knowledge on governance objects such as maritime security, global crime or state fragility remains an open and continuously renegotiated question. Even if actors do not have political motives for favouring some comparative practices over others – which they often have – there are usually several plausible ways of conceptualizing the phenomena and hence producing comparative knowledge on them. It is not only the balance of power that is 'elusive' (Wohlforth, 1993). All governance objects are.

A productive avenue for further probing into how political contention affects the production of comparative knowledge would therefore be to explore how actors cope with the ambiguities. One common strategy that actors employ is to depoliticize comparative practices and to treat ambiguities as something that can be reduced through better data collection or better methodologies (on the depoliticization of knowledge production, see Louis and Maertens, 2021). As part of this strategy, actors may also acknowledge that there are different plausible representations of the issues, as the IISS does for instance by providing more than one set of figures on military expenditures (see Giegerich and Hackett, Chapter 3). This strategy essentially seeks to decouple the mapping tools dimension of comparative practices from their ordering tools dimension. The two dimensions are, however, closely intertwined. Relatedly, at least two politicization strategies can be observed in the practice of security politics: the first politicization strategy is to emphasize the ambiguities. When established comparative practices do not support the policy proposals that actors want to promote, then they can reopen the debate on the best comparative practices by demonstrating that the issues can also be represented differently. Governance arrangements, however, often require some agreement on how to produce comparative knowledge on the respective issues. The second politicization strategy is, therefore, to problematize the ambiguities and to push for a common comparative framework to be negotiated and developed. In global security politics, such problematizations are not uncommon, but have so far led only in some instances – for example during arms control negotiations – to a consolidation and standardization of the epistemic infrastructures. One crucial reason is that the actors know that different comparative methodologies may produce different governance outcomes – in short, that the comparative practices are ordering tools – which means that they usually cannot develop a common comparative framework without resolving the underlying political questions.

How does comparative knowledge become politically relevant?

Actors produce comparative knowledge both in order to influence ongoing debates and to put new issues on the agenda. Instead of asking whether the production of comparative knowledge is spurred by political debates or initiates such debates, it seems more productive, therefore, to adopt a processual perspective and delve into the complex dynamics in which comparative practices are used to increase political attention for issues, prompting debates that then create more demand for comparative knowledge, thus making the comparative practices more relevant politically. Several chapters provide insights into these dynamics, which underpinned the growing political attention paid to relative naval capabilities in the late 19th century (Langer, Chapter 10), the proliferation of epistemic infrastructures on maritime security (Bueger, Chapter 6), the evolving governance of state fragility (Krause, Chapter 7) and supply and demand with respect to statistics on global crimes (Jakobi and Herbst, Chapter 8). Cybersecurity is an example of how a dynamic of this kind can become self-perpetuating, with the producers of comparative knowledge sustaining a narrative of an ever-evolving threat landscape that demands constant monitoring – and hence a continual production of comparative knowledge (see Myatt and Müller, Chapter 9).

These dynamics do not unfold automatically. Rather, they depend on the ability of actors – not necessarily the same actors as those producing the comparative knowledge – to convince relevant constituencies that some issues deserve more political attention and require more or renewed political action. Comparative practices are powerful tools in this endeavour. Actors resort to several strategies to increase the impact of their arguments. They condense the arguments into simple statistics (see Friedberg, 1988: 283), a strategy that works particularly well in policy fields in which governance activities are informed by calls for evidence-based policy making (see Jakobi and Herbst, Chapter 8). They craft special booklets that present and visualize the arguments, as NATO, for instance, did during the East–West disputes over the military balance in the 1980s (see Schlag, Chapter 4). And they use narratives to impose certain frames on developments. One example is the narrative of a tech race between the US and China, which is both substantiated through comparisons and creates further demands for comparisons to track which of the two states is winning the 'race' (see Retzmann, Chapter 12).

However, more research is needed to unpack these dynamics. The chapters suggest several avenues. One is to delve deeper into why particular forms of comparison – rather than comparative practices as such – come to be relevant. Two already mentioned possible factors are, first, the fit to the policy arguments that actors want to make and, second, governance modes that value particular forms of comparison. Notably, evidence-based policy making foregrounds statistical forms of comparative knowledge. Paul Beaumont (Chapter 2) stresses another factor: he shows that US policy makers chose equality in aggregates as the key comparison for the SALT II arms control negotiations because they thought that this comparison mattered most to how audiences would judge the outcome of the negotiations. This suggests that actors choose those forms of comparison that they deem to resonate most with the audiences that they want to influence. Both producers of comparative knowledge and their audiences may re-evaluate the pertinence and salience of particular ways of comparing in the wake of events that confound their expectations. One example, mentioned by Giegerich and Hackett (Chapter 3), is the weak performance of the Russian military in the war in Ukraine, which has led to debates on whether past assessments overestimated the relative strength of the Russian military, with analysts arguing for comparisons that pay more attention to qualitative factors such as morale, cohesion and logistics. Last but not least, Schmidt (Chapter 11) hints at what might be termed a 'form follows function' logic. The negotiations on the CFE Treaty put a premium on the verifiability of the agreed distribution of military power, which meant that dynamic force comparisons (such as complex combat simulations) were unsuitable and made simple statistical comparisons of select major weapon systems the preferred ordering tool for managing the military balance.

The relevant constituencies of actors are another avenue. In a narrow sense, the constituency consists in the politicians, diplomats and experts that partake in the governance of issues. Research on comparative practices tends to focus on how this constituency compares and debates comparisons. In a wider sense, the constituency of actors also comprises the publics that observe global security politics and potentially put pressure on policy makers to adopt, modify or end certain policies. What Paul MacDonald and Joseph Parent (2021: 375) emphasize with regard to status politics holds true for research on comparisons more broadly. More research is needed on this broader constituency, which played a role in the naval competition of the late 19th century, was the target of NATO's Force Comparisons booklets and a factor in the US decision making on the SALT II comparisons. While Beaumont (Chapter 2) teases out that the US government assumed that it knew how its domestic public would assess status, Paul Musgrave and Steven Ward (Chapter 5) show that the US public is in fact pluralistic in its status understandings, with different subgroups using different markers to evaluate international status. This raises a double question: to what extent do the narrow and the broader constituency of actors differ in their prevalent comparative knowledge? Does this matter and, if yes, in what ways?

The final avenue is the comparative ordering of the agenda of global security politics. Several chapters, as mentioned, show how comparative practices were key to the processes through which particular security issues gained in prominence and importance within the agenda of global security politics. What is more, as Anja Jakobi and Lena Herbst (Chapter 8) highlight, comparisons have also been mobilized by actors to debate the significance of different issues of security governance – that is, for attempts to order security issues in terms of their relative salience. Research on comparative practices has, however, so far paid scant attention to the practices that are used in global security politics to compare the evolving salience of security issues as diverse as, say, arms dynamics, global crime and state fragility. Yet, the ordering of the agenda of global security politics involves not only the identification of the security issues that should be addressed as part of global governance. It also involves comparisons about which of these security issues (should) matter and how much. And by foregrounding some issues, these comparisons also make the comparative practices relating to these issues more relevant. One example is the varying salience of naval force comparisons. Debates about world power status made them central to debates about great power competition in the late 19th and early 20th century. During the Cold War, the nuclear balance and the European conventional balance were widely regarded as the most crucial dimensions of the East–West conflict, making the related comparisons more salient than naval force comparisons. In the past two decades, naval force comparisons have become more prominent again in the wake of growing competition between the US and China.

How do comparative practices shape security politics?

Comparative practices are ordering tools. They are, in fact, indispensable for most ordering purposes. When actors compete over power or status, they make comparisons of how much power or status they and other actors have. When actors negotiate governance arrangements, they make decisions on how to allocate rights and duties among themselves (and potentially also to other actors), which – like all matters of distribution – involve comparisons. When actors debate how much some security issues matter or should matter, they make comparisons about the importance of the security issues in question relative to other security issues. The question is, in this sense, not whether the ordering of global security politics involves comparative practices. It does. The question rather is which comparative practices it involves and what effects they have.

Put differently, some particular comparative practices may be associated with a specific mode of governance, for instance indicators and rankings with indirect modes of governance (see Broome and Quirk, 2015; Kelley and Simmons, 2020). But all modes of governance involve – in one way or another – comparative practices. Comparisons are integral to the construction of the governance objects, the debates on how much different actors have to contribute to the governance, the debates on how successful the governance is and, last but not least, the debates on which governance objects should get how much attention in world politics.

For all their differences, research on balance of power politics, status politics and indicators/rankings all associate comparative practices primarily with competitive dynamics in world politics. The chapters in this volume underscore that the effects on these competitive dynamics are variable. Comparative practices may either fuel competitive dynamics (see Langer, Chapter 10; Retzmann, Chapter 12) or be part of governance arrangements that tame them (see Beaumont, Chapter 2; Schmidt, Chapter 11). What determines in these cases which of the effects comes into play is not so much the difference between absolute and relative standards of comparison – the factor that Ann Towns and Bahar Rumelili (2017) emphasize to explain variations in competitive dynamics – but rather the type of ordering that the relevant actors strove for: unilateral ordering through competition versus ordering through joint governance.

That said, the chapters underscore that the modulation of competitive dynamics is only one effect that comparative practices have. They are also integral to the construction of governance objects and influence collective action in at least two ways. The first effect, discussed earlier, pertains to ordering the agenda of global security politics through distinguishing between, and ascribing salience to, policy issues. The second effect consists in steering the governance of the issues. These steering effects can occur in one of two ways: when states – or other governance actors such as international organizations – draw on comparative practices to decide how they deal with the issues, as in the use of state fragility rankings and ratings to decide on the allocation of development aid (see Krause, Chapter 7); or when other actors use comparative practices to put pressure on states or other governance actors to deal with issues in particular ways. This pressure game may have a competitive dimension, notably when the other actors use rankings to suggest that states are in a competition for best performance with regard to the governance of some issues, but it does not have to have one. The pressure can be generated in other ways, for instance through temporal comparisons that highlight and frame some trends, such as increases in piracy attacks, crimes or cyberattacks, as problems that states or other governance institutions should react to and tackle.

There is a strategic dimension to the effects. The fundamental ambiguity of security issues – the fact that they can be represented in multiple ways through comparative practices – gives actors leeway to promote those representations that are most conducive to the effects they prefer. In the CFE negotiations, for instance, the NATO members were able to make their problematization of the balance – the claim that there existed an imbalance favouring the Warsaw Pact – the basis for the arms control measures that entailed far bigger reductions for the Warsaw Pact members than for the NATO members (see Schmidt, Chapter 11). The effects of the comparative practices thus depend to a considerable degree on how successful the various actors involved in global security politics are in making their preferred representations central to the debates on and governance of the issues. This is neither to say that the production of comparative knowledge is always shaped by such strategic considerations, nor that the actors are always able to control the effects that the comparative practices have. The point rather is that the various actors are well aware that different comparative practices have different ordering repercussions and that, as a corollary, the ordering of global security politics often involves battles over the comparative practices that are to inform and guide the ordering.

One argument in research on rankings is that the more the published rankings differ in their representations – that is, the more ambiguous the available comparative knowledge is – the more diluted the ordering effects are (see Sauder and Espeland, 2006; Rumelili and Towns, 2022). If the representations of the issue are too incompatible, then ambiguity can indeed hamper or prevent governance arrangements. Before the CFE negotiations, West and East had been engaged in long and unsuccessful negotiations on conventional arms control since the early 1970s. These negotiations had been stalled by their inability to agree on a common interpretation of the conventional military balance in Europe. That being said, besides preventing collective modes of ordering, disagreements may also fuel more individualistic modes of ordering. Ambiguities about the relative standing of the different great powers were a factor fuelling the late 19th century naval competition (see Langer, Chapter 10). Divergent interpretations of the theatre nuclear and conventional balances in Europe were the engine of the Cold War arms race between West and East (see Müller and Albert, 2021). Moreover, ambiguities seem to prevent some ordering effects, not all. They may make some statistics inadequate as mapping tools, but that has not prevented actors from using them as ordering tools in global crime governance (see Jakobi and Herbst, Chapter 8). And despite their differences the state fragility rankings and ratings have had an impact on the flows of development aid (see Krause, Chapter 7).

Broadening the debate: the comparative ordering of world politics

The main aim of this volume is to foster a common debate in security studies on the use of comparisons in global security politics and to show how integral these practices are to the ordering of the policy field. Global security politics is, however, far from being the only policy field shaped by comparative practices. They are also pervasive features of other policy fields in world politics, such as – to name just a few – economic politics, development politics and climate politics. So, the debate should not remain limited to global security politics. In this spirit, this chapter ends with some suggestions for how to broaden the debate beyond global security politics. There are at least three productive ways for doing so.

The first is to study how comparative practices shape the agenda of world politics. The volume has highlighted how comparisons underpin debates about the importance of different security issues. The uses and effects of comparisons, though, go beyond that. Global security politics is sometimes described as 'high politics' and other policy fields as 'low politics'. That description is itself comparative in that it orders world politics in terms of more and less important policy fields. The comparative ordering of world politics thus has two dimensions: the use of comparisons as ordering tools within policy fields and their use to establish order among policy fields – that is, to differentiate policy fields from one another and to assign political importance to them.

The second is to probe into how different policy fields deal with the ambiguity of comparative knowledge. Ordering is an act of pattering social relations, for instance by sorting actors into a hierarchy. This, however, only works as long as there is some shared understanding among relevant actors of what these patterns are. As the chapters in this volume have shown, the comparative knowledge available on political issues is often ambiguous, though that does not preclude that it has effects on how the issues are governed. This raises questions about the interplay between the level of ambiguity and the ordering effects of comparative knowledge. One crucial aspect of this interplay is that comparative practices can themselves be the objects of ordering, that is, of attempts by actors to make the available comparative knowledge less ambiguous through negotiating and agreeing on common frameworks of comparison. To what extent do policy fields differ in the ordering of comparative practices? For instance, why is the consolidation of knowledge infrastructures happening in some policy fields – think of climate politics and the authoritative role of the IPCC (see Edwards, 2010) – but not in others? Why, to give further examples, has the UN been successful in establishing itself as a key source of comparative knowledge on development politics (think of the Sustainable Development Goals and the related indicators framework, see Tichenor et al, 2022), but not on matters of arms dynamics, despite armaments and disarmament being a crucial dimension of security governance?

The third way is to explore the ecologies of comparative practices that underpin and shape policy fields. The volume underscores that comparisons order world politics in many ways: besides sorting the agenda of world politics, comparisons undergird hierarchies, fuel competition and guide governance efforts. Some comparative practices – for example rankings – potentially combine two or more of these modes of ordering. Still, the ordering of policy fields is not usually the product of one type of comparative practice, but of a combination of comparative practices, some of which enable, and reinforce, or, alternatively, challenge and contest other comparative practices. It seems, therefore, productive to not only study the ordering effects of particular types of comparative practices (such as indicators or rankings), but to delve further into the ecologies of comparative practices that, in their combination and juxtaposition, impart both structure and dynamics – and thus both stability and change – to policy fields.

Such a broadening of the debate will further underscore the point that this volume seeks to make: comparisons are one of many practices used in world politics. But they underpin and shape almost all, if not all, of its aspects, from hierarchies through competitions and the production of knowledge about governance objects to the distribution of (governance) rights and duties. World politics is deeply comparative in nature – and comparative practices are, accordingly, key to understanding and explaining how it is ordered and evolves.

References

Broome, A. and Quirk, J. (2015) 'Governing the world at a distance: the practice of global benchmarking', *Review of International Studies*, 41(5): 819–41.

Edwards, P.N. (2010) *A Vast Machine: Computer Models, Climate Data, and the Politics of Global Warming*, Cambridge, MA: The MIT Press.

Friedberg, A.L. (1988) *The Weary Titan: Britain and the Experience of Relative Decline, 1895–1905*, Princeton, NJ: Princeton University Press.

Kelley, J.G. and Simmons, B.A. (2019) 'Introduction: the power of global performance indicators', *International Organization*, 73(3): 491–510.

Kelley, J.G. and Simmons, B.A. (eds) (2020) *The Power of Global Performance Indicators*, Cambridge: Cambridge University Press.

Louis, M. and Maertens, L. (2021) *Why International Organizations Hate Politics: Depoliticizing the World*, London: Routledge.

MacDonald, P.K. and Parent, J.M. (2021) 'The status of status in world politics', *World Politics*, 73(2): 358–91.

Müller, T. and Albert, M. (2021) 'Whose balance? A constructivist approach to balance of power politics', *European Journal of International Security*, 6(1): 109–28.

Rumelili, B. and Towns, A.E. (2022) 'Driving liberal change? Global performance indices as a system of normative stratification in liberal international order', *Cooperation and Conflict*, 57(2): 152–70.

Sauder, M. and Espeland, W.N. (2006) 'Strength in numbers? The advantages of multiple rankings', *Indiana Law Journal*, 81(1): 205–27.

Tichenor, M., Merry, S.E., Grek, S. and Bandola-Gill, J. (2022) 'Global public policy in a quantified world: sustainable development goals as epistemic infrastructures', *Policy and Society*, 41(4): 431–44.

Towns, A.E. and Rumelili, B. (2017) 'Taking the pressure: unpacking the relation between norms, social hierarchies, and social pressures on states', *European Journal of International Relations*, 23(4): 756–79.

Wohlforth, W.C. (1993) *The Elusive Balance: Power and Perceptions during the Cold War*, Ithaca, NY: Cornell University Press.

Index

References to figures appear in *italic* type; those in **bold** type refer to tables. References to endnotes show both the page number and the note number (231n3).